"Without doubt, Kenny Ausubel has one of the most glorious minds on the planet. Herein he has crafted a dazzling treasury of essays on the destiny of humanity and its place on earth, a rosary of startling truths. His ability to describe the cataclysmic loss of living systems contrasted with the luminous and untold rise of human awakening is unique among living writers and speakers. Read this for its brilliance, but read it also to find joy in the intricate reimagination of what it means to be a human being at this parlous moment in civilization."

—Paul Hawken, author of *Blessed Unrest*;
coauthor, *Natural Capitalism*

"Dreaming the Future proposes a path forward that is both profoundly radical and full of common sense. An excellent read for everyone who wants to build a better future—and for those looking to supplement the many dry technical tomes about today's environmental problems. Ausubel explores the political, cultural, and personal changes needed to chart a sustainable path forward, leaving readers delighted and hopeful."

—Annie Leonard, author and host, *The Story of Stuff*;
codirector, The Story of Stuff Project

"Kenny Ausubel is one of the planet's key people, a kind of hub for the new ideas that will, if we're smart, shape our future. He delivers them with the . . . brio and confidence that will help people overcome their fear and get to work!"

—Bill McKibben, author of *Eaarth*; founder of 350.org

Dreaming the
FUTURE

Dreaming the
FUTURE

Reimagining Civilization
in the Age of Nature

From the cofounder of Bioneers
KENNY AUSUBEL

Foreword by David W. Orr

Chelsea Green Publishing
White River Junction, Vermont

Project Manager: Hillary Gregory
Project Editor: Joni Praded
Copy Editor: Eric Raetz
Proofreader: Susan Barnett
Indexer: Lee Lawton
Designer: Melissa Jacobson

Front cover image by Nils-Udo
Clemson Clay Nest
Botanical Garden of South Carolina, 2005
Ilfochrome on aluminium 124 × 124 cm

Printed in the United States of America
First printing August, 2012
10 9 8 7 6 5 4 3 2 1   12 13 14 15 16

Our Commitment to Green Publishing
Chelsea Green sees publishing as a tool for cultural change and ecological stewardship. We strive to
align our book manufacturing practices with our editorial mission and to reduce the impact of our
business enterprise in the environment. We print our books and catalogs on chlorine-free recycled
paper, using vegetable-based inks whenever possible. This book may cost slightly more because it
was printed on paper that contains recycled fiber, and we hope you'll agree that it's worth it. Chelsea
Green is a member of the Green Press Initiative (www.greenpressinitiative.org), a nonprofit coalition of publishers, manufacturers, and authors working to protect the world's endangered forests and
conserve natural resources. *Dreaming the Future* was printed on FSC®-certified paper supplied by
Thomson-Shore that contains at least 30% postconsumer recycled fiber.

Library of Congress Cataloging-in-Publication Data
Ausubel, Ken.
  Dreaming the future : reimagining civilization in the Age of Nature /
Kenny Ausubel ; forward by David W. Orr.
    p. cm.
  Includes bibliographical references.
  ISBN 978-1-60358-459-3 (pbk.) — ISBN 978-1-60358-460-9 (ebook)
1. Sustainable development. 2. Human ecology. 3. Environmental
protection. I. Title.

  HC79.E5.A9257 2012
  338.9'27—dc23
                            2012019727

Chelsea Green Publishing
85 North Main Street, Suite 120
White River Junction, VT 05001
(802) 295-6300
www.chelseagreen.com

FSC
www.fsc.org

MIX
Paper from
responsible sources
FSC® C013483

For Nina Simons, my beloved wife and endlessly inspired cocreator of Bioneers, and Clay Aster Ausubel Grossman, my grandson, whose recent arrival has made the well-being of future generations intensely personal to me.

CONTENTS

FOREWORD

It's All Alive, It's All Connected!

*T*he greatest discovery of the past century was not in nuclear physics, or biology, or computer science. It was, rather, the discovery (or more accurately the rediscovery) of an ancient premonition—that we are part of a vast web of life, one large evolving system that has many of the characteristics of a living organism. Intelligence, which René Descartes and his heirs believed was a monopoly of *Homo sapiens*, is no such thing. In ways that we cannot fully describe, it is woven through the whole fabric. We live, as Ralph Waldo Emerson once mused, in the lap of great intelligence. We also live within a network of interdependence and obligation that extends back in time to the beginnings of humankind and forward into the future as far as one can possibly imagine.

We are all descended from a common maternal ancestor. We breathe the same air, drink from the same waters, and are fed from the same soils. Our very bodies are a congress of other life-forms on which we are wholly dependent. We are kith and kin to all that was, all there is, and all that will ever be. Our bodies tell the tale of our origins in ancient seas; our minds still have a reptilian core. We are made of stuff from vanished stars and are destined to be food for worms. Life is that majestic and that mundane. But it is also a mystery. D. H. Lawrence put it this way: "Water is two parts hydrogen, one part oxygen, but there is a third thing that makes it water and no one knows what that is." I doubt that anyone ever will know or perhaps ever could know such things. For all of our puffed-up self-importance we are only upstart primates occupying one small booth on the outskirts of a vast, turbulent, ongoing bazaar of living, evolving sentience located on a minuscule planet attached to a third-rate star somewhere in a backwater galaxy in a sea of billions of other galaxies speeding toward some unknown destination. Considering our insignificance in the face of such grandeur and mystery, the prudent response for a species pleased to call itself *Homo sapiens* would be reverence and humility.

The modern world, however, was built on other assumptions. The philosophy of the industrial age is, as designer William McDonough once put it, "If brute force doesn't work you're not using enough of it." And so we muscled our way out of the agrarian world into the industrial age, powered by fossilized sunlight and undergirded by bulletproof certainty that there are no pitfalls or traps ahead nor places where angels would fear to tread. And so we conquered continents, clear-cut forests, dammed rivers, diminished distance and time, and probed the far reaches of space. Admonished by Francis Bacon to "affect all things possible," we conjured substances alien to life and invaded the recesses of the atom and the gene. In the process, as urban historian Lewis Mumford once lamented, we became very long on know-how and very short on know-why.

That is part of the reason that things did not work out as the architects of modernity had hoped. Rather like the sorcerer's apprentice or the curse of King Midas or Marlowe's Faust, ours became the age of paradox—a convergence of power and peril. And stuck in paradox is not where we want to be. In his review of the human prospect, Cambridge University astronomer Martin Rees concluded that at the pinnacle of our success the odds of civilization surviving intact to the year 2100 are at best no better than 50–50 and probably worse.

Given the odds, the only sensible response is to make the task of preserving a habitable planet and creating a fair, decent, and durable civilization in record time "the great work" of the twenty-first century. Anything less or later won't do.

That doesn't mean tinkering with the coefficients of change, but changing the structure of the system that is programmed for disaster. Structural change requires tossing overboard many of the foundational myths of the modern world. There is the myth of lordly human dominance over nature that presumes that we know enough to manage the planet even though we can't manage the back forty. There is the myth that ignorance is a solvable problem, not an inescapable part of the human condition. There is the myth that an economy can grow forever in a finite planet and its corollary that human happiness is a by-product of consumption—a word that ironically once referred to a fatal disease. There is the myth that security is the offspring of a monstrous capacity to kill and cause havoc. Beneath such thinking is a kind of feckless belief that we can tame the demons that we unleash on the world.

In the meantime, in quiet, out-of-the-way, and marginal places and mostly led by unlikely people at the periphery of power and influence, the work of myth breaking and structural change proceeds. Two broad revolutions have been gathering force for centuries but always against long odds and stacked decks. The first began in the Athenian Agora with fledgling steps toward democracy and the concept of human rights based in law. Across the span of nearly 2,500 years the battle for basic rights has gathered force from Runnymede to Rosa Parks; from John Lilburne and the English Levellers in the seventeenth century to Tiananmen Square and children in the Philippines suing on behalf of future generations' rights to nature; from the idea that all men are created equal before the law to Sojourner Truth, Nelson Mandela, and Barbara Jordan. The decks are still stacked and the road ahead will be no less challenging or bloody than that already traveled, but the battle for enforceable human rights and the extension of the rights to "life, liberty, and property" to future generations and eventually the extension of rights to animals and nature will go forward, and some day what Martin Luther King Jr. described as the "arc of history" will indeed bend toward inclusive and dependable justice.

The second stream is still older. It is the knowledge of how to make the human presence in the world on nature's terms, not just human contrivance. It is the art of creating, in ecological designer John Todd's words, "elegant solutions predicated on the uniqueness of place." It first appears in vernacular knowledge: shelter and buildings made from local materials and conforming to site and circumstances; ingenious agricultural practices that build on ecological synergies; indigenous knowledge of the properties of plants and behavior of animals; and the creation of durable economies calibrated to the realities of ecology and physics. Everywhere, its hallmark is the humility to learn from nature and develop partnerships with ecological processes. It is alive and flourishing in our time in the work of Janine Benyus and the Biomimicry Guild, the brilliance of mycologist Paul Stamets, John Todd's living machines, Andy Lipkis's work on water systems in Los Angeles, and Wes Jackson's natural systems agriculture, as well as economists, industrial ecologists, solar engineers, architects and urban planners, restorationists, tree planters, and healers of every kind—all working with nature and posterity in mind.

Interwoven, these two strands are the DNA for what Kenny Ausubel here calls "the reimagining of civilization in the Age of Nature." It is surely a homecoming—in the metaphorical sense of returning to old and familiar ideas and forms that we once knew well, and in the ecological sense implied in the Greek word *oikos* (the root for our word ecology), meaning proper management of the household. But the reimagining of civilization—the blending of indigenous knowledge, science, decent management of our common assets, and practice leavened by compassion and good-heartedness—would be much less likely were it not for the heroic work of Kenny Ausubel and his partner and wife, Nina Simons. Two decades ago they had the foresight, perception, imagination, and courage to create the Bioneers. The result is a hybrid—one part global salon for an ongoing conversation between like-minded but otherwise isolated visionaries and practitioners at the forefront of civilizational change, and one part catalytic organization that takes the many conversations up to a higher level and down to Main Street. Kenny and Nina have helped give birth to a new Enlightenment—this one global but locally applicable; political but beyond left and right; rooted in science, but a companion of indigenous knowledge; a revolution of practice, but contingent on a change of heart and perception. What follows is the remarkable story of the bioneers—the opening chapter in the transformation of civilization and its prospects.

DAVID W. ORR

INTRODUCTION

Slouching toward Sustainability

*S*nail is trucking through Snailville. Turtle comes along and runs right over him. Finally—finally!—the Snail Police arrive. "What happened? What happened?"

"I don't know," groans Snail. "It all happened so fast."

The unfolding globalized environmental and civilizational collapse we're starting to witness today is no overnight sensation. As Paul Gilding observes in *The Great Disruption*, "We've been borrowing from the future, and the debt has fallen due. The science says we have physically entered a period of great change, a synchronized, related crash of the economy and ecosystem. The Great Disruption will ultimately take human society to a higher evolutionary state."

We stand at the threshold of a singular passage in the human experiment: to reimagine how to live on Earth in ways that honor the web of life, each other, and future generations. To move from breakdown to breakthrough, the coming years will be the most important years in the history of human civilization.

At the same time the world faces escalating climate change and extreme environmental and social disruption, we're also witnessing a profound transformation taking hold around the globe. It signals the dawn of a human civilization that honors and emulates the wisdom of nature's design sophistication. It's rooted in values of justice, equity, diversity, democracy, and peace. It's a revolution from the heart of nature and the human heart.

Nature has a profound capacity for healing, and we can act as healers. The good news is that the solutions are largely present, or we know what directions to head in. Around the world in diverse fields of endeavor, social and scientific innovators have been developing and demonstrating far better technological, economic, social, and political models—all inspired by the wisdom of the natural world. Human creativity focused on problem solving is eclipsing the mythology of despair.

This transformation inspires a change of heart that celebrates the unity and intrinsic value of all life. Over and over, it's the story of how great a difference one person can make, and how community makes the difference.

This historic shift to become an ecologically literate and just civilization heralds a declaration of interdependence. Taking care of nature means taking care of people—and taking care of people means taking care of nature. We protect what we love.

Resilience is the grail—enhancing our ability to adapt to dramatic change and restructure our ways of living in concert with natural systems and with respect for human dignity. From here on, the challenge is to alter the "mindscape" and advance the transformation in the shortest possible time. In community lies our resilience. As environmental educator David W. Orr has said, "Hope is a verb with its sleeves rolled up."

In the early 1970s when the prospect of the world's stumbling into an environmental crisis was already staining the horizon, I began asking myself what we could do about it. Were there real solutions? The inquiry ultimately led me to found the Bioneers conference and organization in 1990 with my business partner and wife, Nina Simons. The intent was to bring together leading social and scientific innovators with breakthrough solutions for restoring people and planet.

Over the years, through other work I'd been doing, I'd come across various individuals who appeared to have come up with fundamental solutions to many of our most pressing environmental and social challenges. A pattern emerged. They peered deep into the heart of nature and living systems in search of cues and clues. After all, nature has 3.8 billion years of R&D under her belt. What's here is what works—survivors in an ever-changing evolutionary dance. The most basic question they asked: How would nature do it?

I came to call these explorers "bioneers"—biological pioneers who looked to nature not as resource but as source. They approached the puzzle with systems thinking. Just as everything in the web of life is connected, human systems and natural systems are one system. They took a "solve-the-whole-problem" approach, spanning the rich arc of human endeavor, guided by the intelligence inherent in the natural world.

I had picked up some cues and clues myself along the way. After I suffered a serious health event exhibiting symptoms of a stroke at age nineteen, conventional medicine was unable to help me. As a result, I fell through the rabbit hole into the world of natural medicine around

1970—before the field had a name or existed as a profession. I learned only many years later that my illness likely resulted from a severe chemical exposure.

I moved out of New York City with my first wife and landed in New Mexico in the recognition I needed to be in a healthy environment. After a brief stint in Santa Fe, we moved to a small farm north of town. I figured working hard physically had to be good for me, and I felt like an idiot as an urbanite completely unskilled in basic lifeways such as gardening, building, and the raft of practical earthbound skills most people once knew.

I had the great good fortune to fall into a dynamic nest of hard-core DIY back-to-the-landers, many of them iconoclastic dropouts from successful professional careers. I eagerly apprenticed to learn organic farming, natural building, solar energy, composting toilets, vegetable canning, and tuning up my pickup.

Gradually my health stabilized. And I didn't feel like quite such an idiot, though I'm a terminal failure as a mechanic and the world is better off without me farming.

One evening I got a chilling call from my mom in New York City. My father had cancer. Six months later he was dead at age fifty-six. Two weeks after his death, in the mail unbidden I received a holistic health newsletter with compelling testimonials by terminal cancer patients reputedly cured by a metabolic-nutritional regimen. As sympathetic as I'd become toward natural medicine, I found the claim repellant. I believed what the doctors said: Cancer was largely incurable, and the only effective treatments were surgery, radiation, and chemotherapy.

Long story short, with my father freshly buried and my heart broken, I embarked on a research mission to learn all I could about "alternative" cancer treatments. Ultimately I produced the film *Hoxsey: When Healing Becomes a Crime* and a subsequent book about the corrosive medical politics that have obstructed or suppressed promising unconventional cancer treatments, almost all of them loosely within the realm of natural medicine. (The FDA has yet to approve a single nontoxic cancer treatment.)

The Hoxsey herbal treatment was a classic case history of medical politics—its therapeutic value twice upheld by federal courts while thousands upon thousands of patients claimed to be cured by it. Nevertheless it was denied the fair scientific test for which its founder Harry Hoxsey spent his entire life fighting. Decades after his death, laboratory tests showed all the herbs to have anticancer, antitumor, or immune-boosting properties—and an NIH team later recommended it as worthy of further investigation. Like everything else, I discovered, medicine is political.

I dove deep into researching the netherworld of remarkable remissions and "people who got well when they weren't supposed to," as cancer surgeon Bernie Siegel calls them. I learned that a centuries-old medical civil war had been raging. Apart from the obvious economic war between conventional and "unconventional" medicine, there was also a profound conflict of medical philosophy. It led me to what became an underlying principle for Bioneers.

Allopathic (conventional) medicine grew out of a school called "heroic medicine." The basic premise was that the body had no ability to cure itself. Hence the physician had to intervene in a "heroic" manner with highly aggressive and usually toxic or dangerously invasive procedures (mercury for syphilis, surgery before asepsis and anesthesia). As Benjamin Rush, one of the fathers of American medical education, stated, "I would treat nature as I would a squalling cat: Throw it out in the rain."

To the contrary, the natural ("empiric") medicine tradition posited that nature has a profound and mysterious ability for self-repair and healing. The role of the doctor or practitioner is to support the body to heal itself, using various generally nontoxic, noninvasive methods.

My takeaway from this conflict of medical philosophy was that, given nature's profound capacity for healing, environmental restoration becomes a process of working with nature to heal nature—of helping nature heal itself. Bioneers 101.

Because the Hoxsey treatment is an herbal formula, I became immersed in the world of botanical medicine. Through a daisy chain of connections, I met Gabriel Howearth and filmed his remarkable biodiversity gardens at San Juan Pueblo north of Santa Fe. Although I had lived on our little farm for six years, I had never seen anything remotely like this marvel. Gabriel had gathered rare and endangered native open-pollinated seeds from all over the world, a rich ark of heirloom and traditional varieties that were little known and often under threat of extinction. He apprenticed with many indigenous farmers, principally in the Americas, and learned ancient traditional farming practices that are as endangered as the seeds. It was my introduction to biodiversity and traditional ecological knowledge (TEK).

The old saw that "variety is the spice of life" mistakes the condiment for the meal. In nature, diversity is the very fabric of life, an article of faith. It's nature's fail-safe mechanism against extinction—"diversify your portfolio" is a biological strategy. Diversity is also the sacred tree of life with intrinsic value independent of its use value to people.

Gabriel and I went on to found the company Seeds of Change in 1989 to create a market partnership with backyard gardeners as a pathway for conserving these invaluable seed stocks, along with the traditional knowledge hard-earned over generations. Clearly the company was not the solution to the world's biodiversity crisis in this Sixth Age of Extinctions, but like the Hoxsey remedy, it seemed to offer at least part of a solution and larger strategy. Diversity in all its expressions, both biological and cultural, emerged as another first principle of Bioneers.

Throughout the 1970s and 1980s, I kept encountering this persistent pattern of nature-inspired design across a wide variety of fields and issues. During a visit with Josh Mailman, a friend and investor in the *Hoxsey* film and Seeds of Change, I was alternately enthusing about these visionary innovators modeling solutions on how nature does it, and bemoaning the fact that people seldom heard about such game-changing work. If only the world knew, it could radically leverage the pressure for change. He suggested I hold a conference and bring them together. I shrugged; I'd never been to a conference, and the idea didn't interest me. Then he cheerfully offered, "I'll give you $10,000. Have a conference." We had a conference.

At the inception, Bioneers was an experiment and we frankly didn't know what we were doing. Call it "beginner's mind," to be polite. Nor were these kinds of ideas and approaches prevalent. When we started, forget being on the radar screen—we might as well have been UFOs.

But even under the best of conditions, memory is a shape-shifter and reality is consensual. Were my recollections accurate? On the twentieth anniversary of Bioneers in 2009, I decided to take a trip down memory lane for a reality check.

I'm a research pack rat. I pored over all the old conference programs, media materials, and other artifacts. The original cultural DNA had persisted with surprising consistency, while evolving and coevolving with the world. Tickling the immovable object of isolated silos of "single issues" with the irresistible force of systems thinking, we shook loose rich novelty. We had been exploring biomimicry for eight years when biomimicry master and author Janine Benyus first spoke at the conference and gave the game-changing design science its name with her newly released landmark book *Biomimicry: Innovation Inspired by Nature*. From the outset we accentuated indigenous thinking and traditional ecological knowledge (TEK) as fundamental to environmental restoration, and linked them as the forebears of biomimicry.

We drew the connections between environmental well-being and social and racial justice, creating a space for these generally separated communities to explore common ground. With environmental health researcher and attorney Carolyn Raffensperger and others, we helped develop the idea of "ecological medicine" as the inextricable interdependence of ecosystem and human health. We highlighted the centrality of women's leadership to achieving environmental improvement. We pursued the grail of building ecological and social resilience in the face of radical environmental and social change, including strategies of greater decentralization and relocalization.

A friend once said to me, "It's great to be ahead of your time—like two weeks ahead of your time." Indeed, it appeared we had been ahead of the curve in some ways. Of course that was sort of the point—otherwise, why bother?

Then I came across the unmarked yellowed manila folder that changed everything.

There lay the vintage 1989 *Time* magazine "Planet of the Year" edition. Instead of a standard annual "Person of the Year," the cover featured the "Endangered Earth" with a weirdly beautiful bound-up, shellacked globe by the artist Christo. I remembered it as though it were yesterday.

That summer, *Time* had convened a private miniconference of experts and its reporters to look at the state of the planet. This edition was the result. It detailed the early onset of climate change on the heels of NASA climatologist James Hansen's first urgent testimony before Congress. As the Paul Revere of global warming, Hansen warned the nation's political leaders that we had the decade of the 1990s to start closing out our fossil fuel accounts to avoid runaway climate change.

The magazine waded through the mounting litany of global environmental crises—freshwater scarcity, toxics, the biodiversity crash, public health threats, archaic transportation infrastructures, wealth extremes, and so on—listing suites of possible solutions.

I remembered viscerally the hope I felt when the nation's leading weekly newsmagazine published this bold and reasonably well-informed call to action. Even *Time* knows the time is here, I thought. Society is awakening at the highest levels. Sure, there's a lot they're missing and the thinking itself is often flawed—but a national response focused on solutions may be arising. The space is opening up, and we can run with it. We'll have a wind at our back, for a change.

When Hansen first testified in 1988 about the ominous vector of climate change, he hoped to provoke a national response. He did. It came from Exxon and the fossil fuel industrial complex, which spent the next 20-plus years sowing doubt and cultivating inaction with the biggest and most expensive disinformation campaign in human history. It was a catastrophic success.

As a result, the world has been slouching toward sustainability—at least until very recently. Something began to shift around 2006. David W. Orr calls it a "global ecological Enlightenment" and author Paul Hawken terms it "blessed unrest." Meanwhile, escalating physical realities continue to override delusion, propaganda, and inertia.

In truth, although it's one minute to midnight on the ecological clock and too late to avoid large-scale destruction and disruption, "the shift is about to hit the fan," in the words of filmmaker Tom Shadyac. Around the world, the transition from fossil fuels is irreversibly under way, along with countless other basic changes in how we organize human civilization to operate in concert with natural systems and in a reasonably peaceful coexistence with each other. We're entering the Age of Nature, and there's no turning back.

So it's not so much that Bioneers—and many others—have been ahead of the times. At a teachable moment of wide awareness, powerful interests stole the slim sliver of time we had to jump-start the transformation for how we live on Earth and with each other in a way that lasts. Had things gone differently, we'd all be ahead of our time right now. Maybe even just two weeks ahead of our time.

This collection of essays tracks the arc of big ideas, metatrends, and game-changers that have been brewing in the fertile hatchery and breeding ground of Bioneers over the years. Likely you may encounter some pretty different ways of seeing the world as well as breakthrough innovations still not commonly known.

Nature-inspired solutions occupy the practical center. Systems thinking is the lens, polished by the clear light of humility in the face of how little we know and can ever know. The compass is progressive values reflecting justice, democracy, diversity, equity, and freedom.

Over the years, Bioneers has grown into a community of leadership. The complexity of the world's challenges and problems today is so vast that they can be solved only through extensive interdisciplinary collaboration and a rousing diversity of approaches, cultural perspectives, and ideas. The archetype of the lone inventor or solo visionary has given way to team-based, collaborative models connecting diverse fields, expertise, and teams. Bioneers is a network of networks and movements where cross-pollination is a way of life, where the power of connection generates innovation and greater power in the world. At the end of the day, it's about the symphony, not the soloist.

In these pages you'll stand at the crossroads where the Gaia theory of Earth as one giant intelligent superorganism hooks up with parallel ancient empirical indigenous TEK and the cutting-edge design science of biomimicry. The science of Nature's Operating Instructions meets the Original Instructions of First Peoples for how to live on Earth for the long haul and for how to be a human being. Resilience Thinking responds to ecological regime change. Ecological Medicine anchors public health in the health of ecosystems. National Green Plans illuminate how an entire country can redirect its national purpose to systemic restoration founded in a strong green economy. The once separate social justice and environmental movements converge in the recognition that what we do to each other we do to the Earth, and we'll have peace with the Earth only when we practice justice. The emerging movement for the global Rights of Nature irrevocably expands the very notion of rights to the nonhuman world. Burgeoning democracy movements animate the topography of hope shared by vast majorities of the world's peoples.

Part 1, "It's All Alive . . . ," is a guided tour—the scenic route—through some of these big ideas, breakthrough innovations, and archetypal megaphors of clashing paradigms, as well as a drive-by of the fast-crumbling ruins of a civilization on a collision course with nature, including flashes of the Dim Ages where retrograde interests stalled the progress we might otherwise have made. Part 2, "Hungry Ghost Stories," visits the rhinoceros in the room—corporate power—capped by a foray into arguably the most important democracy work in the world today by the "unlikeliest of people in the unlikeliest of places." Part 3, "Value Change for Survival," brings us up to the present where "the shift is about to hit the fan." We telescope out for a more cosmic view of some of the larger forces at play on human history and consciousness at this watershed moment.

In 1990 Bioneers put forth the proposition that in great measure the solutions are already present. Even where we don't know exactly what to do, we know what directions to head in. Twenty-three years later, it's virtually impossible to keep up with the avalanche of authentic solutions, creative responses, and the radical transformation in global consciousness. There's as much cause for hope as for horror.

Then again, now that we've irrevocably entered the ecological red zone, as author John Michael Greer points out, in some cases we face not so much problems as predicaments. Problems have solutions. Predicaments are by their very nature insolvable and instead require creative, dynamically shifting responses. As the dancer and arts teacher Sarah Crowell puts it, "The way we'll hold it together is to hold it—together."

My father was a historian who often invoked Sir Isaac Newton's remark that, "If I have seen further, it is by standing on the shoulders of giants." For me, being part of the Bioneers community has allowed me to stand on the shoulders of a community of giants. I am inexpressibly grateful, and I invite you to take the journey and meet some of them in these pages.

As this book goes to press in the summer of 2012, the world has just experienced the hottest year since record keeping began. In March in the United States, over fifteen thousand local weather records were shattered, from unprecedented swarms of tornadoes to jaw-dropping temperature highs and lows. Meanwhile, the 99 percent have put the 1 percent on notice. A wildly diverse yet astonishingly values-consistent global movement of movements is converging to create a world that's ecologically healthy and resilient, socially just, democratic, and free.

Time is of the essence, and in these times we're all called upon to be leaders. I hope this book will be valuable to you to help lead this revolution from the heart of nature, and, in so doing, make the seemingly impossible inevitable. Vaya con Gaia.

Part 1

IT'S ALL ALIVE . . .

CLOSE ENCOUNTERS
OF THE BIOLOGICAL KIND

Earth Hospitality

*T*he journal *Science* reported in 2005 that the giant earthquake—the one that caused the Asian tsunami and ruptured more than eight hundred miles of seafloor in the Indian Ocean—also set off a series of temblors felt nearly seven thousand miles away in Alaska. One hour after the quake, Mt. Wrangell recorded fourteen small earthquakes in eleven minutes. Said Michael West of the Alaska Volcano Observatory, "It was pulsing, if you will, in sync with the waves from Sumatra."

In fact, the earthquake's massive shock waves ricocheted around the world, raising the Earth's rocky crust by half an inch. For weeks, the planet vibrated like a bell. Commented West, "We're learning that the Earth is a far more connected place than we once thought it was."

Naturalist author and biomimicry expert Janine Benyus investigated what happened in Thailand before the tsunami:

> Elephants started trumpeting. Lizards, insects and snakes started climbing up into trees. The flamingos that were breeding near there had already gone inland. They were shocked—shocked—to not find any animal corpses besides humans. The animals had moved inland. They had moved up.
>
> Pacinian corpuscles are mechanoreceptors in the tip of an elephant's trunk and in its feet [also found in human skin] that sense what are called Rayleigh waves that move in and through the Earth. They were started by the rupture in the Earth. These Raleigh waves move in the surface of the Earth about ten times faster than the speed of sound. Elephants pick up infrasound. The animals talk to one another with infrasound, very low tones through the air. Their infrasound, we now think, causes Rayleigh waves in

the Earth so that their messages can go even farther. So that an elephant can say, "I'm ovulating, come home."

An hour before the elephants started to wail, and before the first waves hit, elephants who were toting tourists around broke their chains and ran inland. We of course ran towards the sea. We are a young species with a lot to learn. We see through a glass darkly, and when you do that, you should probably borrow some lenses from the organisms that can see much better. I'm tuned these days into survivors.

What if it's all connected? That question arose in the 1960s for scientific researcher James Lovelock. After NASA asked him to design experiments for the Viking space mission to determine if there was ever life on Mars, he began to ponder what makes life different from nonlife. Outer space brought him down to earth.

Lovelock was intrigued that Earth's atmosphere had remained relatively constant over long periods of time. Just a small increase or decrease in the amount of oxygen would either set the atmosphere on fire or kill most life-forms. Why has the ratio of oxygen remained at just the right level? Why have the oceans maintained just the right salt concentration favorable to life? How has the temperature range that life depends on managed to remain relatively constant?

Lovelock's bold hypothesis was that somehow the sum total of living things on Earth has modulated the balance of oxygen and carbon dioxide, the saltiness of the sea, the surface temperature of the planet— just as our bodies know how to regulate themselves.

With microbiologist Lynn Margulis, Lovelock proposed the Gaia hypothesis, the idea that the entire symphony of all living things self-regulates the Earth's conditions to make the physical environment more hospitable for them in an exquisite, dynamic balance. Think of it as a vast "hospitality" enterprise.

Or, in the words of Janine Benyus, "What life does is create conditions conducive to life." There's a mission statement. Of course, for millennia, indigenous peoples, the world's original bioneers, have held exactly this Gaian view. It's all alive. It's all connected. It's all intelligent. It's all relatives.

At this critical moment when—for the first time in history— humanity has the capacity to destroy the conditions conducive to life on a global scale, these are the time-tested processes, dynamics, and recipes that have allowed life to flourish during 3.8 billion years of evolution. Benyus gave this revolutionary design science a name: biomimicry, "innovation inspired by nature." Biomimicry directs our attention to nature's own solutions. It celebrates the biological diversity of the web of life, both for its practical wisdom and its intrinsic value.

For all the chatter about the Age of Information, what we're really entering is the Age of Nature. After all, we didn't invent nature. Nature invented us. Nature bats last, the saying goes. Even more important, it's her playing field. We would be wise to learn the ground rules and how to play by them.

The solutions residing in nature consistently surpass our conception of what's possible. The quest to understand nature's operating instructions is showing us how to design appropriately for human civilization by modeling human organization on living systems and adapting practical ways to serve human ends harmlessly. The very genius of nature that we are destroying is precisely what we now most need to get ourselves through this bottleneck.

These close encounters of the biological kind reveal an intelligence in nature far beyond human intelligence. As James Lovelock elaborates on the Gaia hypothesis: "Gaia theory sees the biota and the rocks, the air and the oceans as existing as a tightly coupled entity. Gaia's evolution is a single process and not several processes studied in different buildings of universities. It has a profound significance for biology. It affects even Darwin's great vision, for it may no longer be sufficient to say that organisms that leave the most progeny will succeed. It will be necessary to add the proviso that they can do so only so long as they do not adversely affect the environment."

What Lovelock describes is an emergent ecological Darwinism that moves beyond the interests of a single organism to the behavior of entire ecosystems and communities.

> These new ecological models demonstrate that as diversity increases so do stability and resilience. We have at last a reason for our anger over the heedless deletion of species and an answer to those who say it is mere sentimentality. No longer do we have to justify the existence of the humid tropical forests on the feeble grounds that they might carry plants with drugs that could cure human disease. Gaia theory forces us to see that they offer much more than this.

Through their capacity to evapotranspire vast volumes of water vapor, they serve to keep the planet cool by wearing a sunshade of white reflecting clouds. Their replacement by cropland would precipitate a global disaster.

A geophysical system always begins with the action of a single organism. If this action happens to be locally beneficial to the environment, then it can spread until eventually a *global altruism* results. Gaia always operates like this to achieve her altruism. There is no foresight or planning involved. The reverse is also true, and any species that affects the environment unfavorably is doomed, but life goes on.

Life will go on. Earth is mighty and resilient, and has several billion years to go until the sun becomes a "red dwarf" and turns out the lights on planet Earth. When people talk about "saving the Earth," we would more appropriately frame it as saving ourselves. Doing so requires us to radically change our relationship to nature, and to see nature very differently—from nonhuman points of view.

"Gaia philosophy is not humanist," Lovelock points out. "I see the world as a living organism of which we are a part: not the owner, nor the tenant, not even a passenger. To exploit such a world on the scale we do is as foolish as it would be to consider our brains supreme and the cells of other organs expendable. Would we mine our livers for nutrients for some short-term benefit? Gaia works from an act of an individual organism that develops into global altruism."

It's worth remembering that until the 1960s universities did not even have biology departments, only botany and zoology, reflecting our ludicrously limited perspective on the natural world. It also betrays our deep cultural bias toward charismatic species such as animals and plants. In the decades since, Margulis helped dramatically expand our knowledge of the five kingdoms of life, which may well number twenty or more before we're done. Multicellular organisms like us are latecomers, a budding tip of just one branch on the tree of life.

From Margulis's perspective, the real news of twentieth century science is that the greatest diversity of life is in the microcosmos, which requires a microscope to see. Her work illuminates life as most fundamentally bacterial and symbiotic. On a planet where microbes represent the vast majority of life and maintain the conditions necessary for life, there is only one conclusion: bacteria rule.

Human history is a small footnote in the bacterial evolution of life on Earth. Calling bacteria "lower" organisms is a folly of our anthropocentrism, as we begin to understand just how precariously megafauna such as we humans hitch a ride on an incredibly complex web of life.

It's a web we know little about. Scientific estimates of life's diversity of living species, including bacteria, range from 1.4 million to 200 million. We don't know the number even to within an order of magnitude. It's a myth that scientists pop the champagne cork when they discover a new species. They just add it to the towering stack of the ten thousand or so species of plants and animals alone we find each year, give it a name, and file it with the growing inventory of strangers. But we do know we stand to lose 10 to 25 percent of species in the next fifty years at the current rate.

In light of this Sixth Age of Extinctions—called the Anthropocene Age to acknowledge the geologic chronology of an age when human activities have become a dominant force of nature affecting Earth's ecological systems—the Encyclopedia of Life project set out to record and genetically sample every living species on Earth. Many new tools are at our disposal, from globally wired, decentralized networks of naturalists, biologists, and ecologists to genetic identification procedures and micro–video recording techniques. For all the fever dreams of genetic engineering, scientists have never invented a new gene, and the first order of business is the conservation of the living treasure of the world's biological diversity and keeping that knowledge in the public domain.

The Gaia theory of Earth as a self-regulating adaptive system may be the most important scientific concept advanced in the twentieth century. The Gaian idea has become a living symbol, helping mobilize efforts to address global environmental issues—though some folks get a bit over-enthusiastic with the metaphor beyond what the actual scientific theory proposes or has shown. The Gaia hypothesis is exactly that—a provisional work-in-progress. As evidence mounts, we learn how little we know.

The solutions to our problems are present in the wisdom and genius of the sentient symphony of life that creates conditions conducive to life. What greater gift could we have? To paraphrase the Western naturalist writer Wallace Stegner, our challenge is whether human civilization can live up to the majesty of the landscape.

THE REENCHANTMENT
OF EARTH

A Cocreation Story

*W*hen the Europeans first came to Turtle Island—the name Native Americans of the Northeast gave North America—they thought they had found a luxuriantly fertile and abundant wilderness. It was a wonderland of diversity and cornucopia of plenty.

As described by California historian Malcolm Margolin and others, ships entering Golden Gate Bay sailed past enormous pods of whales and flashing waves of smelt. There were so many salmon in the straits that you could just about walk across the water on their backs. Vast flocks of geese and ducks blackened the sky, mingling with abundant eagles and giant condors.

As the Europeans made their way inland, they paused to rest in verdant open lawns amid wide groves of large oak trees. For miles and miles, it could only be compared to a park, as if planted like a fine English garden. There was little undergrowth except for the thriving herbs, wild oats, and high grasses. The huge herds of grazing elk and antelope seemed tame, lazing curiously on sunny hillsides. As the newcomers moved on, they encountered an entire plain covered with giant swatches of rose, yellow, scarlet, orange, and blue flowers in distinct communities. Patches of a single color ranged a mile or more across.

To the Europeans, this was obviously a wilderness, the natural state of grace of a blissfully undisturbed land. The numerous Indians living there were environmentally inconsequential, living freely off the fat of the land. The newcomers could not have been more wrong.

If you leave forests alone, you do not get forests that look like natural parks, or huge meadows, or endless expanses of flowers. It was actually a vast cultivated landscape carefully tended by the indigenous peoples living there. They understood that human beings are a keystone species on whom many others depend. They were consciously and superbly managing a coevolutionary landscape, deliberately affecting the health and well-being of the greater web of life and in turn enhancing their own place within it.

The California Native Americans knew that when a certain wren began to tweet, the salmon would be there in four days. They knew that when the elderberry ripened in the fall, you could start collecting shellfish again. They knew that everything was connected in a vast circle of continuous creation, and they knew how to play their part in a way that enriched the web of life for themselves and future generations.

The early Europeans frowned on the Natives' "addiction" to burning the land—at certain times the air looked like LA smog—and they soon made laws against it. But it turned out the natives had good reason to burn. It cleared the understory and removed undesirable trees, thus preventing catastrophic large-scale forest fires and revitalizing the overall health of the forest. Burning fostered certain kinds of grasses with large seeds that were useful. It improved the habitat for game. Burning at a certain time of year was good for the acorns people liked to eat because it prevented oak moths from hatching and infesting the trees.

As Margolin recounts, even up until the 1920s the Bay Area was legendary for its mammoth beds of clams and oysters. The Coast Miwok people would still come, gather the clams, and sell them. When the state wildlife managers took over, they clamped down and radically limited their harvest. The Coast Miwok protested, saying that taking the clams was keeping the beds alive. They told government officials, "It's because the clams know we're coming that they're growing, and we have a long relationship with them." The government said, "No, you're depleting this resource." They banned them from coming anymore.

Within five years, only one of eleven clam beds was still viable and alive. The officials did a scientific study and found that the act of taking these clams out, especially the larger ones, was aerating the beds and making room for others, like weeding a garden. Their study concluded that what they thought was a wild resource was actually a cultivated garden kept alive and well by sophisticated caretakers.

Early Native Americans had a widespread system of rules and regulations, and they recognized some limited land ownership. The thinking was that owning something brought with it a responsibility to the land and provided an incentive for moderation. You'd show restraint, because you knew you would have to come back to it next year.

They also had shared lands. The fishing season was regulated up and down entire river drainages across many cultures speaking different languages. These were in effect the first international fishing treaties. If you broke these kinds of laws, there were grave penalties—and spiritual consequences as well.

As Margolin has said, "It's really important to get a view of humanity as not living apart from the world or destructive to it. People by their way of living can actually be a blessing to the world. But to be a human being, you need more than one generation to take this stuff up."

Native American restoration ecologist Dennis Martinez observes that because human beings are a keystone species in natural ecosystems, when they're removed—when the top predator is absent—certain things begin to unravel within that system and fall apart. He says, "It's not just top-down—it's also bottom-up. Everything is in a cycle. Everything is connected in circles and intersecting in all dimensions. All levels of energy flow through every ecosystem."

He cautions against romanticizing the accomplishments of First Peoples, who also made serious mistakes and paid the price. The extinction of numerous large animals—what biologist E. O. Wilson called "the large, the slow and the tasty"—that occurred many thousands of years ago is testament to how easy it is to disrupt the balance.

Humility is our constant companion as we realize how little we really know and how little control we have over an unpredictable and incomprehensibly complex living environment. Restoration is largely a lost art and a new science, and we have never before faced the scale of destruction now confronting us. As Martinez points out, "That means that not only do we have to go back to Traditional Ecological Knowledge (TEK), but we need to bring in Western science too. We don't heal the land. We intervene no more than necessary to allow natural processes to heal the land. It's about relationship. You have to love the natural world—the plants and the animals—and take care of them as you would your own family. It's about our responsibility as human beings to participate every day in the re-creation of the Earth. It just goes on and on."

As we face a host of unnatural disasters caused by centuries and millennia of land mismanagement and the absence of a land ethic, one of our best hopes is that today we have both traditional wisdom and modern science to help us learn again to lovingly and patiently attune our hands to the heartbeat of the land, teaching us anew the ancient ways. Beckoning us onward is the reenchantment of Earth.

TWENTY-FIRST-CENTURY BLUES

The Dim Ages

I've got the twenty-first-century blues.

As the new millennium kicks into its second unstable decade, threats of terrorist attacks with weapons of mass destruction continue to stalk our national security. But in fact, perhaps the greatest security menace clouding the millennial dawn is going to be the deteriorating environment. Or so say some CIA analysts.

They warn that the wars of the future—the *near* future—will be fought over water, not oil. Water tables are sinking faster than the promise of economic growth—and unlike oil, there's no substitute for water. They caution against global pandemics and new deadly infectious diseases. They see tidal waves of desperate environmental refugees on the horizon. They anticipate widespread political destabilization and cascading financial crises.

The skid marks of industrial civilization are everywhere to be seen. Let's take the scenic route.

These are biblical times indeed, but it's no longer a miracle to walk on the water of the Sea of Galilee. Its level has dropped to the lowest ever recorded. Over in Mexico City, an aquifer plummeting eleven feet a year is making the famed National Cathedral "bend and droop like a reflection in a funhouse mirror."

Which might remind locals up in Alaska of their "drunken trees" sagging into the once-upon-a-permafrost. Alaska got ahead of the global warming curve. Roads are buckling. Rupturing sewage lines are spawning a return to the old reliable outhouse. But even citizens grateful for those oil royalties are speechless at the death of *millions of* acres of spruce forest, the biggest loss ever of trees to insects in North America. Nobody much wants to talk about the thawing tundra beneath the eight-hundred-mile trans-Alaska oil pipeline either.

By as early as 1999, the hottest decade in a century-and-a-half of record keeping had included December grass mowing at the New York Botanical Garden and massive floods ravaging Europe. Moaned one of Prague's fifty thousand evacuees, "We were prepared for a hundred-year flood, but this was a thousand-year flood." Then again, those epic forest fires sure could've used some of that rain that year in the twenty-nine U.S. states strangled by long-term drought. Global weirding was kicking in, with each passing year setting new records—not the kind of record book you want to be in.

Even Rip Van Bush's EPA woke up to smell the climate change. Yup—it's for real and it's caused by fossil fools. But hey, now that we've waited so long, there's nothing to do about it. It's inevitable, get used to it, and say *adios* to Rocky Mountain meadows and coral reefs. This is about economic growth.

Of course the insurance industry wasn't buying it. The global giant Munich Re estimated the price tag for global warming at some $300 billion a year a ways down the buckling pike.

But for now the climate suits West Nile virus just fine. In the blink of an eye, it hitched a ride with mosquitoes up to the northern hemisphere and clear across the country, so we sprayed the little suckers good. Problem is, when researchers did an autopsy of dead birds in New York, they found lots more birds dying from the pesticides than from the virus.

And now it turns out that just when we thought we had the ozone hole licked, new research shows it's a prodigious contributor to global warming, and the UV rays it lets through are already mutating nasty new viruses we've never seen before in those algal blooms off the coasts, the ones that are feeding on all that abundance of sewage and farm runoff. But I dare you to prove the connection, because it could also be from also the millions of pounds of antibiotics downstream from those factory farms and giant fish farms.

So let's not jump to conclusions. The first-ever government report on pharmaceutical drugs in the water said those antibiotics are competing for ecological shelf space with prodigious amounts of hormones. Chalk that up to the estrogen-replacement industry and its once-formidable marketing department. And then there are all the other meds now showing up in the majority of U.S. streams that are tested—anticholesterol drugs, antidepressants, chemotherapy agents, Viagra, and caffeine—*lots* of caffeine.

Maybe this pharmaceutical pollution has something to do with all those intersex fish. Seems to be feminizing them, and I don't mean that in a Robert Bly kind of way. Alligators with shrinking penises, human sperm counts dropping, about half the men at risk from a cluster of new reproductive disorders menacingly called "testicular dysgenesis syndrome."

Same deal in water taps from the bayous to Berlin. Pretty soon those profit-maximizing drug companies will be inserting special charges in your water bill.

Which doesn't sound fishy if you're Percy Schmeiser, the Canadian farmer who got busted by Monsanto for illegally growing its genetically engineered canola without a license. The thing is, he didn't plant it. Must've volunteered when some seed fell off a farmer's truck, or pollen drifted over and contaminated his fields. After Percy won a couple of rounds in the Canadian courts, Monsanto settled for a pittance and headed off to sue farmers across the Midwest and Canada. This game of toxic trespassing tag enlarged their sputtering sales with a captive market. Talk about going to seed.

But of course convincing courts is a far cry from convincing animals. Cows put into fields of genetically modified (GM) corn stubble wouldn't touch the stuff. One farmer said his cows just waltzed right through large fields of Monsanto's GM Roundup Ready corn to break through a fence to eat some good old conventional corn. An Iowa farmer swore that rabbits, squirrels, and mice wouldn't go near GM corn even when he left it in an open bin in the barn. Ravenously omnivorous raccoons gave the cold shoulder to warm fields of GM corn and trucked down the road a piece to feast on that premium-priced organic corn. Maybe animal testing isn't always a bad thing after all.

Which brings us to some other hot potatoes, the spuds in the Moscow farmers markets where Geiger counter–toting officials were confiscating radioactive produce, seeing as Chernobyl's only four hundred miles down the road. Or the three Japanese nuclear plants that temporarily closed after the companies admitted falsifying safety data about cracks in their aging reactors. But folks just didn't believe the government when it said there's no relationship between aging and accidents. At least not until a tsunami opened their minds.

It's a terrible thing when trust in government breaks down. Just ask the guards at U.S. nuclear reactors. They know why half the country's nuke plants have failed mock terrorist attacks. What do you expect with wages the same as those of custodians? And those floodlights management installed—heck, they shine on the guards instead of on the terrorists! But hey, it's just those whining workers again—I mean, where is Homer Simpson when you really need him?

Homer's probably gorging himself on junk food, and calling in sick with the 76 million Americans who get food poisoning every year from a food supply more dangerous than it was fifty years ago. Or maybe he's at Weight Watchers with the 60 percent of Americans who are overweight or obese. All that super-size fat and sugar has gotta be what's behind the diabetes epidemic, too.

Unless the scientists who now say air pollution causes diabetes are right. So we'll have to study that two-mile-thick brown cloud hovering over south Asia, which might help explain the half-million people dying from respiratory problems in India every year. Or what about that bubble-gum-pink haze showering record amounts of pollutants over Hong Kong? Not great for business either. It's hurting tourism and making Honda shrink-wrap its cars so they don't all look that same weird yellow color in the showroom.

It's enough to make a government delete all this anxiety-inducing data off official websites, and plug up the Freedom of Information Act. I mean, what if it fell into the wrong hands! Could be dangerous. Italy's former prime minister, media magnate Silvio Berlusconi, had the right idea. His company bought up nearly all the country's TV stations. No news is good news. He must've taken a pointer from Bush Lite when he quipped, "You can fool some of the people all of the time—those are the ones to concentrate on."

It's got to send you lunging for the Prozac. Lots of Wall Street traders did, even before that 1990s dot-com market bubble burst into a national recession. Jim Cramer, the TV financial pundit and former hedge fund manager, knows firsthand why those bubble-headed Wall Streeters never saw it coming: "Prozac and all those other drugs banish the 'This is the end of the world' thoughts, which means you are not as anxious as you should be about an obvious downside." Hey, things could be worse. At least he's not one of the 3 billion people living on less than $2 a day. Let 'em eat placebos. Which are proven to often work about as well anyway.

But if Prozac doesn't make you feel more secure, try war. Take out Iraq! More cheap oil for our national security. So what if improving fuel efficiency by 2.7 miles a gallon would eliminate the need for Gulf oil? Grab the sunscreen and relax. Relax environmental standards, that is, and get with the program. National security. Economic growth. Banish those "this-is-the-end-of-the-world" thoughts.

Hmmmm. Drunken trees. Sinking cathedrals. Thousand-year floods. Intersex fish. Testicular dysgenesis. Financial meltdowns. Petrowars. Climate chaos. End-of-the-world thoughts.

Welcome to the twenty-first-century blues.

I don't know about you, but I don't feel real secure. Neither do Gregory Foster and Louise Wise, formerly at the National Defense University in Washington DC, who concluded, "The environment is the most transnational of all transnational issues. It respects neither national boundaries, nor traditional conceptions of sovereignty and territorial integrity."

They say we must confront two questions of fundamental strategic import: whether humanity's role is to be nature's master, servant, or steward; and whether nature's commons, in affecting us all, demand sustained collective international attention and tending. They envision the military becoming an environmental exemplar, turning its attention to disaster relief, ecological restoration, and the vigorous enforcement of environmental law. They see the biggest factor in the environment's future as the universalization of democracy. The environment demands global, multilateral cooperation.

We simply do not know how close we are to a flash mob of tipping points. Precaution is the byword, changing from managing harm to preventing it. The precautionary principle being adopted around the world echoes grandma's time-tested common sense, better safe than sorry, an ounce of prevention is worth a pound of cure, look before you leap. As precautionary maven and executive director of the Science and Environmental Health Network Carolyn Raffensperger has said, maybe we should call it the "Duh Principle."

"What were they thinking?" future generations will ask. The book *Why Smart People Can Be So Stupid* suggests that smartness is *not* the opposite of stupidity. The opposite of stupidity is wisdom, defined as the ability to apply knowledge to achieve the common good. Duh.

One antidote to the twenty-first-century blues is a Declaration of Interdependence. We have a pretty good idea how to lighten our footfall, by 90 percent or more. The enterprise of restoration promises an unparalleled economic boom and global jobs creation, starting with a Marshall Plan for clean energy and food security.

Ecological medicine teaches us that human health security depends on restoring the health of our ecosystems.

Genuine social security hinges on mutual aid, community, and cultural diversity.

The Gulf war to focus our efforts on is to end the gulf between rich and poor.

This is where to find *sustainable* security.

Time is of the essence. The worst failure we could have is a failure of the imagination.

THE CLASH OF CIVILIZATIONS

Disposability or Sustainability?

*Y*ou have to figure the Force is with you when Yoda gets on board. In this case, Yoda is the Pentagon's term of endearment for Andrew Marshall, a revered military oracle who headed up an elite military think tank that envisions future threats to national security. After reading a 2002 National Academy of Sciences report on global warming, the octogenarian sage decided that indeed the sky is falling. He commissioned two master futurists to produce an analysis.

Their report, titled *An Abrupt Climate Change Scenario and Its Implications for United States National Security*, draws on historical research showing that dramatic climate change can be very sudden, occurring in a matter of a decade or two. This has occurred frequently in the distant past and at least twice that we know of in Earth's "recent" history—about 8,000 and 11,500 brief years ago.

The report laid out several possible scenarios, ranging from worse-than-we-ever-imagined to unthinkable. By 2020 we could face megadroughts and megafloods, mass starvation in many regions, hordes of desperate ecological refugees, and war over scarce resources of food, water, and energy. Or, the report said, if climate change is really abrupt, the world could melt down in a period of three to five years, then flip the switch into an ice age. Think snow for hundreds of years on end.

Yoda concluded that the force of global warming is definitely with us. Call it actionable intelligence. So he decided to do an end run around the political top brass by leaking the unclassified report to *Fortune* magazine. His hope was that the business world would get the picture and move decisively to alter the course of civilization. Pentagon spokesmen later confirmed that indeed they had not bothered to pass Marshall's report on to his higher-ups in the Defense Department or White House.

The report demurely suggested that "alternative fuels, greenhouse gas emissions controls and conservation efforts are worthy endeavors." It concluded by posing the alternative: "Abrupt climate change is likely to stretch carrying capacity well beyond its already precarious limits. Disruption and conflict may well be endemic features of life. . . . Every time there is a choice between starving and raiding, humans raid."

Some choice.

As reporter Andrew Zaitchik summed up the Pentagon's response, "The Department of Defense and Energy have recently installed photovoltaic panels atop the enormous building's five-sided roof. And if a solar-powered Death Star isn't the perfect symbol of humanity's two possible futures, then I don't know what is."

Indeed there's a clash of civilizations, but in this case it is not between Islam and the West, or tradition and modernism. It's between a disposable civilization and a sustainable civilization. We have created a civilization that is a suicide bomb. We need to start disarming it right away.

Einstein famously said that "God does not play dice with the universe," but we are. All bets are off when you're gaming the Earth. The house always wins. And the awful truth is that global warming is just the tip of the melting iceberg. We are running evolution in reverse, shattering the very mirror of nature that can show us who we are and how to live in this place in a way that lasts. The jagged shards are so dreadful to contemplate that most people don't want to go there. The problem is, we're already there. Denial and neglect are only going to seal the deal.

As painful as it is, it's imperative that we grasp what's already happening on the ground in order to shift our course immediately. Here's a symbolic fractal of the times. We won't linger.

One of the best ways to see what's happening is to watch the animals. In Scotland's northern isles, home to some of the world's richest bird life, ornithologists called 2004 the "year without young." Birds by the millions did not hatch eggs, if they laid them at all. This unprecedented nesting failure was caused by starvation from the overnight disappearance of the small silvery sand eels the birds feed on. The ocean warmed, the sand eels went north, and a massive ecosystem crashed that had functioned stably for a very long time.

The oceans themselves are becoming increasingly acidic from absorbing all that CO_2 from the bonfire of the fossil fuels. The more acidic environment is contributing to the decline of coral reefs, shellfish, and plankton, the basis for nearly all marine life.

All over England (as well as in many other places, including the United States), some wildlife seems to be exhibiting a feminization process that could interrupt evolution itself. An estimated third of the male fish tested in some British rivers were found to be growing female reproductive tissues and organs. Seals, sea otters, peregrine falcons, and honeybees are among the species that may be heading for what reporter Mark Townsend calls a "uni-sex" existence, which could mark a beeline for eventual extinction. The culprits are gender-benders, endocrine-disrupting chemicals that scramble the body's subtle hormonal growth signals and that are now pervasive globally.

Pollution and ecological disruption are also triggering bizarre behavior in animals, reported the *New Scientist*: "Hyperactive fish, stupid frogs, fearless mice, and seagulls that fall over." Not to mention the fact that increasing numbers of animals in some species no longer seem to know how to mate, parent, build nests, learn, forage, or dodge predators.

People seem to have forgotten that we're animals, too. Do the math. All life is connected, and we're in this together.

As the big wheels keep on turning, the environment will increasingly set the agenda. Nature is deregulating human affairs faster than a lobbyist can buy a politician, and we are so not ready. Just ask New Orleans, Haiti, Fukushima, or the flooded river valleys of Pakistan. We face a perfect storm of environmental degradation and the ongoing collapse of a rickety, misbegotten infrastructure that in most cases is provoking the very conditions that will topple it.

What makes matters especially confusing at this crucial juncture is the toxic political cocktail of delusion and deceit. It's one thing to be blind to the fact that we are one with the environment. It's another to cover it up. For the eight catastrophic years of George W. Bush's Dim Ages, the legacy of which continues to haunt us, we faced arguably the most secretive, deceptive, and crooked political administration in American history. But make no mistake: They were also true believers. It was faith-based politics of delusional grade, and it whacked the world with the hangover from hell.

So-called "sound science" has been the sound of one hand clapping. The suppression of science for ideological and political ends in the United States reached such epic dimensions so as to drive sixty of the world's most influential scientists, including twenty Nobel laureates, to go public with documented charges of distortion, misrepresentation, and outright lying. Such a broad-based response to a government's manipulation of science policy by normally disinterested, apolitical scientific professionals is exceedingly rare.

Hey, faith is great. But as they say in the world of science, "In God we trust. All others must provide data." At this pivotal moment in the fate of the Earth, we cannot afford anything less than a clear-eyed view of how the world actually works, as best we can glean it.

As ecological reality intrudes thunderously on human delusion, it's clear we're dealing not only with ideological extremists looped on belief systems; they're also jacked up on greed. There is a dark wind howling across these dis-United States. It's polarizing us with one hand and picking our pockets with the other. A more faithful characterization would be, "Let us prey"—on the public, that is.

Cleaning up the environment depends on cleaning up politics. Democracy is key to restoration. In words often attributed to the Italian fascist dictator Benito Mussolini: "Fascism should more accurately be called corporatism, because it is the merger of corporations and the state." To achieve real democracy, we need to enforce the separation of corporations and the state.

Perhaps the greatest weapon of mass destruction is corporate economic globalization. Its purported benefits, too, are more based on theology than fact—an article of faith that is discrediting itself as much of the world becomes ever more impoverished and ravaged, even as some regions do become more prosperous.

We stand on the edge of a vast historical discontinuity in our most fundamental relationship with nature and each other. It's going to be a long way home. Educator David W. Orr reminds us of this: "In Irish folklore, the salmon is regarded as the wisest of creatures because it knows how to find its way home. That, in a way, is our challenge. Can we find our way back to a future in which our best traditions, highest values and a sense of connection with place and posterity prevail?"

Biomimicry expert Janine Benyus puts it this way:

> The criterion of success is that you keep yourself alive and you keep your offspring alive. But it's not your offspring—it's your offspring's offspring's offspring ten thousand years from now. Because you can't be there to take care of that offspring, the only thing you can do is to take care of the place that takes care of your offspring. That's why the one nonnegotiable policy that we need to write into law is that life creates conditions conducive to life.

There is a great awakening around the globe today. Unprecedented numbers of people are affirming that our destiny is inextricably tied to the well-being of the web of life. But as the worldwide movement for restoration gains traction, we will increasingly confront the relentless demons of rationalization. They will tell us, "We can't get there from here. We need to go slower. We need to stick with what we've got or face economic ruin." But we cannot compromise on what is non-negotiable from nature's point of view. That is sound science. That is sound policy and economics.

We, too, have a preemptive strategy. It's called precaution, preempting harm before it happens or can happen again. In German, the word for the precautionary principle, *Vorsorgeprinzip*, means "forecaring" or caring into the future. That is our charge.

Precaution also engenders a profound sense of humility at how little we know. As the Native American restoration ecologist Dennis Martinez observes, "Indigenous people have recognized that you can't control the environment to the extent humanity is trying to do without serious repercussions. So ethics have been developed which teach us that, if we ignore the needs of our relatives in the natural world, we will suffer serious repercussions. It's no accident that tricksters like Coyote and Raven are often the creators in tribal stories in North America, because it's the nature of the universe to be real iffy. You work with chaos, you work with change, you work with the unpredictable, and you work with humility. Restoration is a community-based intergenerational endeavor. It is more a process than a product."

Perhaps our greatest faculty as human beings is our ability to reinvent culture rapidly. Around the world today people are spontaneously spawning a culture dedicated to creating conditions conducive to life. It reflects the unique convergence of the global peace movement, the global justice movement, and the global environmental and health movements. This convergence has never happened before. It marks a historic turning point in human civilization.

The brilliance of the group mind is on the loose. People everywhere are stepping into the breach with real solutions and the social strategies to allow these solutions to take root. It's a culture of restoration, of reconciliation, of healing.

Ecologists say the surest way to heal an ecosystem is to connect it to more of itself, and this movement is rapidly connecting up a globally decentralized nervous system. The environment is the ultimate transnational issue, and solutions on the ground are poised to spread worldwide at the speed of text messaging. But here in the United States, we have a very special responsibility both to our own country and to the world because, for good or ill, our actions make an outsize impact.

David W. Orr reminds us that the framers of the Constitution never imagined the destruction of the biosphere—"extermination without representation," he calls it. "No good argument," he says, "can be made for the right of one generation to deprive subsequent generations of the ecological requisites for the pursuit of life, liberty and the pursuit of happiness. Constitutional rights in such conditions would be worth little more than legal entitlement to an apartment in a demolished building."

Orr has proposed a constitutional amendment guaranteeing the right to a healthy environment in the recognition that we are trustees poised between our forebears and posterity, that we are one species in one web of life. The American Revolution is a work in progress.

Even in these darkest of times—no, especially in these darkest of times—we gather to celebrate life. Some call it "crazy wisdom." As Tom Robbins writes:

> Crazy wisdom is the wisdom that evolves when one, while refusing to avert one's gaze from the sorrows and injustices of the world, insists on joy in spite of everything. Ancient Egyptians believed that when a person died, the gods immediately placed his or her heart in one pan of a set of scales. In the other pan was a feather. If there was imbalance, if the heart of the deceased weighed more than the feather, he or she was denied admittance to the afterworld. Only the lighthearted were deemed advanced enough to merit immortality.

Once we held an evening roundtable on ecological medicine at the Bioneers conference. A midwife got up from the audience to speak. She said that she viewed the state of the world through the lens of her work. There comes a moment during labor when a woman knows she cannot possibly draw another excruciating breath—cannot endure even one more agonizing contraction. Right then, said the midwife, she knows the baby is about to be born.

The baby is being born. These are birth pains. Keep the faith.

HONEY, WE
SHRUNK THE PLANET

Regime Change and Resilience Thinking

*T*he nature of nature is change. Sometimes it hurtles into fast-forward, tripping radical shifts. Think of it as nature's regime change. For the first time, people are causing it on a planetary scale.

Andrew Revkin reported in the *New York Times* that "the physical Earth is increasingly becoming what the human species makes of it. The accelerating and intensifying impact of human activities is visibly altering the planet, requiring ever more frequent redrawing not only of political boundaries, but of the shape of Earth's features themselves."

Mick Ashworth, former editor-in-chief of the annual *Times Comprehensive Atlas of the World*, said his staff of fifty cartographers updated their databases every *three and a half minutes*. Commented the editor, "We can literally see environmental disasters unfolding before our eyes."

Environmental disasters are almost always human disasters as well. Satellite pictures of Myanmar over the past few decades have recorded the displacement of over three thousand villages of the indigenous Karen, Kachin, and other peoples, dislodging a half million people. The main culprit is the corporate hunger for oil and gas, backed by the ruling murderous military junta (which mercifully seemed to soften its grip on power in 2012).

Google Earth can leave you google-eyed. An overrun resource base is visibly shrinking at the same time our population keeps growing. Honey, we shrunk the planet. The bottom line, of course, is that we're living beyond our means. Nearly two-thirds of the life-support services provided to us by nature are in decline worldwide and the pace is quickening. We can't count on the ability of the planet's ecosystems to sustain future generations. This is new territory.

The big wheels of ecological governance are turning. "Regime shift" is the technical term some ecologists use—for instance, when the climate flips from one state to another. It can be irreversible, at least on a human time frame. These evolutionary exclamation points unleash powerful forces of destruction and creation, collapse and renewal. During these cycles of large-scale creative destruction, we do have a sort of compass. As Charles Darwin observed, "It is not the strongest of the species that survive, nor the most intelligent, but the ones most responsive to change."

Change is not linear, and sudden shifts sometimes remake the world in the blink of an eye. We know we're approaching mysterious thresholds that mark the tipping points of ecological regime change, and we may have already crossed some. The closer we get to each threshold, the less it takes to push the system over the edge, where the degree of damage will be exponentially greater. Societies slide into crisis when slammed by multiple shocks or stressors at the same time. Climate change is propelling both natural and human systems everywhere toward their tipping points.

When huge shocks transform the landscape, structures and institutions crumble, releasing tremendous amounts of bound-up energy and resources for renewal and reorganization. Novelty emerges. These times belong to those who learn, innovate, and adapt. Small changes can have big influences. It's a period of creativity, freedom, and transformation.

The name of the game is resilience. It means the capacity of both human and ecological systems to absorb disturbance and still retain their basic function and structure. Resilience does *not* mean just bouncing back to business-as-usual. It means assuring the very *ability to get back*. But if ecological regime change happens, resilience means having sufficient capacity to transform to meet the new management. A network of ecologists and social scientists called the Resilience Alliance outlined some of the rules of the road in their book *Resilience Thinking*.

The first principle of resilience thinking is systems thinking: It's all connected, from the web of life to human systems—"You can only solve the whole problem," says Huey Johnson of the Resource Renewal Institute. Manage environmental and human systems as one system. Taking care of nature means taking care of people, and taking care of people means taking care of nature. Look for systemic solutions that address multiple problems at once. Watch for seeds of new solutions that emerge with changing conditions.

Resilience thinking means abandoning command-and-control approaches. We're not remotely in control of the big wheels of ecological governance or complex human systems. Greater decentralization can provide backup against the inevitable failure of centralized command-and-control structures. Think decentralized power grids, more localized food systems, and the Internet. Redundancies are good fail-safe mechanisms, not the waste portrayed by thinking focused on industrial efficiency.

The heart of resilience is diversity. Damaged ecosystems rebound to health when they have sufficient diversity. So do societies. It's not just a diversity of players; it's "response diversity," the myriad adaptive strategies for responding to myriad challenges. Each one does it slightly differently with specialized traits that can win the day, depending on which curveball comes at you. Diverse approaches improve the odds. Diverse cultures and ideas enrich society's capacity to survive and thrive.

Ecological governance is also operating on much grander time frames than quarterly reports and midterm elections. Think dozens, hundreds, even thousands of years. Sustainability means staying in the game for the long haul.

We know some other keys to resilience.

- Build community and social capital. Resilience resides in enduring relationships and networks that hold cultural memory the same way seeds regenerate a forest after a fire.
- Empower local communities to solve their own problems. Governance usually works best when it's closest to the ground and includes all stakeholders across all levels.
- Beware of systems being too tightly connected, because one shock to a system can cause multiple ones to crash at once.
- And above all—learn, experiment, and innovate.

The one non-negotiable is to face our vulnerabilities clearly and collaboratively. Windows of opportunity are finite and fleeting. As Yogi Berra said, "I knew I was going to take the wrong train, so I left early."

Fortunately the climate is changing in more ways than one. A starburst of creativity is also warming the globe with what ecological designer John Todd calls "human ingenuity wedded to the wisdom of the wild." With any luck, we may be able to avoid catastrophic ecological regime change by embracing societal regime change.

Some of the most inspiring models are the National Green Plans well under way in the Netherlands, New Zealand, Sweden, Singapore, and the European Union. Holland has led the way. The Dutch National

Environmental Policy Plan made sustainability and environmental recovery a national goal. Since its inception in 1989, it has achieved a formidable 70 percent of its mission. This new societal regime aligns business with biology and the state with the public good.

The Dutch took the solve-the-whole-problem approach and had strong political leadership. In 1989 Queen Beatrix used her traditional Christmas Eve speech to appeal to the nation. She reported that—although the Netherlands had some of the best environmental regulations in the world—scientists were warning her of the real possibility there would be no Dutch great-grandchildren. In a country where 27 percent of the country lies below sea level and holds 60 percent of the population, the threat of rising seas from global warming is up close and personal. The Green Queen's speech precipitated a political sea change.

The Dutch mobilized around a bold goal: *total environmental quality recovery in twenty-five years*. They welcomed new ideas. They built on the successes of others, saving loads of time and money. They generated rigorous transparent data unpolluted by special interests. They've made it freely available to the world because no country can do it alone.

But the process really kicked in only after business got on board and took the lead. Fate lent a hand. Following the collapse of the Soviet Union, some Eastern European nations were eager to establish market economies. They asked a few key Dutch business leaders to advise them on how they achieved the excellence of Dutch public education, health, and housing, all within a robust business climate.

Upon arrival, the Dutch business leaders literally could not breathe from the out-of-control pollution left by an unaccountable one-party state. Seeing children condemned to grow up in these bereft conditions vaporized their opposition to independent government regulation.

They returned to Holland with a surprising proposal: Have government set the standards, and let business figure out how to achieve them. While business proved pivotal for the first step in the national plan, government became the key player. Together they developed the twenty-five-year plan, as well as annual plans that report on progress and challenges. If business fails to meet the specific voluntary goals, government will intervene with mandatory controls. To guarantee transparency and accountability, the government funded environmental NGOs as watchdogs to transmit their findings to the media and the public.

The European Union, representing over 500 million citizens in twenty-seven nations, has begun to adopt some of the same approaches.

While The Netherlands and other European governments do at times backslide in the pace of their environmental commitments depending on which parties are in power, there's a broad societal and political consensus on the need to achieve sustainability.

"What planet are we on?" you might wonder from here in the Wild West of Western civilization. Isn't it time for a U.S. National Green Plan? We have a golden opportunity to regenerate our waning economy at the same time as we seriously repair environmental degradation and rampant social injustices. We're a brittle superpower bedeviled by an aging infrastructure so decrepit the American Society of Civil Engineers gives it a pitiable grade of D. We're ill prepared to deal with disasters, especially the natural and industrial disasters that present greater threats to the nation than terrorism. Our declining public health and educational systems rank among the lowest in developed countries. Even before the 2008 economic crash, real wages had been stagnant or declining for decades. Extremes of wealth and poverty rival the Gilded Age of the robber barons, while the military economy is fast bankrupting our future.

The reinvention of a green economy can begin to solve our bundle of economic and social ills simultaneously. We can create abundant jobs, prosperity, equity, and hope. Our new declaration of independence is from fossil fuels and imperial entanglements. We can make the urgent transition to renewable energy at the same time we renew the higher angels of what it means to be an American.

In fact, the seeds are sprouting everywhere. In the absence of federal leadership, large numbers of cities and states are banding together to lead exactly these kinds of changes. It's a metatrend called *new localism*. Political power is decentralizing to effectively address bioregional realities of people and place.

Political boundaries are also morphing. A historic convergence of the environmental and social justice movements is crystallizing in the shared recognition that we can achieve environmental well-being only when we achieve social justice. The environmental community is increasingly embracing social justice as central to its mission. Indigenous communities, our old-growth cultures, are providing visionary leadership as guardians of their "original instructions" for how to live in peace with the land and each other.

Environmental justice pathfinder Carl Anthony has suggested that low-income communities and communities of color are the environmental canaries in the coal mine, and that addressing the deep injustices responsible benefits everyone. The data support his conclusion. When hazards between groups are lower—in other words, the disparities of environmental pollution and harms are less between communities—the overall environmental risk declines. The ability to put hazards in some-one else's backyard results in creating more hazards for society as a whole.

Historically when we talk about sense of place, we're usually imagin-ing an ancient redwood forest, a thriving coral reef, a desert at dawn. But for the first time in history, half the world's people now live in cities. As currently organized, these cities are unsustainable, but how we transform them could be the make-it-or-break-it factor for the world's environment. Urban landscapes of poverty, violence, drug abuse, and illness are increasingly divided into zones of have-nots and have-a-lots. Low-income inner cities predominantly populated by people of color are the first to be written off as sacrifice zones of environmental degra-dation and social disintegration.

As author Paul Hawken observes,

> It is critical to realize that underlying the extermination of nature is the marginalization of human beings. If we are to save what is wild, what is irreparable and majestic in nature, then we will ironically have to turn to each other and take care of all the human beings here on Earth. There is no boundary that will protect an environment from a suffering humanity.

The divide is compounded by inequities in the distribution of toxicity in the environment that is manifesting in radical behavioral effects. Though it's certainly not the only factor, an interesting recent study draws a possible direct correlation between exposure to lead in early childhood and national violent crime rates. Lead poisoning associated with the widespread use of leaded gasoline after World War II corresponded closely with the rise in juvenile crime in the 1950s. The problem was especially acute among children in the inner city, where lead paint was common. The unexpected decline of violent crime in the mid-1990s closely tracked the generation growing up after leaded gasoline was banned. However, universally pervasive industrial chemicals, including endocrine disrupters, are associated with behavioral disorders such as aggression.

As Anthony points out, the truth is that, although low-income communities and communities of color are the canaries in the coal mine, we're all subject to the now globally distributed sauce of poisons.

The wounds are more than physical and environmental. Entire generations brutalized by ceaseless war and privation are profoundly traumatized in much of the world. Globalization is dislocating a permanent force of unemployable young men and women who see no future. Street wars are raging. Gangs have globalized from El Salvador to Los Angeles, from Russia to Rio, Paris, Lagos, and Omaha. A global prison-industrial complex bent on punishment only binds the ties tighter and provides universities of crime, and what has been an urban phenomenon is now spilling out into the countryside as well.

As Ernest Hemingway wrote, "The world breaks everyone, but some people become strong in the broken places." Studies about social resilience—why some people recover from trauma and abuse—show that perhaps the most important factor is reaching out to helpers and mentors. Often these allies are not the immediate family, but aunties or neighbors or teachers. The more help a person gets, the more they're encouraged to keep reaching out. Social ties save lives.

This next wave of environmental consciousness embraces civil rights, social justice, and environmental health to heal our wounds. It is led by courageous visionaries who know what the solutions are because they have lived the life. They know that the work of restoration is necessarily the work of peace and justice.

Majora Carter, founder of Sustainable South Bronx, has taken resilience thinking to the streets. She grew up in the very tough neighborhood of Hunts Point in New York City's notorious South Bronx during some of its roughest years. At the time, it was a poster child for urban disintegration. She had countless gifts that could readily have allowed her to leave it all behind and find success nearly anywhere in any walk of life. Instead, she refused to abandon her neighborhood to the forces of racist neglect, environmental injustice, and entropy. She organized and cajoled and negotiated, and she has had a very substantial impact in a relatively short period of time.

The Sustainable South Bronx project has had exceptional success, creating riverfront parks and a green-roof demonstration project atop its offices. The group is close to achieving one of its main goals, pressuring the city and state to dismantle the underused Sheridan Expressway, a destructive highway right through the heart of the neighborhood, in favor of community-based restoration and a green economic development zone. It's successfully implementing a Bronx Environmental Stewardship Training program as part of the Green the Ghetto project to seed the community with a skilled green-collar workforce that has both a personal and economic stake in the neighborhood's environment. Leaders in the African American community such as Harlem's Peggy Shepard of WE ACT for Environmental Justice, Van Jones (who founded Green For All), and Omar Freilla of the Green Workers Cooperative are effectively organizing around a green economy founded in green-collar justice and the relief of poverty and racial inequality. Networks of networks are getting connected, collaborating, and innovating across divides in unprecedented initiatives to solve the whole problem. From systems thinking to decentralization and authentic diversity, it's resilience in action.

As David W. Orr puts it, "Hopeful people are actively engaged in defying the odds or changing the odds."

A successful U.S. National Green Plan depends on our doing *all* this—together—with respect, justice, and dignity for all people and the circle of life.

The Mayan people call this epic threshold the "Time of No Time." Ohki Siminé Forest, a Canadian wisdom keeper of Mohawk descent who lives and works with the Mayan people in Chiapas, describes the Mayan vision in this way. From here on, we're on Earth time. Mother Earth is shaking to her core. It's a time of madness, disconnection, and hyperindividualism. It's also a time when new energies are coming into the world, when people are growing a new skin.

The Mayan vision says that we in the West will find safe harbor only if we can journey past a wall of mirrors. The mirrors will surely drive us mad—unless we have a strong heart. Some mirrors delude us with an infinity of reflections of our vanity and shadows. Others paralyze us with our terror and rage, feeding an empire that manufactures our fear into resignation.

But the empire has no roots and it's toppling all around us. In this time everyone is called to take a stand. Everyone is called to be a leader.

To get beyond the wall of mirrors, the final challenge is to pass through a tiny door. To do this, we must make ourselves very, very small. To be very humble. Then we must burrow down into the Earth, where indigenous consciousness lives. On the other side is a clear pond. There, for the first time, we'll be able to see our true reflection.

In this Time of No Time, we can go in any direction we want—by dreaming it. Our dreaming can shift the course of the world.

That's our deepest well of resilience.

It's going to be a long and winding trek across generations. We're already making some of the paths others can walk toward the dream, toward our many dreams. Countless more dreamers will blaze luminous new trails. The dreams are already within us. One day we may awaken to find ourselves living in our wildest dreams.

NATURE'S OPERATING INSTRUCTIONS

The True Biotechnologies

*W*hen soil biologist Elaine Ingham started testing for the ecological impacts of genetically modified organisms at her Oregon State University lab in the early 1990s, it looked like a ho-hum affair. Tasked with anticipating their possible effects in the "real world," she examined fourteen species of engineered microorganisms, bacteria, and fungi. None proved capable of surviving in natural habitats. She likened any potential environmental impact to dropping a penguin into LA's La Brea Tar Pits.

Based on that data, the USDA's Animal and Plant Health Inspection Service, which is responsible for setting federal regulatory policy on genetically modified organisms (GMOs), concluded that engineered organisms posed no greater risk than the parent organism.

Then number fifteen arrived. *Klebsiella planticola* is a bacterium that lives in soils everywhere in the world in the root systems of every plant species (It has since been reclassified as *Raoutella planticola*.) It decomposes plant litter. The engineers inserted genetic material from another bacterium to make *Klebsiella* produce alcohol. They wanted to put an end to the postharvest burning of farm fields and create valuable products from the waste. By inoculating field residues, they could alter the biomass to produce 17 percent alcohol content—then sell it for gasohol, cooking food, or cleaning your windows. The remaining sludge would make an organic fertilizer. Not a bad proposition—valuable products from the elimination of waste, and air you can breathe in the fall.

Too good to be true? You bet. You've spread live alcohol-producing *Klebsiella planticola* on your fields and into the plants' root systems where it will produce alcohol. What's the level of alcohol that's toxic to plants? One part per million. The GMO *Klebsiella* produces how much alcohol? Seventeen parts per million. Likely result: drunk, dead plants.

Drunk, dead plants is what Ingham's lab got in every experiment. There are some riparian and wetlands plants in the world with mechanisms for dealing with alcohol production in their root systems. But in the worst-case scenario, we could lose virtually all terrestrial plants. Oops.

As world-renowned geneticist David Suzuki observes, the very nature of science at the cutting edge is that most of our ideas will turn out to be wrong. It's the way science progresses. So why the big rush to apply every incremental insight, as the biotechnology industry relentlessly demands?

The obvious answer is money, honey. But it's more than that. It's a way of seeing the world and how the world works.

Surely John D. Rockefeller never dreamed that making a killing pumping oil in Pennsylvania would one day result in a global cancer pandemic or cause the North Pole to melt. The chemists who first cracked petroleum molecules to release "better living through chemistry" didn't imagine that Teflon would stick to just about everything, especially the molecules in living tissue.

Nuclear scientists failed to predict how their handiwork would catalyze a chain reaction that would indirectly lead to support for a police state to try to stop terrorists from exploding a dirty bomb. Nor did they anticipate that potential terrorists could most easily obtain those nuclear materials from a hospital radiation ward.

Monsanto scientists failed to envision monarch butterflies dropping dead after pollinating its GM corn. Or the genetic pollution of ancient landraces of Mexican corn that hold the precious genetic diversity used by breeders as the first line of defense against mass starvation.

As Andrew Kimbrell, the executive director of the Center for Food Safety, points out, "Technology is legislation." As deeply as the fate of our lives and the planet have been informed by technological decisions made without full disclosure or public consent, you'd think by now we'd understand the history of technology as the nail-biting drama of unforeseen consequences, many of them dreadful. Over and over, the scent of money trumps humility and precaution.

Petrochemicals, nuclear energy, and genetic engineering—the three central technologies of the twentieth century—have proven at least very dangerous and at worst catastrophic. Centralized command-and-control structures, top-down toxic high technologies, and globalized monocultures characterize a dysfunctional civilization at odds with the decentralized intelligence of living systems. We have reached the biological high noon of a losing confrontation with our planetary habitat. We cannot afford any more big mistakes, and we urgently need to clean up the ones we've made.

Techno-utopians say technology will get us out of this technological nightmare. Luddites say technology *is* the nightmare. The dichotomy is a false one. Technology is here to stay, and most people want what it offers, but not the "side effects"—which are actually effects. Where to turn?

The answers are hiding in plain sight. As the biologist Janine Benyus suggests: "When I look at technology these days, I don't say, 'Technology: yes or no?' I ask how well adapted a particular technology is. How well adapted is that product, that process, that policy to life on Earth over the long haul?"

Biomimicry, the design revolution that Benyus terms "innovation inspired by nature," starts with the no-brainer that as human beings, we *are* nature. There is no separation between people and the environment. We *are* the environment. And, says Benyus,

> Our biological elders have been here much longer than we have. Compared to them, we just arrived, and have everything to learn about how to live gracefully on this planet. Bacteria bootstrapped themselves up out of the chaos and in the 3.8 billion years since then, life has learned to do some amazing things. Life has learned to fly, circumnavigate the globe, live at the top of mountains and the bottom of the ocean, lasso solar energy, light up the night, and make miracle materials like skin, horns, hair, and brains. In fact, organisms have done everything we want to do but without guzzling fossil fuels, polluting the planet, or mortgaging their future. In the process of meeting their needs, organisms manage to fertilize the soil, clean the air and water, and mix the right cocktail of atmospheric gasses that life needs to live. What life in ensemble has learned to do is to create conditions conducive to life. And that's what we have to learn too. Luckily, we don't need to make it up. We need only step outside and ask the local geniuses that surround us.

To create conditions conducive to life, nature has operating instructions that Benyus has distilled as "Life's Principles." Life optimizes rather than maximizes—it designs for the good of the whole system, whereas maximizing for just one element skews the overall system. It designs for multiple functions, creating efficiencies. It matches form to function.

Life leverages interdependence by recycling all materials, fostering cooperative relationships, and creating self-organizing systems. Life uses benign manufacturing with "life-friendly" materials, water-based chemistry, and self-assembly.

Life also constantly adapts and evolves. It's keyed to the local and it's responsive. It's resourceful and opportunistic. It uses feedback loops to keep learning and responding. It integrates cyclic processes. It cross-pollinates and mutates. It builds resilience through diversity, decentralization, and redundancy, allowing for failure and building in safeguards to avoid the possibility of crashing the whole system at once.

The principles appear simple. Nature runs on current sunlight. Nature banks on diversity. Nature rewards cooperation. Nature builds from the bottom up. Nature recycles everything. Life creates conditions conducive to life.

Biomimicry seeks to apply "Life's Principles" by studying organisms in the context of local habitat and whole systems embedded at every level of nested ecologies. Rather than viewing them as raw materials or a physical resource, we view them as teachers, mentors, and guides. Instead of their bodies, we want their recipes.

As biomimicry has begun to enter the mainstream, startling examples of applying the genius of nature to human affairs are taking shape. A German company studied the physical design of the immaculate white lotus, which lives in the muck yet whose rough self-cleaning surface sheds dirt readily when wetted. The shape is the key. The company designed a paint that stays clean for five years without sandblasting or detergents. The Ormia fly is being studied for its ability to find crickets, which are master ventriloquists that disguise their location by their chirping. The fly has the biological equivalent of a directional microphone to detect crickets, which may lead to advances in hearing aids. The bathing suits worn by Olympic champion Michael Phelps and the U.S. team were modeled on sharkskin, the most hydrodynamic substance we've yet found.

Indeed, Benyus points out, people are learning to "grow food like a prairie, harness energy like a leaf, weave fibers like a spider, find cures like a chimp, compute like a cell and run a business like a redwood forest. Quieting human cleverness is the first step in biomimicry. Next comes listening, then trying to echo what we hear. This emulating is hard and humbling work. When what we learn improves how we live, we grow grateful, and that leads to the last step in the path: stewardship and caretaking, a practical thanksgiving for what we've learned. The practice of biomimicry requires community, not just with other organisms, but with people in other disciplines."

The basic question of biomimicry—"how would nature do it?"—offers a rich opportunity. Research shows only a 12 percent similarity between the way biology and human technology currently solve problems—in how our design imitates nature's design. Biology solves 95 percent of challenges through the structure and organization of organisms' body parts and behavior. Only 5 percent of organisms manipulate large amounts of energy to achieve their purpose in the way we do.

Jay Harman is one of our most gifted biomimics and a self-described strategic optimist. He brings a new set of eyes to ecological design and clean technology. As a small child in Australia, Jay became a student of the sea. He passed endless hours entranced by the way water moves. He began to notice the way kelp swirled into spiral patterns in turbulent currents and, though you can easily break it with your hands, withstood the extreme stress and did not break. He came to realize that nature's favorite form is the spiral.

> It's easy to think of nature's movements as chaotic, but there is a common shape underlying all of that chaos. The First Peoples of the world all recognized how common spirals are in nature and believed that they were a reflection and a representation of the divine, the Creation, fertility and genius. In fact, the spiral is the most common shape and symbol for the great mystery of life across many ancient traditions.
>
> Now with the benefit of modern science, we can see that these spirals are everywhere, from DNA to particle decay in quantum mechanics to the growth of every living thing. From the atomic level to the very largest structures in our universe, movement wants to follow the same path as the whirlpool that you see when you pull the plug from your bath. It's the path of least resistance.
>
> I saw these beautiful shapes in nature when I was a boy, but I didn't see them as my life's work for many years. I love nature, and I've always loved using tools to fix things—a broken-down bike, a wrecked boat, some neglected land. As a young man, I was happy working in nature in the Fisheries and Wildlife Department in Australia, but felt increasingly frustrated and powerless seeing the destruction of the wilderness and being unable to fix it.

> One day, very depressed about the state of the world, I was walking on the beach and I picked up a spiraling seashell. Suddenly, with a rush, it all came together. I could apply my lifelong fascination with spirals to make more benign tools, and hopefully prove to the world that it is more profitable to protect nature than to destroy it. That recognition was one of the most exciting moments of my life. It didn't make life less challenging—in fact, quite the opposite. But from that moment on, no one and nothing could talk me out of it.

Little did he know that his enchantment with nature's movements flowed into a long lineage of cosmic explorers, from indigenous peoples to Leonardo Da Vinci, who have sought to grasp nature's deepest pattern language. From the shape of galaxies to the flow of blood in your veins, to how air moves through your lungs, to how plants and flowers unfold, the spiral rules. It correlates with the fabled golden mean and the Fibonacci sequence, viewed by many as an ideal mathematical representation of aesthetic beauty.

Harman is a naturalist, inventor, and entrepreneur. Following his first career as a captain and field officer for the Western Australia Department of Fisheries and Wildlife (today the Department of Fisheries), he went on to found companies in fields including electronics, bioscience, and transportation. His first biomimetic designs surfaced in the 1980s when he built highly efficient and beautiful boats with hulls mimicking the shapes of dolphins and fish. In the 1990s, the shapes of sea creatures suggested to him more effective designs for propellers, which are at the core of all marine transportation, an abominably polluting and environmentally destructive industry.

Harman is indeed now demonstrating that it's more profitable to copy nature than to destroy it. As CEO of PAX Scientific, a Marin County industrial-design firm that he operates with his wife and partner Francesca Bertone, he develops energy-efficient and ecologically friendly technologies. PAX Scientific is revolutionizing industrial design, working with companies in businesses as far-ranging as refrigerators, ships, and computers.

A computer simulation illustration tacked on the wall of the PAX office shows vividly what happens to water when a standard propeller moves through it. The shape the water makes exiting the propeller is a tangle of conflicting currents. The water coming off Harman's "impeller" is a spiraled braid of elegant ease. The mission at PAX is to dramatically reduce the use of energy in the industrial world through the application of biomimicry.

"It seems obvious that energy-efficient technology would be designed with this in mind," he says. He continues:

> Well, guess what? Virtually no industrial product in the world today pays any attention whatsoever to nature's optimized geometries, even though the greatest scientists in history were enthralled by these spirals—Plato, Pythagoras, Da Vinci, Descartes, Newton, Kelvin, Einstein. It was never of interest to the Industrial Revolution. Why was that?
>
> The Industrial Revolution was about mass production, making thousands and then millions of exactly the same forms out of flat plates of metal and square building blocks. The Industrial Revolution was also about cheap and plentiful power. If you needed more speed, you didn't look to nature to find a more efficient shape, you just shoveled in more fuel and blasted your way forward.
>
> That actually worked well enough until the side effects began mounting—ugly cities, polluted lands, fossil-fuel power no longer cheap and plentiful, and global warming. Nature works on an entirely different principle. It doesn't stamp out flat plates. It doesn't do straight lines at all.
>
> For example, the human cardiovascular system has 60,000 miles of plumbing and there's not a straight pipe in there, yet it is beyond compare when it comes to energy efficiency. How many machines do you know that can drive anything 60,000 miles on one and a half watts?
>
> In nature, survival of a species depends on optimal use of energy, so how is the human species doing? Technology guzzles it, nature sips it. I wanted to show industry that there's an enormous amount we can learn from nature about efficiency and that it's more profitable to protect and copy nature.

In a quest to realize the PAX vision to apply "nature's core design principles to engineer energy efficient products that enhance and sustain life on earth," Harman has logged thousands of hours studying the flow patterns of ocean and air currents, and was astonished by the incredible effectiveness of natural flow systems. From these observations he developed a hypothesis: "Fluids always want to follow a particular path." He made a fundamental discovery he calls the PAX Streamlining Principle, which permitted him to design systems that replicate highly efficient natural flow systems. Harman researches some of PAX's designs aboard the four-hundred-ton research vessel *Pax*, a sister ship to Jacques Cousteau's *Calypso*. Harman also possesses numerous patents in marine craft design and friction reduction technologies. The shipping industry, which has until recently been very feebly regulated, is responsible for huge amounts of pollution and energy use, and global shipping traffic is slated to grow radically in the decades ahead.

Given the degree to which the biosphere and our entire socioeconomic enterprise are completely dependent on water and other fluids, and the fact that freshwater shortages present one of our most important looming global crises, the potential applications of Harman's discoveries are almost limitless in an astonishingly vast array of technologies.

The first area PAX began to commercialize was fans. Believe it or not, there are over 30 *billion* fans turning every day that use 18 percent of the world's electricity. The PAX fan uses 30 percent less power and the difference in noise is audible—a reduction of half. From computers (an older Mac has sixteen fans) to air conditioners, refrigerators, and range hoods, PAX is aiming for radically reduced energy usage in mass markets.

The first product created by PAX Water Technologies is designed to circulate water in the very, very large public drinking water systems and storage tanks that you see throughout the country. Along with the copious use of chemicals, energy-intensive pumps regularly have to circulate water between enormous tanks to keep them from growing bacteria because the water stratifies into heat layers that provide friendly conditions for bacterial growth. Instead PAX uses an impeller whose spiral design is so beautiful that it's displayed in New York City's famed Museum of Modern Art. What looks like a miniaturized version in the museum is the actual size of an impeller used to mix volumes of water 200 feet in diameter and 40 feet tall—using as little energy as three light bulbs.

"We're bringing this to utilities," says Harman,

> and enabling them to manage their water quality with a reduction or elimination of the need to add chemicals in the field, and we're helping them circulate their tanks using, in some cases, less than 10 percent of the energy for pumping.

The impeller is like a frozen whirlpool, and it's creating a similar pattern in the water. Once it sets up, the entire water body becomes a ringed vortex like a smoke ring, which is by far nature's most efficient flow structure. This is one of the reasons that we can impact very large volumes of water with such a small device and so little energy. It can also oxygenate water. It pulls air down from the surface. Once it stops, the water continues to mix for several hours afterwards.

PAX Water is also developing solutions to improve water quality in lakes and ponds that have been degraded by agricultural runoff and to counteract mosquito breeding, particularly in lesser developed countries where around four million people die each year from mosquito-born diseases.

The PAX industrial mixing technology also addresses other major industrial processes you've probably never thought much about, but Harman has. "So many things that we do each year in our lives involve mixing. Just about every processed food in the world goes through some sort of mixing. The total use of energy in the world for mixing is quite enormous. We've created a company around industrial mixing that can be used in pharmaceutical production and industrial products such as paint mixing and mining slurries. PAX Mixer has been granted some funding from the Advanced Research Projects Agency–Energy (ARPA–E) program of the U.S. government to develop its mixer for pharmaceuticals and other solutions. The striking thing about that is that the federal government is now supporting biomimicry research, and I think this might be the first time."

As you would expect, PAX is also developing a boat. It can be made entirely of recycled plastic and uses much less energy for manufacture and propulsion. It's designed for human power or an electric motor. It's highly stable and can carry a large payload. It can be designed to be up to a hundred feet in length. It's optimal for fishing communities in less developed countries where trees for wooden boat construction are being decimated and other boatbuilding materials are too expensive. There's an old boatbuilders' saying that if it looks good, it is good. It follows the lines of orcas and dolphins, masterpieces of drag reduction. And then of course there's the personal watercraft, a fishy-looking "Wild Thing" prototype that has won awards worldwide and has been sponsored by Coca-Cola in international boat shows.

PAX has also entered the windmill market with radically redesigned windmill blades whose spiral shapes provide far better drag and flow, and can turn and generate power with just the whisper of a breeze. ARPA–E also funded this project.

Its most controversial project is a geo-engineering experiment. As climate change bears down, predictably the traditional engineering mentality of extreme interventions into the biosphere, such as blowing huge clouds of smoke into the atmosphere to dim the sun's rays and dumping iron filings into the oceans to remove CO_2, is picking up momentum. There's a growing inevitability about such potentially reckless ventures. For one thing, there are no international laws to stop them; any buccaneer billionaire could pull the switch at will. Given our grim technological history of dire unintended consequences, it's scary stuff.

On the other hand, we're facing mounting prospects of climate doom. What to do? Harman believes he has a possible geo-engineering solution: the "atmospheric heat sink." Basically, he's exploring the option of setting up a large impeller or series of impellers to mix the atmosphere. Like the water tanks, the atmosphere in a greenhouse effect becomes stratified into thermal layers. Blend the atmosphere by doing what nature does generating vortices, Harman says, and we could buy ten or twenty years to play catch-up and stop dumping CO_2 into the atmosphere. He believes it will also mitigate tornados, which are more frequent and severe with climate change. He proposes to engage a leading atmospheric science team to investigate the potential of vortex-based impellers as atmospheric heat sinks.

There's no question, he admits, that there will be unintended consequences, including the likelihood of very intense rains. A risk, yes, but arguably far less of a risk than some of the other ideas that are moving from geo-engineering concept to reality at a brisk pace. What would you do?

PAX has spun off multiple companies, and is now working with a fistful of Fortune 500 companies. The PAX water mixers are now selling in the United States and Canada, with sales doubling yearly. PAX has been awarded prestigious and highly competitive grants from the US Department of Energy and the California Energy Commission. It expects to break into the mass market with various products soon. But innovation is a tricky business. You're up against embedded costs in existing infrastructure, complacent vested interests, and the "NIH syndrome"—"not invented here."

"That moment on the beach was decades ago," Harman recalls wistfully. "It took years to translate this insight into design tools, and even longer to make headway in the industrial world. It's hard work, but when you see how things could be, it's agonizing when the world doesn't change. But I want to encourage you, if you find something you love, stick to it. If you've found the work that gives life meaning, surround yourself with good people who remind you of what's possible. Accept that there will be frustration, but don't let that stop you. And remember the whirlpool, it may seem for a long time that nothing is happening, and then, suddenly, the system will coalesce and with a rush the flow will carry you faster and faster. I think we can all feel that more than just efficient industrial design is picking up speed. There's a global movement happening for environmental and social change that is like water. It's almost invisible, and like water, has tremendous force. It's a great privilege to be part of the swirling whirlpool of hope and action."

Along with mimicking nature's operating instructions, innovators are applying nature's own true biotechnologies directly for environmental restoration.

You'll likely never know how mesmerized you are by mushrooms and fungi until you encounter mycologist Paul Stamets. He's the quintessential bioneer who has looked to the natural world for guidance on how we can not only preserve the diversity and integrity of the natural world, but also apply this knowledge to restoration. His work developing fungi-based "mycotechnology" has illuminated some of the most hopeful and wildly imaginative strategies anyone has conjured up.

Fungi are some of the fundamental decomposers, digesters, and recyclers of the food web. Yet we are largely clueless about their broader ecological functions. Of all the diversity of the world, the fungi and the bacteria are among the least studied, although they are among the most ancient and ubiquitous keystone systems for all life on Earth. Recent molecular research suggests the fungi appeared on land over 1 billion years ago and set the stage for the evolution of land plants about a few hundred million years later. Science has described just 75,000 fungi from a kingdom that contains upward of 1 million, according to the best current guesses.

We know that fungi and mushrooms can be powerful medicines. Stamets identified one mushroom, the turkey tail, which is now in advanced tests at the National Institutes of Health for breast cancer.

When his elderly mother developed terminal Stage IV breast cancer and was essentially given up to die by her physician, she agreed to try turkey tail. Within several months, she began to make a complete recovery.

Given such potentially profound healing power for people's bodies, Stamets had long wondered as an ecologist if his beloved fungi were also in some sense medicines for the land. In a succession of experiments and demonstrations, he has shown remarkable results. Mushrooms can purify soil contaminated with diesel oil, leaving virtually no trace in either the soil or the flesh of the mushrooms. The bioremediation of soil occurs in a matter of weeks and months, not years or decades.

In one experiment, after Stamets's oyster mushrooms detoxified some diesel-contaminated soil, the onset of dynamic natural processes colorized what restoration can look like in action. As the mushrooms decayed, worms and maggots appeared and ate them. Birds came to eat the insects and worms, carrying seeds on their feathers. Within a matter of weeks, the formerly contaminated dead dirt turned into a thriving oasis of life. This is restoration in fast-forward, radically accelerated by fungi.

An obvious arena for the large-scale application of mycotechnology is the conversion of conventional farmlands to organic cultivation. Large swaths of farmland are severely polluted by decades of use of agricultural chemicals, virtually all of which are made from petroleum. Appropriate fungi could be applied as soil amendments to help detoxify millions of acres of chemically farmed land and dramatically accelerate the process very inexpensively.

Stamets has further demonstrated how certain fungi are able to defeat and digest harmful *E. coli* bacteria, which present a major public health problem that often originates from factory farms. Obviously, we'd be better off without factory farms in the first place, but the fungi could be an important intermediate step to prevent the *E. coli* from contaminating groundwater and sensitive estuaries.

An additional advantage of such mycotechnologies is that they can be relatively simple in application. As often as not, they require a gardener, not an engineer.

In backyard experiments, Stamets surmised that fungi and garden-variety vegetables have coevolved over time in a symbiotic relationship. He adapted the standard organic gardening practice of companion planting—cultivating certain plants together that enhance each other's growth. He companion-planted his garden with fungi, and saw yields increase as much as 150 percent. While experiments have shown that organic gardening produces equal and greater yields than chemical farming, myco-companion gardening could afford decisive advantages to small farmers and gardeners around the world while actively restoring the soil.

As word spread about Stamets's magical mushrooms, one day he got a call from the Department of Defense. The U.S. government has the world's largest stockpiles of chemical weapons, many decaying after thirty or more years, with no good ways to destroy them without dispersing them into the environment (such as incineration). Could his mushrooms help remediate them?

Sure enough, two varieties of mushrooms were able to completely metabolize and transform Sarin nerve gas, among the most lethal and durable toxins on the planet. Stamets co-authored a patent with Battelle Laboratory, which works extensively with the Department of Defense, on myroremediation of chemical and biological warfare agents (U.S. Patent Application 09/259,077). As Stamets wrote, "One of the active mushrooms is a resident in the old-growth forest and my clone gave rise to mycelium that denatured VX... In one of many tests, two of my strains neutralized 'very close surrogates of chemical weapons such as sarin, soman and the VX family of compounds' [as reported by the Jane's Information Group in 1999]." As the mycologist told the military, since one of his active strains is native to the Pacific Northwest old-growth forest, protecting our national forests is a matter of national security.

As a roving bio-ambassador on behalf of fungi, Stamets is a dedicated teacher, inoculating the culture and broadcasting spores far and wide. When it comes to nature's operating instructions, he has shown how fungi provide radical and authentic biotechnologies.

The field of phytoremediation is blossoming. Plants that act as pollution sponges are decontaminating tens of thousands of toxic sites on factory grounds, farms, and military facilities. As reporter Andrew Revkin described, they represent botanical detox centers: sunflowers that capture uranium, ferns that thrive on arsenic, alpine herbs that hoard zinc, mustards that lap up lead, clovers that eat oil, and poplar trees that metabolize dry-cleaning solvents. It's now a several hundred-million-dollar industry so cost-effective that it can be employed for the countless sites where Superfund is not in the cards.

Hundreds of plant species are in use commercially to accumulate metal to clean up abandoned mine sites. The late Rufus Chaney of the USDA pioneered the breeding of hyperaccumulator plants that suck metals from the soils of contaminated mining sites so that some "farmers" can now grow profitable crops of copper or other metals. Microbiologist Randall Von Wedel developed a biosolvent made from vegetable oil that separates oil from water and became the only state-approved agent in California for eating up ocean oil spills.

Ecological designer and granddaddy of biomimicry John Todd asserts that these kinds of true biotechnologies could allow us to reduce the human footprint by 90 percent or more and return large portions of land to the wild. What might that look like?

Dave Foreman of the Rewilding Institute knows that ecosystems regulate from both the bottom up and top down. Usually the key is the role of the top predator in the system. Removing the top predator generally produces cascades of catastrophic effects. That's why when sea otters disappear, kelp forests also disappear—the sea otters' main prey, the sea urchin, is a ravenous predator of the kelp on which hundreds of other species depend. Similarly, a healthy population of wolves maintains a healthy population of moose, which means that the balsam fir forest is healthy. Remove the wolves and it unravels. When you eradicate wolves and mountain lions, migrant songbirds decline because raccoons, skunks, and foxes multiply and eat baby birds and their eggs. When you remove predators such as coyotes, house cats go wild gobbling more songbirds than any other natural predator. It's all connected.

Ecology is the exquisite art of relationships. As rangeland restorationist Dan Daggett points out, restoring the environment is about creating and sustaining healthy, functional relationships—both between people and nature and between people and people. As in any long-term relationship, we have to honor old agreements and responsibilities.

Hooved animals known as ungulates have coevolved over long periods of time with grasslands and are essential to their ecological processes and well-being. By studying the ancient patterns of buffalo on the Great Plains, biologists and ecologists have been able to understand how the behavior of the hooved animals cocreated these huge grasslands, as well as the weather that coevolves with them. By mimicking those patterns and using cows instead of buffalo (we have *lots* of cows to spare) some innovative ranchers are successfully bringing back grasslands, biodiversity, and ecosystem health—and saving their ranches.

One of nature's tricks that people have adapted for rangeland management and restoration is called "move 'em and mob 'em." It mimics the ancient migration patterns of buffalo across the plains, where they never stayed too long in one place and therefore did not overgraze an area or eat the green shoots so early in the growth cycle as to kill the perennial grasses permanently. Predators such as wolves, as the saying goes, "put the lightning in the step of the deer." In the absence of wolves to keep the herds moving, modern portable electric fences and ranch hands can substitute for predators, and keep the cows moving from place to place at exactly the right moments. The result—healthy, abundant grasslands and well-fed cows.

Apart from the ecological benefits, there are other gifts in Dan's work. I live in New Mexico, where bullets have literally flown between ranchers and environmentalists over grazing on public lands. In truth, these apparent enemies have real and vital mutual interests. Family ranchers often have a long lineage of living on the land, and care as deeply about the land as environmentalists do. Yet corporate agribusiness keeps driving family ranchers off the land with economic ruination, leaving the land vulnerable to development. When these ranchers leave, their private properties (which can be quite large) often end up as subdivisions—which no one except developers want to see.

Acting at the highest level as a citizen diplomat, Dan has brought these polarized camps together in the hope of recognizing their common interests and developing viable alternatives based on ecological management practices and creative business strategies. He broke the ice in the tense first meeting with a simple request. He asked the ranchers and environmentalists alike to recognize the difference between values and opinions, and leave their opinions at the door. As people went around the room speaking to their deepest values, the response was universally about the care of the land. For ranchers, in many cases their families had been on the land for several generations, and they feared deeply for its future, especially losing it to developers because of economic pressures. No one in the room wanted that to happen. Once people established this literal common ground, Dan steered the conversation to best management practices (BMPs) and presented what restoration ranching was learning about how nature's tight interdependence of ungulates and grasslands had flourished for centuries.

The result is that the ranchers who use BMPs are doing better economically because they now promote special premium-priced "wolf-friendly beef," and host ecotourism cabins on their ranches where guests can experience the renewed biodiversity of birds, wolves, foxes, and other critters. Home on the range can look real different these days as a result of this kind of conflict mediation, which is among the most important and overlooked aspects of restoration.

Another iconoclastic citizen diplomat has been patiently working to transform Los Angeles, the very poster child of environmental destruction. Talk about a tough gig. When Andy Lipkis was growing up in LA in the 1950s and 1960s, it hurt to breathe the air. His parents sent him away from the escalating smog to a summer camp in the nearby mountains. There he fell in love with the forests, and had his heart broken when he learned they would all be dead in twenty years from the growing smog below. At the age of fifteen, he began planting trees to clean the air and rehabilitate the smog- and fire-damaged forests. He challenged the California Department of Forestry and Fire Protection (today CalFire) to hand over its surplus stock of eight thousand seedlings—and the California Conservation Project was born. He went on to found the now legendary group TreePeople, where he has served as president since 1973.

Andy started raising funds and pushing to restore LA's dying forests in myriad ways. By the end of 1977, TreePeople had planted fifty thousand trees, and fifty thousand children had taken part in environmental education programs. Today TreePeople has forty-two employees and thousands of volunteer "citizen foresters," a term Andy coined. Many people credit Andy with inventing the citizen forestry movement.

In the years that followed, TreePeople guided the development of the city's Community Forest Advisory Council, and led the effort to bring millions of dollars to community groups in the aftermath of 1992's civil unrest. The group worked with an alphabet soup of city agencies to plant trees in the mountains surrounding LA and to educate youth on environmental issues. More than 1 million children and teens are now a part of that effort each year. More than 2 million trees have been planted.

But all that was prequel. In partnership with a constellation of public agencies and other groups, TreePeople's visionary TREES project—Trans-Agency Resources for Environmental and Economic Sustainability—is developing a retrofit of the entire LA landscape to manage the city as a living ecosystem. This may be the most exciting, large-scale attempt in the history of the world to green a giant urban area. One reason for its success to date has been its successful marriage of ecology and economics. Another is Andy's supreme skill as a citizen diplomat who can bridge many worlds.

You may remember the old cartoon where the hapless Wile E. Coyote chases the Road Runner and corners him against a big wall. The Road

Runner seems trapped—until he paints a door on the wall behind him and escapes through it. That's sort of how Andy approached the ecological wall that the city of LA had run up against. Like all cities, LA was built before people understood ecology. The City of Angels epitomized the scourge of resource-gobbling, pollution-spewing, out-of-control megacities devouring the planet. And now that the majority of the world's population lives in cities that consume three-quarters of the planet's resources, transforming cities is a non-negotiable condition of environmental well-being.

The door Andy painted on LA's wall of ecological limits showed how the urban and biological webs can fit together in healthy, beneficial ways. He did it by overlaying a map of LA with an ecological map of the city's original forest ecosystem, which in turn revealed the underlying watershed on which everything depends. By using integrated resource management, he demonstrated how to eliminate huge amounts of waste, save money, and dramatically improve the quality of life. He boldly proposed that the ecological goals could be met just by recovering water that the city was wasting.

But what Andy found above all was that restoring the natural ecology first required restoring the social ecology. He had to connect all the fractured agencies and people.

Andy has brought together a fragmented bureaucracy to achieve an integrated approach to cleaning up an ecology which until then was organizationally siloed into separate domains of obtaining water, channeling storm water, controlling floods, conserving energy and water, improving air quality, reducing waste, improving human health, and creating jobs.

The project bred changes in bureaucratic mind-set so profound that the two key LA agencies, the largest public works agencies in the nation, changed their names and missions. The LA County Flood Control Division became the Watershed Management Division, and the Stormwater Protection Division is now the Watershed Protection Division. The city is saving money and water, getting greener, providing green schoolyards and vital watershed education for kids, and mitigating the effects of climate change.

Along the way, Andy and TreePeople created a curriculum called Schoolyard Explorers that turns kids into watershed managers. As he points out, kids can lead—after all, they led TreePeople's massive LA recycling program, now among the biggest in the country with almost

700,000 homes and small apartments in the program, and the city is ranked number one in solid waste management and recycling.

The process that Andy catalyzed over thirty years ago in LA has led to a far greater understanding of how to manage cities as part of an ecosystem. That, he says, is why poster-child LA is now living up to its promise as the City of Angels, a beacon for other cities where he now consults—such as Portland, Seattle, and London, as well as countries including China and Israel.

As Paul Hawken, social entrepreneur and coauthor of *Natural Capitalism: Creating the Next Industrial Revolution*, points out, "Today we have an expanded sense of what nature is: a flow of services which cannot be commoditized, services which are not bought or sold but which absolutely influence and dictate the quality of our life on this planet, from whence all so-called economic value is derived. These flows of services, which we mostly take for granted, include pollination, oxygen, global climatic stability, riparian systems, fisheries, soil fertility, topsoil, control of erosion, flood catchments, and so on. What natural capitalism is saying is that the limiting factor to human wellbeing and development is no longer human-made capital in the developed world; it is life itself. As more people place greater strain on living systems, limits to prosperity are coming to be determined by scarcities of natural systems rather than industrial prowess."

Companies practicing natural capitalism are demonstrating that we can already achieve a radical increase in resource productivity and efficiency. The solution is to use less stuff and more people, the exact reversal of the first Industrial Revolution. This formula produces more jobs and better jobs, and higher profits through the elimination of waste and liability.

The greatest gift of true biotechnologies is ultimately a human one, what biologist E. O. Wilson calls biophilia, the resonance that life has for life. As Janine Benyus sees it,

> You enter into deep conversation with organisms, and this student-elder dialogue absolutely fills you with awe. Seeing nature as model, measure and mentor changes the very way you view and value the natural world. Instead of seeing nature as warehouse, you begin to see her as teacher. Instead of valuing what you can *extract* from her, you value what you can *learn* from her. This shift changes everything.

When we finally realize that unencumbered evolution is more precious than any vein of oil, the rationale for protecting wild places will become self-evident. After all, it's not a new gadget that's going to make us more sustainable as a culture—it's a change of heart and a new set of eyes, a new way of viewing and valuing the world in which we are embedded and on which we depend. We're a young species, but we're very adaptable, and we're uncanny mimics. With the help of our 30 million planet-mates, I believe we can learn to do what other organisms have done, which is to make of this place an Eden, a home that is ours, but not ours alone.

Perhaps that's where we went so wrong, forgetting old agreements and abandoning old relationships. As the late Seneca historian John Mohawk pointed out, "It's true that humans have to go to the tree and say, 'I have to build a house.' But once we've broken the one-on-one relationship so that the thing that appears to you is never a tree, but only a board, you have separated yourself from that which was the relationship to the spirit of things. The same thing is true about our relationships to plants and animals, to food, fibers, and everything else. They've become commodities and we've become consumers. If there's an essence to what the problem is in the world is, that's it."

As educator David W. Orr suggests, the ultimate object of ecological design is the human mind. For the most part, solutions exist for the vast majority of our problems, and the solutions residing in nature consistently surpass our concept of what's possible. It is not ultimately a technological issue, but a human perception issue. The real environmental crisis is between our ears.

Luisah Teish, an initiated elder in the Ifa/Orisha tradition of southwest Nigeria, sees it this way:

> In the West African tradition, Oya, the goddess of fall, is the queen of the winds of change, the boss lady of the cemetery, the mother of catastrophe. Whenever I talk about Oya, the mother of catastrophe, people shudder. But the proper definition of catastrophe is a sudden structural change. Oya doesn't move the furniture around in the house; she blows the roof off and knocks down the beams, and reduces the debris to compost so that we can start all over again. At this

point at the turn of the century, this is what we have to do in terms of the way we think about our relationship to nature.

The Earth is the mother and we are the children. We are the ones that come out of her. We are the ones who are learning from her and through her, and we are the ones who are going to return to her. Our alienation from this indigenous mind is what allows us to poison ourselves, kill each other and poison the environment.

In this time of change, take note of the place in nature where you are regenerated, and go there. If you're a child of the river, or the forest, or the mountain or the thunder—wherever it is in nature that regenerates you—go to that place. Declare yourself one who learns from that place and is nurtured by that place, and is a defender of that place and that energy. Then live it.

Let's live it.

ECOLOGICAL MEDICINE

One Notion Indivisible

*I*caught a few minutes of an old Star Trek movie recently, the one where the crew of the starship *Enterprise* travels back in time to prevent the extinction of humpback whales. During the mission, one of the crew is shot and captured and taken to a hospital. Bones, the starship doctor, gets a panicked look on his face and mutters, "We'd better hurry—you remember what twentieth-century medicine was like. He may be dead already."

In a biological world whose hallmark is interconnectedness, and now a globalized human society that is endlessly interconnected, human health cannot hide from the storm in gated communities. Our success or failure as a civilization may well hinge on how ingenious, nimble, and socially just our public health systems can become.

We're living at a time when vast social and biological forces are interacting in complex ways—and with unpredictable impacts. War, famine, and ecological damage have caused great human disruptions, which in turn have transformed tuberculosis, AIDS, and other modern plagues into global pandemics. As we alter Earth's basic life-support systems—climate, the ozone layer, biodiversity—and pour gargantuan quantities of toxic chemicals and wastes into the biosphere, we are finding a mounting number of human health crises intimately coupled with environmental factors. We are all involuntary subjects in a mass medical experiment, and there's no control group.

The very emblem of industrial civilization is cancer. Large-scale cancer studies with twins show that only 10–30 percent of cancer is genetically determined. In other words, from 70–90 percent is caused by environmental and occupational exposure, which means it's preventable.

The living biological truth is that human health is dependent on the health of the environment. Therefore the first step toward a healthier future lies in *ecological medicine*. Pioneered by a global movement of concerned scientists, doctors, public health advocates, and others, ecological medicine is a loosely shared philosophy based on advancing public health by improving the environment. It proposes a medicine that simultaneously treats individuals *and* reshapes how our entire industrial civilization operates.

As Carolyn Raffensperger, who coined the term and is executive director of the Science and Environmental Health Network, says, "A truly holistic medicine extends beyond the mind-body connection to the human-planet whole." Here are some basic tenets of ecological medicine she helped outline:

- The first goal of medicine is to establish the conditions for health and wholeness, thus preventing disease and illness. The second goal is to cure.
- The Earth is also the physician's client. The patient under the physician's care is one part of the Earth.
- Humans are part of a local ecosystem. A disturbed ecosystem can make people physically ill.
- Medicine should not add to the illnesses of humans or the planet. Medical practices themselves should not damage other species or the ecosystem.

In keeping with the Hippocratic Oath to "first do no harm," ecological medicine suggests first doing no harm to the environment, then creating a medical practice that minimizes its own harms. Like virtually all earlier healing traditions, it emphasizes prevention, strengthening the organism and the environment to avoid illness in the first place.

Ironically, medicine itself is a highly toxic enterprise. The health care industry emits nearly half the known dioxin and dioxinlike compounds and around a quarter of the mercury released into the environment. To that you may add IV bags that leach endocrine-disrupting chemicals into patients; nuclear medicine and its deadly wastes; toxic chemotherapy drugs that are classified as hazardous wastes; and the flood of pharmaceutical drugs now polluting water and land, contributing to mutations among wildlife and turning up in our tap water.

In the eye-opening book *The Coming Plague*, Laurie Garrett reveals how embedded we are in an inescapable, incredibly complex web of relationships with our entire ecosystem, especially the microbiological world.

One clear warning signal is the dramatic change in our relationship with infectious disease. TB and malaria, once thought to be largely eradicated, have returned with a vengeance. Endemic corruption, neglect, poverty, and prison overcrowding in countries such as Russia and Thailand have produced hotbeds of mutating drug-resistant TB and HIV strains that can spread worldwide, greatly aided by globalization and decrepit public health systems in many nations. There is also the fact that 95 percent of our expected population growth of another 3 billion people will occur in less developed countries, whose public health systems are strained and underfunded.

It's well proven that the overuse of antibiotics has bred widespread resistance and precipitated a global medical crisis. But what few realize is how much of the source is factory farming, which uses an estimated 29 million pounds a year in the United States alone at last count—on top of the 3 million used for people. About 70 percent of all antibiotics sold in the United States are given to healthy food animals as a nontherapeutic treatment to artificially speed up their growth and compensate for the effects of unsanitary conditions on the farm. Then the antibiotics migrate into land and water to breed even wider resistance.

Our entire system of industrial agriculture is a prime culprit in creating conditions conducive to disease. It reduces insect diversity, skewing populations that may harbor deadly viruses. The massive amounts of animal wastes from factory farms that pollute waterways give rise to toxic algal blooms that harbor dangerous pathogens. North Carolina's hogs outnumber its citizens and produce more fecal waste than all the people in New York and California combined. Across the United States, animals raised for food produce almost 90,000 pounds of waste *per second*.

Deforestation and ecosystem disruptions turn out to be the primary drivers in diseases such as Lyme disease, hantavirus, and Ebola. Some of the main disruptive forces are war, massive urbanization, and polluted water. Waterborne diseases are the most widespread, affecting over 2 billion people, often as a consequence of large dam projects.

Then stir the toxic stew with climate change, which appears to be causing even more rapid mutation among deadly bacteria and viruses, some never seen before. Add human sewage and the chemical stew of immune-damaging pollutants to cook up tidal blooms that breed algal vectors that produce outbreaks such as cholera. Then load it in the bilge of a ship heading halfway around the world from Bengal to Peru. You get the drift.

Meanwhile ecological disruption and local wars are creating masses of refugees. Tens of millions more people in the developing world could be on the move because of disasters. Bacteria produce new generations in thirty minutes and they trade genetic material as feverishly as traders on the floor of the stock exchange, as microbiologist Lynn Margulis quipped. They develop drug resistance and spread the information with lightning speed. They are constantly evolving one hundred times faster than we are. It is their world more than ours. If we are waging a war against bacteria, they will win.

Even the rich may lose on this one if they gamble that drug companies can stay ahead of the curve. No one is immune to mobile global epidemics. Pile on the specter of bioterrorism if you have any question left that what we really need is a healthy environment and robust public health system, not a fee-for-service business model banking on curing just prosperous individuals.

Only a new medical paradigm that approaches human health with these biological and social truths in mind can succeed in the long run in a world where human activities are now radically disrupting microbial ecology on a large scale.

In a world primarily made up of relationships, we've been mostly focused on negative feedback loops, the endless ways that disruptions to ecosystems can engender cascades of destructive repercussions. But there are also complementary sets of beneficial feedback loops. Ecological restoration sets in motion synergistic dynamics that promote stability and health, and we can contribute positively to that process.

Now don't get me wrong: Nature is not warm and fuzzy, and there's plenty of competition and violence, but a very important part of the picture that usually gets left out is symbiosis, or in cultural terms, mutual aid. Margulis called Earth a "symbiotic planet," and she inspires us with a different vision for how to apply symbiosis toward a new ecological view of health and infectious disease.

Margulis suggested that as human beings we're here by the grace of the microbes because we make such world-class, multicellular hosts. An adult body is estimated to carry up to 200 trillion microbes, ten to twenty times the number of cells in our bodies. In effect, we constitute "prime real estate." The microbes that have coevolved with us are well suited to colonizing the most intimate niches of our body's sprawling ecology. They can crowd out so-called bad bacteria, to which they surely do not want to lose their tenancy. Location, location, location.

An ecological view of health suggests that a relentless war on germs may be self-defeating. People in the industrialized world are cleaner today than at any time in history, yet paradoxically our antimicrobial campaign can disrupt microbial balances, often giving rise to bacteria that we famously don't get along with. People live more or less harmlessly with certain germs as long as the germs are ubiquitous. In this case, a lack of familiarity can breed contempt.

Researchers have found that the best protection from allergies was associated with large families with older siblings, shared bedrooms, and growing up with a dog. In other studies, lower allergy rates are associated with children who attended day care in their first year. Contact with real dirt and soil—and other people—is a positive influence on building immunity.

Rather than a war on germs, we might instead be looking to supply foreign aid to friendly microbial ecologies in exchange for a reasonably peaceful coexistence. In the big picture, strengthening planetary immunity and restoring ecological balance are the most sensible strategies for promoting long-term health, resilience, and stability.

A 2005 ad in *National Geographic* by the American Plastics Council celebrated plastic as the sixth basic food group. According to some researchers, Americans are now consuming an estimated average of 5.8 milligrams a day of DEHP, a phthalate plasticizer used in everything from food wrappings to children's toys, medical devices, and ubiquitous PVC products. It's an endocrine disrupter, a gender bender that can have adverse health effects at parts per *trillion*. (The EPA's legal limit in drinking water is six parts per billion.) Such estrogen-mimicking chemicals are associated with early puberty in girls. In infants and children, they can produce measurable neurological deficits and changes in temperament such as not laughing and smiling as much and more fear and agitation under stress. As Theo Colborn (founder and president of the Endocrine Disruption Exchange) has said, these chemicals have the potential to change the very character of human societies.

Blood tests from the umbilical cords of newborns have found an average of 200 foreign synthetic chemicals. Almost 4 billion pounds of toxic chemicals were released into the environment in 2010. The number of dead zones in the oceans from chemical and human pollution has doubled every decade since 1960. A 2008 study counted 405 dead zones worldwide. Plastics and their toxic components permeate even the seabed. In some parts of the ocean some sea animals that eat krill get a ratio of one part krill to five parts plastic.

It's bioterrorism on a daily basis. A US Army Surgeon General's analysis suggests that a worst-case scenario of an actual terrorist attack on a major urban chemical plant could kill up to 2 million people.

The burden of proof for these kinds of harms is on society. Close to 90,000 synthetic chemicals now percolate through our land, water, air, and bodies, while the industry turns out 1,000 new chemicals a year. By the time one finally is proven to be harmful, the patent has run out—and it's on to the next one.

Of all the environmental problems we face, changing the industrial chemical metabolism is one of the most doable in the near term. Profound breakthroughs are occurring in the burgeoning field of green chemistry. By modeling nature's recipe book, we're learning to do everything we want to do without poisoning people or planet.

Pathfinding scientists such as Paul Anastas are lighting the way to benign practical alternatives. Known, alongside John Warner, as one of the two "fathers of green chemistry," Anastas coined the term. It means not only designing a harmless molecular architecture of the chemicals we develop, but also designing production processes that generate less waste and hazardous materials.

In 1989 Anastas went to work in the EPA as chief of the industrial chemistry branch and director of its program in green chemistry. He also served as a member of the White House staff. Trained as a conventional chemist in industry and academia, over twenty years ago he began challenging assumptions about how we make molecules and practice molecular architecture. In 1991, he established the industry-government-university partnership Green Chemistry Program and the Presidential Green Chemistry Challenge Awards. In 1997 he helped found the Green Chemistry Institute in Washington DC, serving as its director. Then he joined the faculty at Yale as professor of green chemistry and director of the Center for Green Chemistry and Green Engineering; in 2009 he rejoined the EPA to advance green chemistry.

Today the Green Chemistry Institute has chapters in twenty-five countries. The National Academy of Sciences is actively exploring the field. China has opened its sixth Green Chemistry Research Center. The Nobel Prize for chemistry was awarded to two green chemists in 2005.

Anastas says that green chemistry boils down to a design issue. He helped devise "the Twelve Principles of Green Chemistry." Thankfully, business leaders and big companies are discovering that following nature's lead benefits the bottom line, produces superior products, and reduces harm and liability—among other benefits, including enhancing environmental justice and national security. Green chemistry is true alchemy that can create good chemistry with people and planet.

Business is awakening, too. When the European Union passed legislation called REACH (Registration, Evaluation, Authorization, and Restriction of Chemical substances) to require extensive safety testing of the thirty thousand most common chemicals in commerce, the U.S. chemical industry saw it as the shot across the bow. The EU policy proposed to require all manufacturers to test industrial chemicals for their impact on public health before selling them in Europe, instead of the usual waiting to count the dead bodies before regulating. Under previous European Union and current U.S. rules, *about 99 percent of chemicals have not been tested.*

There is a profound difference of philosophical orientations at stake. The United States uses a cost-benefit formula, reducing regulatory decisions to an economic equation weighing the speculative cost of regulations against their monetized benefits. The Europeans employ the precautionary principle, prioritizing the prevention of harm.

With annual revenues of over $700 billion as of 2010, America's chemical industry is among the nation's biggest exporters and is accustomed to dictating the rules. In the face of REACH, it enlisted the intervention of its big brother, the U.S. government, including no less a figure than then Secretary of State Colin Powell, to wage the fiercest and biggest lobbying effort in the European Union on record. Call it "Nightmare on K Street," exported to Brussels. The bullying tactics served to royally piss off "Old Europe," as the general's colleague Secretary of Defense Donald Rumsfeld contemptuously called it, but in the end the sheer power of the industry managed to dilute the European legislation significantly and industry continues to try to weaken it further. Nevertheless, REACH exists, and should advance in years to come.

As a spokesman from the AeA (formerly the American Electronics Association) said, "The moment the ink hits the paper in Europe, it becomes a global piece of legislation." Globalization is generally a race to the bottom, but in this case it can mean a race upward. Companies can't afford to lose a primary market like the European Union and they don't want to manufacture fundamentally different products for the global market. Indeed, the good word is spreading. In 2008, California enacted two laws that establish a "Green Chemistry Initiative" in the state. Maine and Washington took legal steps to keep dangerous chemicals out of products designed for children.

According to business strategist Gil Friend, the smartest companies are seeking "regulatory insulation" by setting their internal standards so high that "regulations become an afterthought."

But won't all this regulation cost too much? Nonsense. After Massachusetts passed a Toxics Use Reduction Act, 80 percent of the nearly one thousand companies that filed plans implemented alternatives that brought about significant reductions in the amounts of chemicals they used. Not only did it *not* harm their businesses, their production increased by one-third and they saved $15 million in operating costs.

The centerpiece of ecological medicine is the precautionary principle. At a landmark retreat in Wingspread, Wisconsin, in 1998, a visionary group of scientists, environmentalists, philosophers, and others defined the Precautionary Principle: "When an activity raises threats of harm to human health or the environment, precautionary measures should be taken, even if some cause and effect relationships are not fully established scientifically. In this context the proponent of an activity, rather than the public, should bear the burden of proof. The process of applying the precautionary principle must be open, informed and democratic, and must include potentially affected parties. It must also involve an examination of the full range of alternatives, including no action."

Some communities, governments, and companies are putting the precautionary principle into practice in highly creative ways. In Oregon, the Portland City Council and Multnomah County Board of Commissioners passed a resolution to reduce toxics by applying the principle to county and city government operations. Denton, Texas, used it to stop the use of pesticides in public spaces, while the process of rigorously examining alternatives revealed the economic benefit that the waste corn gluten abundant in the region makes a viable nontoxic natural pesticide. The Hawaii Supreme Court invoked the principle to enforce the state's public trust responsibility for protecting its surface water from harm for future generations.

California has led the way. San Francisco earned bragging rights as the first city in the country to pass precautionary legislation. The city and county applied the principle to their annual purchasing budget, prioritizing not the cheapest alternative, but the safest. They've developed an approved products list and are challenging businesses to meet the opportunity.

California's Environmental Protection Agency instituted the use of the precautionary principle as state environmental justice policy. The purpose is to equip low-income communities and communities of color to enforce equal rights to a clean and healthy environment.

Kaiser Permanente—the nation's largest nonprofit healthcare system—instituted on-site farmers markets programs at many of its hospitals. Kaiser recognizes that healthy, nutritious, locally grown, and organic foods can both prevent illness and improve human health. Kaiser also knows its action enhances environmental quality and the economic vitality of local communities. Meanwhile, in 2009 the *Los Angeles Times* reported that "more hospitals in the U.S. are offering organic produce and hormone- and antibiotic-free meats and dairy foods in response to a trend toward healthier eating habits." Green Jell-O is out, green apples are in.

In the face of potentially catastrophic global warming, cities and states are taking the precautionary lead. Seattle's utility became the first in the nation with no net emissions of greenhouse gases. Portland, since starting on the same track in 1993, has reduced per capita emissions by 13 percent by virtue of strong investments in public transit and by an innovative suite of incentives for green building. Tom Potter, Portland's mayor from 2004 to 2009, said, "People have looked at it the wrong way, as a drain. It's economical. It makes sense in dollars." In other words, precaution pays.

Meanwhile, groups such as Health Care Without Harm, a coalition now operating in over fifty countries, have systematically begun the elimination of toxics such as mercury and dioxin from hospital incinerators and the medical waste stream. Laws in Canada are going after dental mercury.

In truth, it's principally hugely profitable big business interests that continue to fuel environmental destruction that threatens public health and sustains a highly toxic medical system.

Earlier in the twentieth century, the American Medical Association (AMA) controlled the business of medicine. Along with fiercely opposing national health insurance, the AMA fought domination by corporations. For well over half the century, it was remarkably effective at preventing corporate competition from offering health care services, except for sectors such as the emerging drug business and medical supply companies.

Laws enacted around 1900 forbade corporations from engaging in the commercial practice of medicine because, unlike a doctor, a corporation could not be licensed to practice medicine, and the commercialization of medicine conflicted with "sound public policy." Most hospitals were nonprofit enterprises until the 1960s.

Morris Fishbein, the powerful head of the AMA in that era, characterized the prospect of corporate medicine as "racketeering." Although in truth the AMA's real horror of corporations was the specter of their relegating doctors to the status of employees—becoming just another labor input on a corporate balance sheet—Fishbein diagnosed the situation accurately.

By the 1970s, however, the critical condition of medical economics presented an irresistible growth opportunity for corporate medicine. The AMA's failure to deliver affordable, effective health care to a large plurality of Americans opened the gate wide for corporate privatization. Large corporate ventures seized the opportunity, promising efficient business management to control costs.

Fishbein's worst fears about the corporatization of medicine have been realized. U.S. health care costs have reached the highest per capita of any developed nation in the world, while our health care quality is in many regards dismal compared with other developed nations—and, as of 2009, over 50 million Americans were uninsured.

According to medicine's own standards, *85 percent of prescribed standard medical treatments lack scientific validation altogether.* Conventional medicine is often not safe either. Over 100,000 Americans are killed each year by the *appropriate* use of pharmaceutical drugs just in hospitals, the fourth leading cause of death. Not to mention the fact that *JAMA* (the AMA's journal) reports that a patient has only twenty-three seconds on average to state her concerns to a doctor before being interrupted.

Managed care has more accurately become "managed profits" on an increasingly concentrated playing field. A handful of conglomerates controls nearly all medical insurance, and a parallel trend is shrinking the number of managed-care corporations. With poignant irony, Paul Ellwood, the architect of HMOs, dramatically reversed his position and criticized the "unacceptable" quality of American health care, calling for universal health coverage.

The economics of health care are unsustainable, which is one reason that the use of natural medicine is becoming more widespread. From the perspective of ecological medicine as well as that of tens or hundreds of millions of patients, natural medicine is safer, cheaper, and often effective. Given burgeoning market demand for alternative treatments, large insurance companies have added them to their mosaic. The potential cost savings from alternative therapies are emerging as a decisive factor.

Until recently, conventional medicine made a blanket condemnation of alternative therapies as snake oil (some are, of course). Ironically, snake oil, the favorite archetype of medical charlatanism, seems to have gotten a bad rap after all. Contemporary research has found it has important therapeutic value, possibly even against cancer. Its long history of medical usage continues today in China, where it is successfully employed to treat arthritis and skin disorders.

When researcher Richard Kunin bought snake oil from a Chinatown herb shop in San Francisco and subjected it to laboratory analysis, it proved to have *even higher levels* of key therapeutic fatty acids than fish oil. Kunin went on to test two U.S. species of rattlesnakes against the principal variety used in China. It turns out the Chinese species has at least *five times* the active constituents of the others. How did Chinese healers know?

Studies by the National Cancer Institute have found the occurrence of drug activity higher in plants reported in folk literature than in plants collected at random. Of the over 120 drugs on the market today that are derived from plants, three-quarters have a history of medical usage by indigenous peoples. How is it that traditional medicine systems have consistently prefigured and predated innumerable scientific "discoveries"?

The natural (empiric) medicine tradition is a way of knowing based on direct observation and experience. Outcomes are its first measure of success, emphasizing pragmatic results over theory or understanding. Or as one wag contrasted it with conventional medicine's reverse paradigm, "Sure it works in practice, but what about in theory?"

Among the most ancient expressions of the empiric tradition are herbs. Medicinal herbs have been found with the remains of humans dating back sixty thousand years. The very word *drug* derives from the Dutch *droog*, which means "to dry," since people have historically dried plants to make medicinal preparations.

Botany endures as the cornerstone of pharmacy. About 25 percent of prescription drugs contain at least one plant constituent, and another 25 percent are modeled on plants. Over 80 percent of the world's population still relies on plant-derived medicines for basic health care needs.

Germany leads the developed countries in its acceptance of botanical medicine. The German equivalent of the FDA collated all herbal folklore as well as scientific studies into a reliable database, and now an estimated 70 percent of German doctors prescribe herbs, accounting for over half the country's $3 billion annual herb sales. The late Varro Tyler, Distinguished Professor of Pharmacognosy Emeritus at Purdue University, called the system "rational herbalism." For the better part of the twentieth century, conventional medicine dismissed herbs as a bunch of weeds. But as Ralph Waldo Emerson said in *Fortune of the Republic*, "What is a weed? A plant whose virtues have not yet been discovered."

Health care advances in the twenty-first century will be about looking back as well as forward. The great health advances of the nineteenth century had little to do with medical care and everything to do with public health measures. Diseases were dramatically controlled by a variety of societal and environmental changes, like maintaining clean water supplies and quarantining the sick. The result was a steep decline in diseases such as TB, cholera, and diphtheria before there were drugs to treat the illnesses or vaccines to prevent them.

Around that time there raged a fundamental conflict of medical opinion between Louis Pasteur and his scientific rival, Antoine Béchamp. Where Pasteur identified pathogenic germs as the cause of disease, Béchamp contended instead that, "The terrain is everything." In his view, it is principally an imbalance in the body's ecology that allows dangerous germs to gain dominance or stimulates otherwise harmless germs to mutate and turn malignant. A healthy terrain, he proposed, defeats pathogens or holds them harmlessly in check in a dynamic balance.

In other words, the medium is the message in biology as well. These kinds of ideas are finding their way into practice around the world. The city of Munich in Germany pays local growers around its watershed to farm organically. The Vienna Hospital Association contracts with a large network of local organic growers for hospital food, thereby also creating a stable long-term organic farming infrastructure. By heavily taxing pesticides, Sweden reduced their use by 65 percent.

These are all harbingers of the coming era of ecological medicine. Ecological medicine shifts the emphasis from the individual to public health; from nutrition to the food web and farming systems; from a human-centered viewpoint to one of biodiversity and the ecosystem services that are the foundations of health and healthy economies. It is founded in the precautionary principle, and it calls for a new social contract with both the human family and the web of life. Now that we have had a national debate about health insurance, maybe we're ready for a debate about health *care*.

Both the imperative of sustainability and the desire to protect what we love and hold sacred are embodied in the precautionary principle. As David W. Orr wrote,

> We are co-members of one enterprise stretching back through time beyond memory, but forward no further than we are, plain members and citizens of the biotic community. This awareness carries both an imperative and a possibility. The imperative is simply that we ought to pay full and close attention to the ecological conditions and prerequisites that

sustain all life. That we seldom know how human actions affect ecosystems or the biosphere gives us every reason to act with informed precaution. The possibility is that in the long gestation of humankind we acquired an affinity for life, earth, forests, water, soils and place, what E. O. Wilson calls "biophilia." It is the best hope for our future that I know.

DREAMING THE FUTURE

Empire Crash in the Age of Nature

*D*reaming the future can create the future. We stand at the threshold of a singular opportunity in the human experiment: to reimagine how to live on Earth in ways that honor the web of life, each other, and future generations.

Then again, in the immortal words of Yogi Berra, "The future ain't what it used to be."

We also stand at the brink of worldwide ecological and civilizational collapse. We face a reckoning from the treacherous breach in our relationship with nature. We've been acting like a rock star trashing a hotel room, and it's the morning after. But this hotel is planet Earth. The guest rules are non-negotiable. If we don't change our ways fast, management may vote us off the island.

We're entering the Age of Nature. It calls for a new social contract of interdependence. Taking care of nature means taking care of people, and taking care of people means taking care of nature.

The ecological debt we've incurred is dire. We've precipitated climate change that's within 1°C of the maximum temperature in the past million years. As NASA's chief climatologist James Hansen warns, "Beyond that, we will likely see changes that make Earth a different planet." Think *Jurassic Park*. Hansen and many other leading scientists say we have until 2020 at best to make a massive global shift, an extreme carbon makeover. It's showtime.

There's a Gary Larson cartoon pertinent to our current predicament. A crowded lifeboat filled with dogs is floating away from a sinking ship. The lead dog says to the assembly, "All right—all those in favor of eating all the food all at once—raise your paws." It's a dog's world all right.

As historian J. R. McNeill concluded in *Something New under the Sun: An Environmental History of the Twentieth-century World*, the sun has set on the biblical observation that there's nothing new under the sun.

- The century was unusual for its intensity of environmental change and the centrality of human activity in provoking it.
- Our ways of living are specifically adapted to our current circumstances, such as climate, the abundance of cheap energy and cheap freshwater, rapid population growth, and even more rapid economic growth.
- These preferences are not easily adaptable if and when our circumstances change.

For long-term biological success, the best survival strategy is to be very adaptable, pursue diverse sources of subsistence, and optimize resilience. Yet we've limited our adaptability to a very narrow set of parameters whose intrinsic nature is to create instability and undermine the brittle structures of human affairs on which we now depend.

If there's one essential fact to know, it's that all the basic life support systems of the planet are in serious and accelerating decline, and we're going to have to be more adaptable than ever.

Ecology is founded on limits, yet the single most important idea driving this destruction is the ideology of unlimited economic growth. As McNeill points out,

> Economic growth became the indispensible ideology of the state nearly everywhere. Like an exotic intruder invading disturbed ecosystems, the growth fetish colonized ideological fields around the world after the dislocations of the Depression: It was the equivalent of the European rabbit. After the Depression, economic rationality trumped all other concerns except security. Those who promised to deliver the Holy Grail became high priests. One American economist in 1984 cheerfully forecast five billion years of economic growth—only the extinction of the sun could cloud the horizon.

Meanwhile war and perceived threats to defending national security generated the world's military-industrial complexes, whose environmental consequences have been almost unimaginable in scale and scope. Ironically the disturbed environment is itself creating the ultimate national security threat, a kind of hostile power provoked by our own security anxiety, a golem made from the clay of our fears.

The reality of nature is continuous cycles of creation and destruction, of birth and death. Sustainability, as author Paul Hawken points out, is the dynamic midpoint between destruction and restoration. In light of the severe damage and depletion, we need to tip the scales by putting our thumb on the side of restoration. Fortunately Earth has a profound capacity for self-repair. Just not on a human time frame.

The world situation that's spontaneously combusting is a perfect storm of environmental degradation and rolling infrastructure collapse. It's by no means the first time. Several prior human civilizations have bought the farm of self-induced environmental calamity.

As Jared Diamond points out, prior civilizations have met their demise by cutting down forests, eroding topsoil, and building burgeoning cities in dry areas that ran short of water. Sometimes hastened by climate change, the ensuing disintegration has occurred suddenly—in a matter of a decade or two after a society has reached its pinnacle of population, wealth, and power. The climax of maximum resource consumption and waste production has produced unsupportable environmental impacts.

When Diamond examined the demise of the Mayan civilization in Mexico, he teased out the final thread from the unraveled tapestry: political leadership. "Their attention was evidently focused on the short-term concerns of enriching themselves, waging wars, erecting monuments, competing with one another, and extracting enough food from the peasants to support all these activities." Sound familiar?

As we enter this drastic period of ecological regime shift, we're going to be busier than a cat in a room full of rocking chairs. Although global warming is getting all the ink, other intimately interdependent issues equal its magnitude: the mass extinction of 30 to 50 percent of Earth's biological and cultural diversity, freshwater shortages that will lead to wars, the universal poisoning of the biosphere, and the greatest extremes of inequality in modern history—a world that's 70 to 80 percent poor.

These epochal periods of creative destruction also present trans-formative opportunities to make the world anew. The quest is to build resilience—strengthening the capacity of natural and human systems to either rebound without losing their structure and function or to transform completely. The conundrum is that the whole world is going to need to transform at once.

The driving force behind today's unprecedented globalized collapse is financial. Futurist and economist Hazel Henderson has characterized conventional economics as "a form of brain damage." It rationalizes the insatiable predation of nature and people, while disappearing environmental and social costs from the balance sheet. It concentrates wealth and distributes poverty. It exalts greed and self-interest. It conflates free markets with democracy. It merges corporations and the state. Its foreign policy is empire. It has been a catastrophic success.

As author and scholar Kevin Phillips has chronicled, every major empire over the past several hundred years has undergone a depressingly predictable cycle of collapse, usually within ten to twenty years of its peak power.

The hallmarks are always the same:

- the financialization of the economy, moving from manufacturing to speculation;
- very high levels of debt;
- extreme economic inequality; and
- costly military overreaching.

The Dutch, Spanish, and British empires followed this pattern. The United States is repeating it. But as the oil magnate J. Paul Getty said, "Every time history repeats itself, the price goes up."

Yet there's an even deeper story behind empire crash.

Energy is a nation's master resource. Each empire has had an idiosyncratic ability to exploit a particular energy source that propelled its rise to economic power. The Dutch learned how to tap wood, wind, and water. The British empire fueled its ascendancy on coal. The American empire has dominated with oil. The cautionary tale is this: No empire has been able to manage the transition to the next energy source. The joker in the deck this time around is the climate imperative to transition off fossil fuels worldwide. It requires the most complex and fiercely urgent transition in the history of human civilization. Nothing like it has ever been done.

As Paul Hawken observes, "Historically few civilizations have reversed their tracks with respect to the environment, but rather have declined and disappeared because they forfeited their own habitat. For the first time in history, a civilization—its people, companies, and governments—is trying to arrest the downspin and understand how to live on Earth, a watershed in human existence."

Ecological regime change demands political regime change. As the environmental analyst and founder of the Worldwatch Institute Lester

Brown wrote, "Socialism collapsed because it did not allow prices to tell the economic truth. Capitalism may collapse because it does not allow prices to tell the ecological truth. We are in a race between tipping points in nature and our political systems."

Just as economics is driving the destruction, it needs to power the restoration. The charge is to transform the global economy from a vicious cycle to a virtuous cycle.

As the late senator Gaylord Nelson, principal founder of Earth Day, said, "The economy is a wholly owned subsidiary of the environment." Real wealth creation is based on replenishing natural systems and restoring the built environment, especially our infrastructure and cities. It's based on investing in our communities and workforce. It's been shown to work best when done all at once. According to Storm Cunningham, the author of re*Wealth!*, restoration could become an estimated $100 trillion market. There's plenty of work to do, plenty of people to do it, and abundant financial incentive. Every dollar we spend on predisaster risk management could prevent seven dollars in later losses.

The rules of virtuous engagement aren't that complicated. As Fred Block wrote in "The Moral Economy," "The essential idea was brilliantly expressed in the title of a 1980s bestseller, *All I Really Need to Know I Learned in Kindergarten*. The guiding principles are familiar rules such as: don't hit, take turns, play by the rules, listen to the teacher, don't waste food and art supplies, and be prepared to share. These principles produce order in the elementary school classroom, and they can also assure order and prosperity in our nation's economy."

The question is—will we change our old bad habits fast enough to beat forbidding odds?

There is cause for hope. A large movement is building. David W. Orr calls it a "global ecological Enlightenment." A big bang of brilliant, effective work is meeting with increasing receptivity. Yet still the pace of destruction outstrips our response. Real success will require a giant leap across the abyss on visionary currents of bold action. It will take skillful means. It will take a big heart. And in times like these, as Albert Einstein said, "Imagination is more important than knowledge."

Game-changing innovations in design and technology as well as social innovations are surfacing constantly. Global digital media can spread them at the speed of text messaging.

At the forefront is biomimicry, the art and science of mimicking nature's design genius. The biomimicry company Novomer looked at excess CO_2 in the atmosphere and asked "What would a plant do?" It would treat it as food. Novomer figured out how to use CO_2 as a feedstock to produce biodegradable green plastics. That's just one glimmer of what's possible.

Biomimicry is arguably the single most important design strategy to shoot the rapids of the next ten years. But it transcends gee-whiz technology. Biomimicry inspires us with nature's genius, and celebrates our kinship with the web of life. Among Navajo people, the worst insult you can say is, "You act like you have no relatives." Biomimicry invites us to act again as if we have relatives.

A riptide of capital is mainstreaming biomimicry and clean tech, now the third largest domain of venture capital investment. In Silicon Valley, the "watt.com" era has dawned. The Internet was in 2010 roughly a $1 trillion industry, while the worldwide energy market is roughly $6 trillion. In 2009 Google put forth a $4.4 trillion clean energy plan that proposed by 2030 to slash its fossil fuel use by 88 percent and CO_2 emissions by 95 percent. In 2010, Google teamed up with a large venture capital firm to build a giant $5 billion undersea transmission cable along the Atlantic coast to serve offshore wind farms up and down the Eastern seaboard (the Atlantic Wind Connection).

The smart money is hot on the trail of the next Industrial Revolution. There's mounting pressure on Uncle Sam because government policies make or break markets.

Astoundingly, the United States has no national energy policy, much less a plan for a post-oil world other than drill, baby, drill. Since World War II, the U.S. military has become a global oil protection force. It's no coincidence that the map of terror and the map of oil in the Middle East are almost the same. As clean energy expert and longtime consultant to the Department of Defense Amory Lovins points out, "We also pay a half trillion dollars a year to sustain military forces whose primary mission is intervention in the Persian Gulf. We have, of course, other national interests in the Persian Gulf than just oil, but it's hard to believe we would've invaded there twice if Kuwait and Iraq just grew broccoli. This military cost of our oil dependence and oil defense missions in every combat and command around the world—not even counting the corresponding military cost—add up to 10 times what we're paying for oil from the Persian Gulf, and they rival our total defense spending at the height of the Cold War. What's wrong with this picture?" The Iraq War not only failed to corner one of the last great reserves, it radically drained the treasury. As of 2012, the United States remains mired in the quicksand of Afghanistan and at risk of war with Iran.

The current oil economy transfers massive amounts of wealth to the ever more unstable Middle East, while our escalating debt indentures us to China and other foreign creditors. Oil dependency exposes the United States to perilous vulnerabilities in global power politics, and, as peak oil looms, China and India compete for supplies from Latin America, Africa, and Asia. Potential global flashpoints metastasize, spurring faster global warming.

Meanwhile, Germany seizes the solar high ground. Denmark rides the wind future. Japan leads on conservation technologies. China institutionalizes higher fuel efficiency standards with the stroke of a pen and moves to take the lead on clean technology development.

National energy policy, anyone?

But for now in the United States, the real action is happening at local and regional levels.

California, which would be the world's eighth largest economy if it were an independent country, in 2006 passed Assembly Bill 32, arguably the world's first comprehensive climate change legislation, and has been busy installing many square miles of solar panels. Massachusetts passed the nation's most far-reaching package of legislation on renewables and green jobs, and launched the first major offshore wind initiative after navigating federal approval. Texas is building some of the biggest wind installations ever, helping the United States recently surpass Germany as the world leader in total wind power.

Multicity and multistate collaborations are spreading nationwide. At least five states and over a hundred cities are collaborating on policy innovations in formal coalitions. In the coal-fired Midwest, RE-AMP's eight-state network has helped accomplish serious state-level renewables and efficiency targets. The collaboration has also stopped all but one of twenty-four proposed new coal plants from being built.

Enough municipalities are competing for "greenest city" status to start a new sports league. Mayor Michael Bloomberg of New York, who produced the Big Apple's 2030 green plan, PlaNYC, said: "Shrinking the world's carbon footprint is a pro-growth strategy, indeed the only pro-growth strategy for the long term." Tellingly, the nation's greenest cities are the ones with the most active citizenry—where bottom-up meets top-down. Municipal governments often do best by contracting with effective local nonprofits rather than trying to reinvent social services.

Demand for a green-collar workforce is rising far faster than the supply of workers. In the United States, where income inequality is the highest of any industrialized country, these jobs pay $16–30 an hour at entry level—$33,000–$62,000 a year. The green-collar restoration economy could help address economic, racial, and political injustice while healing the atmosphere.

But the deeper underlying impetus behind such local initiatives is to reboot Uncle Sam because national laws and policies can severely restrict or undermine local activities. And of course, the federal government is where the *real* money is.

Will Uncle Sam get on board, or at least get out of the way? Will the nation devolve into a radically decentralized, regionally governed country? Both? A decentralization of power seems almost inevitable, and it could become organized by bioregions according to how nature functions.

Our current sprawling society is built on the premise of cheap oil, which is so five-minutes-ago. This shift means a radical reorganization of everyday life, including many more locally based watersheds, foodsheds, and energysheds. Nature is organized by bioregions, and bioregional planning is the way of the future.

Around the turn of the eighteenth century, James Madison, a designer of the U.S. Constitution, wrote to Thomas Jefferson expressing his deep concerns for the fate of the republic. Although he favored a United States rather than autonomous states, he worried that if the nation grew too large, elites at the center would exploit the new country's size. He feared they would divide and conquer a widely scattered population and produce "tyranny."

At 300 million people, the United States may simply be ungovernable. As the political economist Gar Alperovitz observes, "No nation can be managed from the center once it reaches a certain scale. Sooner or later, a profound, probably regional, decentralization of the federal system may be all but inevitable." In fact, many other nations are devolving power to regions in various ways, including Germany, Britain, Brazil, Canada, China, France, Italy, and Spain.

Given the fact that the federal government has been MIA or obstructionist on countless critical issues, including climate change and infrastructure, cities and states are rolling up their sleeves to actually try to solve these problems on the ground at the local level. They're forming alliances, compacts, and networks to improve their performance and strengthen their political power.

It's almost impossible to keep up with the exploding trend toward localization worldwide, from the burgeoning Transition Towns movement that originated in Britain and is spreading worldwide to the Business Alliance for Local Living Economies (BALLE) in the United States. Whatever the vicissitudes of the big wide world, we can all try to take care of our own community, and many are. At the end of the day, most people are connected and committed first and foremost to their own place.

Which is not to say there's any easy fix or romanticized local solution for the complex challenges we face. We are ensnared by byzantine and often archaic governance structures both locally and nationally. Local control has brought us abominable shadows such as genocide against First Peoples, the Ku Klux Klan, religious oppression, and institutional discrimination against women.

In the end, as David W. Orr points out, only national governments have the power to set rules for the economy, enforce the law, levy taxes, ensure the fair distribution of income, protect the poor and future generations, cooperate with other nations, negotiate treaties, defend the public interest, and protect the commons and rights of posterity. Even a design revolution won't remake public policy and the tax system, or move public investment into R&D, or provide basic services, health care, emergency services, or basic fairness.

In truth the environment is a "globalocal" issue, and there's significant movement internationally as well. Germany, with fewer sunny days than Michigan, is the world's solar leader because of government policies that have already resulted in 20 percent renewable energy as of 2011. Spain, France, Italy, and Greece are copying some of Germany's policies. The European Union is aggressively trying to drive new markets forward with CO_2 caps and strong incentives for clean energy entrepreneurs.

Resource-poor Japan, the gold standard of energy efficiency, is making a play to market its radically advanced conservation technologies worldwide. China has made top-level commitments to large-scale R&D on renewables and clean technology.

We need to take this work to scale during this decade. Breakthrough technological innovations have to spread rapidly, as do the government policies that drive these markets. Of equal importance are social innovations and political regime change.

The e-Parliament in Europe began reaching out directly to national lawmakers across Europe and the Mediterranean to accelerate the spread of policy best practices, model legislation, and parliamentary tool kits. Now reoriented as the Climate Parliament with an energy and climate focus, it's pushing to build a large-scale multinational green grid within the next decade. It has been instrumental in disseminating Costa Rica's successful forest policy. By incentivizing the support of ecosystem services, Costa Rica has helped protect and restore much of the country's forest cover, almost 90 percent of which had been denuded during the twentieth century, and ecotourism is roaring.

The newly constructed national constitution of Ecuador turned property law on its head in 2009 as it became the first country to institute legally enforceable rights for nature and ecosystems. Working with Tom Linzey's Community Environmental Legal Defense Fund (CELDF), the Ecuadorian government modeled its policy on Linzey's similar groundbreaking work with one hundred local communities in the United States.

The global North owes a massive ecological debt to the global South. In part because it's politically remote that developed countries will seriously consider any form of reparations or large-scale debt forgiveness, the global restoration economy will go a long way toward healing the ravages of empire, genocide, and racism among nations. While the governments of Australia and Canada have initiated national reconciliation through formal apologies to their First Peoples for past harms, the larger issue is practical: how to lift people out of the poverty that's part of that legacy of colonialism.

These are landmark successes. But as Michael Kinsley of the Rocky Mountain Institute says, "We've got to go from success stories to systemic change." It's going to take epic cooperation among business, government, and civil society—and among nations. We need to play big and aim high.

It begins with a dream. In the words of David Oates in an essay called "Imagine" in *High Country News*:

> To imagine is difficult. It takes courage—encouragement; it takes opportunities carefully constructed (by me or the Fates). Then something magic happens: A key turns in a lock, eyebrows ascend on foreheads—and a new world is glimpsed, a 3-D moment that dazzles.
>
> A vision predicates an imaginative leap: that we are—after all—fundamentally *connected* to each other—that my fate and happiness are not private matters only, but a shared project. A tax cut takes no imagination: It's a few more bucks in your

pocket. But seeing one's ownership in a community, one's own face in someone else's child, that takes imagination.

Imagine—combining our resources to relieve suffering and to open up dead-ends of poverty and hopelessness. Imagine knowing that our fate is each other.

Imagine: knowing that our fate also swims with the salmon and grows with the trees.

Imagine living beyond yourself—finding the thing you're good at and in love with, even if it doesn't pay so well. That would be like coming back to life, wouldn't it? It would be like grace.

Imagine.

Part 2

HUNGRY
GHOST STORIES

THE STING

The Role of Fraud in Nature

*B*iomimicry, the design science of "innovation inspired by nature," is unearthing untold treasures from nature's playbook that we can emulate for our technological and industrial recipe book. But naturally, as human beings we're meaning-making creatures who are suckers for a good story or metaphor. It's seductive to search the biomimicry database for lessons we can apply to human social relations. Some call it "social biomimicry."

After all, who can resist the metaphor of geese that fly in a V formation and rotate the lead goose to lighten the load of bucking the most severe wind resistance?

Or the Seven Sisters oak trees in Louisiana that can withstand fierce hurricanes because their roots grow together to make an entire community of resilience?

These natural-world metaphors are "megaphors"—archetypal ecological parables for how we might better organize ourselves as societies and with each other.

The problem is that every species is unique and uniquely fitted to its context, place, and time. People are not geese or oak trees. And frankly, even as seriously weird species go, human beings are . . . well . . . special.

Yet we are amazing mimics, and surely we can learn a riff or two from the symphony of life. But looking around at the wretched state of the world, you have to wonder: Is there some deeper form of social biomimicry already in play that we're not seeing? Indeed, it's cannily hiding in plain sight. You might call it the role of fraud in nature.

Nature wrote the playbook on deceit. From viruses to Wall Street, nature is a hall of mirrors of lying, cheating, and camouflaging. After all, if force doesn't work, trickery can do the trick. Shady practices can give any organism a winning edge in the ruthless struggle for survival and reproduction that powers evolution and adaptation.

As David Livingstone Smith observed in his book *Why We Lie*, "Lying is a natural phenomenon. The biosphere teems with mendacity. Deception is widespread among nonhuman species, perfectly normal and expectable." Human beings, says Smith, evolved to be "natural born liars."

Among our closest cousins the monkeys and apes, deceit is pervasive. Their brains grew in direct correlation with the size of their groups. Smith suggests "double dealing and suspicion might have been the driving forces behind the explosion of brainpower." In turn, the prized neocortex of the *Homo sapiens* brain—our much vaunted thinking capability—also grew in direct correlation with the size and social complexity of our groups. Then came language.

Nonhuman primates use extensive grooming rituals to establish stable social bonds, cliques, and power structures. With *Homo sapiens*, language replaced public grooming with private gossip. As the psychologist and cognitive neuroscientist Merlin Donald suggests, we may have developed language because we "needed to gossip, forge alliances, win friends and neutralize enemies." We spend 80–90 percent of our conversations talking about other people, two-thirds of that about our immediate social networks. The war of words exponentially escalated the arsenal of deceit, espionage, and manipulation. Evolution has favored these traits.

As Smith observes, "From the fairy tales our parents told us to the propaganda our governments feed us, human beings spend their lives surrounded by pretense. . . . The founding myth of the Judeo-Christian tradition, the story of Adam and Eve, revolves around a lie . . . Eve told God, 'The serpent deceived me and I ate.'"

From faked orgasms to infidelity, breast enhancements to financial fraud, the white lies of social graces to political spin, *Homo sapiens*—Wise Man—might more accurately be dubbed Wise Guy in a Tony Soprano kind of way. After all, humans are a predatory species, and our main prey is our own kind—for the usual suspects of sex, food, survival, or status.

Mimicry is one of the best tricks in the book, and perhaps we're hardwired to mimic nature's bag of tricks without even knowing it. So let's go back to nature for some master classes on the sting.

If you want to observe one classic sting in nature, check out bee orchids. To attract male wasps to pollinate them, the orchids not only look like an insect Marilyn Monroe, they exude a fragrance even more bewitching than the real sexual attractant of the females they're mimicking. The male wasps, which mature a month before the females, lurch from orchid to orchid, looking for love in all the wrong places. Meanwhile they spread the wily orchids' pollen in fruitless grand rounds of "pseudocopulation" that don't get no satisfaction, at least not for them.

That pseudocopulation brings to mind those supposedly AAA-rated bundled mortgage CDOs packaged by the financial masters of the universe to look like the sexiest investment on the Street. Then they turned out to be pseudoinvestments that spread the nectar of wealth among only the rarefied orchids of high finance.

Back a little closer to home with our nearest primate cousins, Smith observes, "Nonhuman species have their own version of fire and brimstone preaching." Called "ritualized signals of displays," we seem to be aping our ape kin to manipulate others. We use the same techniques of "redundancy, rhythmic repetition, bright packaging and supernormal stimuli"—rerunning a relentless sensory overload of brassy ads for cars, toothpaste, and political candidates.

Take bright packaging. Recent research has identified conspicuousness as a key strategic defense against predators. It's called "signal extravagance." Flashy conspicuous prey are flaunting the fact they've survived encounters with predators, who therefore tend to avoid them. A bright butterfly that's toxic or distasteful to birds soon generates imposters among its kind who imitate its colors and patterns in a kind of visual identity theft. Perhaps it brings to mind toxic Lehman Brothers and AIG, and the opportunistic mimics from Goldman Sachs, J. P. Morgan Chase & Co., and the phenotypical bank fraudsters who assumed the poisonous colors of the too-big-to-fail defense.

Another popular form of mimicry in plants and animals is crypsis, the art of concealment. Keeping a low profile also has potent advantages. Many plants and creatures have evolved to blend in with their surroundings—mimicking a stone, piece of coral, branch, or bird droppings.

Perhaps it brings to mind the American Legislative Exchange Council (ALEC). Or perhaps it does not—because the ploy was to keep ALEC invisible. Funded by big corporations and the oil- and chemical-dependent Koch brothers, this secretive shadow government of sorts brings together corporate chieftains and legislators to manufacture bills to rewrite state laws. ALEC bills undermine worker and consumer rights, roll back environmental regulations, privatize education, and deregulate major industries. This clandestine public-private partnership has helped pass stealth legislation across the country, including nearly identical resolutions now legislated in a dozen states to force the EPA to stop regulating carbon emissions. In 2012 ALEC's crypsis strategy collapsed following its exposure as the factory for the "Stand Your Ground" gun laws that seized the national spotlight with the Stand Your Ground defense in the fatal shooting of the young unarmed African American boy Travon Martin in Florida.

Then again, going back to nature, you can also trick the tricksters—as does the highly intelligent octopus *Thaumoctopus mimicus. T. mimicus* is able to shape-shift and shade-shift into a Gaga wardrobe of disguises. It can disappear itself into the exact pattern and coloration of its surroundings. It can scare off predators by taking on the appearance of the highly toxic lionfish. If attacked by a damselfish, it morphs one of its arms into the visage of the fearsome sea snake that eats damselfish.

Which may bring to mind the Yes Men, those notorious shape-shifters who assume the identity of corporate predators for fun and social profit. In 2011 they spawned the Yes Lab to go forth and multiply in the inexorable Darwinian tradition. The Yes Lab sent out a faux press release announcing that General Electric would repay the $3.2 billion tax credit it got last year despite its huge profits. When the Associated Press took the bait, the market immediately carved $3.5 billion off GE's stock price before the hoax was discovered. And in Canada, a Yes Lab team of students and Greenpeace activists launched a humbug campaign that made folks briefly believe the huge new *Hobbit* movie was saving money on sulfurous scenes of infernal Mordor by filming them in the straight-from-central-casting oil-infused tar sands.

Of course, from an evolutionary perspective, lying is a double-edged sword. On the plus side, self-deception is especially valuable when lying to others because we convincingly believe our own hokum. We also lie to ourselves to diminish stress. Inevitably, we're the heroes of our own stories, and of course we all know that every one of us is above average. Research on depressives has found they may suffer from a *deficit* of self-deception.

On the downside of self-deception, take the Fukushima nuclear catastrophe.

The tightly coupled Japanese government and nuclear industry colluded for decades to spin the myth that nuclear energy is as safe as milk. After Chernobyl, they ramped up lush public relations buildings and tourist attractions to promote its safety, especially to resistant young mothers and women of childbearing age. In the elaborately tricked-out Alice in Nuclear Wonderland theme park, the White Rabbit moans, "It's terrible, just terrible. We're running out of energy, Alice," whereupon a

Dodo robot chimes in that nuclear is an "ace" form of energy that's safe and renewable. For a hundred thousand visitors each year, the Caterpillar has pacified Alice about radiation dangers. In the land that coined the term *tsunami*, the word never came up in Nuclear Wonderland. Until, of course, it happened. Then a famous Japanese singer rewrote one of his previous songs with protest lyrics to create the anthem that swept the country, "It Was Always a Lie."

The conundrum is that the Japanese nuclear establishment ultimately deceived itself by fatally believing its own press releases. Nature does not gladly suffer fools, errors, and mistakes. Self-deception may prove to be our evolutionary Achilles' heel.

Yet some part of our brain seems designed to act as an unconscious mind reader, picking up reality-based signals even as we up the ante in the escalating Olympics of deceit and self-deception. Deep inside, we all possess a bullshit detector, and that may be what saves us.

Nature is sending us extravagant distress signals these days. We'd better get really good really fast at reading her mind. The stakes are too high to keep drinking the collective Kool-Aid.

You can't fool Mother Nature. Trust me. That ain't no lie.

THE ROBBER BARONS

Déjà Vu All Over Again

*I*n his book *Thoughts Without a Thinker*, Mark Epstein describes the classic image of the hungry ghost drawn from various schools of Buddhism: "The Hungry Ghosts are probably the most vividly drawn metaphors in the Wheel of Life. Phantomlike creatures with withered limbs, grossly bloated bellies, and long thin necks, the Hungry Ghosts in many ways represent a fusion of rage and desire. Tormented by unfulfilled cravings and insatiably demanding of impossible satisfactions, the Hungry Ghosts are searching for gratification for old unfulfilled needs whose time has passed. They are beings who have uncovered a terrible emptiness within themselves, who cannot see the impossibility of correcting something that has already happened. Their ghostlike state represents their attachment to the past." They are often depicted as having huge stomachs, pencil-thin necks, and tiny mouths.

The more things change, the more they stay the same. Hungry ghosts are among us. Their ravenous hunger can never be satisfied, no matter how much they eat and consume. Like hermit crabs, they've inhabited the shells of corporations over the past centuries. It's the old shell game, and looking backward to the original robber barons will help us see around the crooked corners yet to come.

The term *robber baron* originated as a literal descriptor for the predatory aristocracy of medieval Europe. Both lords and Church archbishops collected tolls from ships on the Rhine River, in principle only by the explicit authorization of the Holy Roman Emperor. However, aristocrats abused their privileged positions by stopping passing merchant ships and demanding tolls even without Church approval. Sometimes they hung chains across the river. Those who came to be known as robber barons charged higher tolls than the normal going rate or operated as free agents. With or without the authority of the Church, the message was the same: "Stand and deliver."

The moniker resurfaced in the nineteenth century when the Industrial Revolution uncorked breathtaking opportunities for vast new wealth, first epitomized by the railroads. Whoever controlled the railroads would control commerce. This unprecedented industrial-scale commercial opportunity led directly to the mass marketing of stocks, to stock bubbles, the wholesale picking of investors' pockets, and the fabulous enrichment of insider scoundrels.

The genesis is revealing. The railroad boom erupted with the Civil War, when building the transcontinental railroad became a matter of national security for the North to win the war. It also presented an unparalleled and irresistible gravy train. The new robber barons engineered the really great train robbery.

A group of California merchants known as the Big Four seized on this most golden apple of the Gilded Age. But Collis Huntington, Leland Stanford, Mark Hopkins, and Charles Crocker were not visionaries. They were petit-bourgeois merchants who well understood the danger to their businesses if a competitor got control of transportation and did to them what they were doing to their captive customers.

Huntington and Hopkins had already made a small fortune by cornering the market on nails, shovels, and blasting powder—then selling them to miners during the Gold Rush for "all the traffic would bear." Monopoly was the name of the game, and Huntington realized that whoever controlled the railroads could corner the market on commerce in the West and grab a piece of all the action. He organized the Big Four to do just that.

Huntington's motto was, "Anything that's not nailed down is mine, and anything I can pry loose is not nailed down." Your generic corporate mission statement.

Huntington traveled to the nation's capital toting a suitcase filled with $200,000 in cash. He returned with a sheaf of federal contracts, though no receipts. He got a package deal so rich that even he was surprised: the monopolistic right to build the railroad line connecting West to East; 12 million acres of free land grants; cheap federal loans for his own company to build the railroad (known today as self-dealing and highly illegal); and the right to set his own freight rates.

Meanwhile Huntington's political partner Leland Stanford captured the governorship and quickly floated a $15 million railroad bond subsidy to the voters. On election day his brother Philip Stanford rattled through the streets of San Francisco in a wagon carrying a trunk filled with gold coins, dispensing them to eager voters. The bond issue won handily by a margin of two to one.

The Big Four systematically began a shopping spree for state politicians and judges. Their nemesis, the famous muckraking reporter Ambrose Bierce, dryly commented, "With the generous help of the deep-pocketed lobbyists of the Big Four, a two-headed calf called the Democratic-Republican party has seized control of the state legislature." Infuriated by Bierce's journalistic bayonets, they started doling out large newspaper advertising contracts in direct exchange for sunny editorial coverage.

Huntington spent most of his time back East, raising the bottomless capital essential for constant expansion and playing backroom politics in Washington DC. As the wealthy Republican political boss Mark Hanna commented, "There are two things that are important in politics. The first is money, and I can't remember what the second one is."

The Big Four built opulent mansions on San Francisco's Nob Hill, acquired European art treasures wholesale, planted vast vineyards, and raised racehorses. But somehow their company, despite making its directors the wealthiest men in California, never did manage to pay out any dividends to shareholders.

By now the Western railroad was universally reviled as the "octopus" whose iron tentacles strangled all of Western commerce. Farmers shipping their goods to market were quoted one price at spring planting, then a higher price at harvest. When they protested, the railroad demanded to see their bookkeeping, then charged them to within pennies of bankrupting them. It had the highest freight rates in the nation—except of course for the "rebates" (i.e., kickbacks) it secretly gave to large customers such as John D. Rockefeller's Standard Oil, methodically wiping out smaller competitors.

In industry after industry, the monopolists seized control: Rockefeller's oil, Carnegie's steel, J. P. Morgan's banking. As one political cartoon of the era portrayed, "The citizen today is born to drink milk from the milk trust, eat beef from the beef trust, be illuminated by the oil trust, and die with the coffin trust."

"Competition is a sin," grumbled John D. Rockefeller, as the incorrigible railroad barons still competed mercilessly with one other. Until, that is, J. P. Morgan called an urgent meeting, a kind of monopolists' summit.

Morgan bluntly reprimanded them: desist in this thieves' quarrel over the spoils and face the common enemy—the public. The real business at hand was the System: extracting high prices for stocks and bonds from the masses of investors. The System was one of integration—steel, oil, iron, timber, mines, factories, ships, railroads, and above all banking—all working together. He summoned them up to the mountaintop to see the coming age of integration—of huge profits, eternal prosperity, billion-dollar corporations!

As the premier monopolist of the banking industry, Morgan warned that whoever stepped out of line would see his investment capital dry up, a death sentence in the cash-intensive, grow-or-die death match. Facing an equally fatal form of capital punishment, they belatedly embraced his vision—especially in light of violent labor strikes (the biggest populist movement in American history) and the 1905 revolutionary unrest in Russia. There's nothing like class war to sober the mind.

Huntington finally met his demise when he went to Washington DC to lobby Congress for the Pacific Railroad Funding Bill to forgive entirely the railroad's gargantuan $76 million debt to the government. For thirty-five years, he had never paid back a nickel of principal or interest on Uncle Sam's prodigiously generous loans.

But Huntington's luck finally ran out. He had made the unfortunate mistake of writing a damning set of private letters to a partner detailing the exact prices it had cost him to "convince" various public officials of the merits of his position. He had made the mistake of chiseling the widow of a partner out of stock coming to her, whereupon she accidentally discovered her late husband's cache of damning letters and released them for the world to see.

Confronted by Congress with the letters, Huntington said flatly, "Sometimes a man won't do right unless he is bribed to do it." In fact, his letters complained bitterly about the rising inflation rate of bribes to congressmen.

When challenged by Congress to produce the financial records of his construction company's actual building costs, he revealed that he had advised the bookkeeper to avoid unnecessary storage costs by burning the documents.

The Pacific Railroad Funding Bill sank in scandal, and Huntington, the last of the Big Four, died a year later. Only Rockefeller's empire was big enough to swallow his swollen kingdom.

But the system Morgan envisioned lived on. Karl Marx was correct in identifying monopoly as the ultimate logic of capitalism, but he was dead wrong (at least so far) in predicting that the workers of the world would rise up in solidarity against it. It has been capital that successfully organized and globalized, not labor.

Here's a parting thought from the Gilded Age book called *The Passing of the Idle Rich*:

> Among my own people I seldom hear purely political discussions. When we are discussing pro and con the relative merits of candidates or the relative importance of political policies, the discussion almost invariably comes down to a question of business efficiency. We care absolutely nothing about any other political question, save inasmuch as it threatens or fortifies existing conditions. Touch the question of the tariff, touch the issue of the income tax, touch the problem of railroad regulation, or touch the most vital of all business matters, the question of general federal regulation of industrial corporations, and the people amongst whom I live my life become immediately rabid partisans. It matters not one iota what political party is in power, or what president holds the reins of office. We are not politicians or public thinkers; we are the rich; we own America; we got it, God knows how; but we intend to keep it if we can—by throwing all the tremendous weight of our support, our influence, our money, our political connection, our purchased senators, our hungry congressmen, our public-speaking demagogues, into the scale against any legislation, any political platform, any presidential campaign, that threatens the integrity of our estate.

Enron? AIG? Goldman Sachs? The robber barons are alive and, well, eating us for breakfast. The more things change . . .

SURVIVAL OF THE FATTEST

The Mythology of Greed

*W*hen Thabo Mbeki, then president of South Africa, opened the Johannesburg World Summit on Sustainable Development in 2002, he deplored the avoidable worldwide increase in human misery and ecological degradation, including the gap between North and South:

> It is as though we are determined to regress to the most primitive conditions of existence in the animal world of the survival of the fittest. It is as though we have decided to spurn what the human intellect tells us, that the survival of the fittest only presages the destruction of all humanity.

Poor old Darwin. When he published *On the Origin of Species* in 1859, it revolutionized our understanding of evolution. His theory of natural selection described the survival of the most fit, sending shock waves through every prevailing ideology and philosophy of the era. It instantly became a Rorschach onto which people projected their belief systems.

Because his theory emerged during the epoch of the ravenous robber barons, they adeptly distorted "survival of the fittest" into an intellectual cover to justify their predatory monopolistic feeding frenzy: survival of the fattest. As industry after industry fell under the concentrated greed of giant cartels, the robber barons rationalized Darwin's theory of natural selection as but a mirror of nature, in Alfred, Lord Tennyson's words, "red in tooth and claw." They painted an amoral struggle for existence where might makes right—where the ruthless pursuit of self-interest automatically cleaves to the greatest good of society. To act otherwise would contradict evolution itself.

Their vision of the struggle for existence applied to human relations meant that nature would assure that the best competitors in a dog-eat-dog world would win, leading inexorably to continuous improvement. This convenient logic underwrote their categorical denial of the need for any social safety net or government regulation. Values and emotions were banished to the gulag of sentimentality.

Here's the kind of conversation the social Darwinists were carrying on. Said John D. Rockefeller, "The growth of a large business is only survival of the fittest. It is merely the working out of a law of nature and a law of God." Remarked the motivational minister Russell Conwell, "To sympathize with a man whom God has punished for his sins is to do wrong. Let us remember there is not a poor person in the country who was not made poor by his own shortcomings." The nineteenth-century English biologist, sociologist and philosopher Herbert Spencer, who actually coined the term "survival of the fittest," opposed state aid to the poor because "the whole effort of nature is to clear the world of them, and make room for better."

Here is how the leading antimonopoly crusader of the era, Henry Demarest Lloyd, portrayed the ideological conflict: "The golden rule of business is: There is no hope for any of us, but the weakest must go first. There is no other field of human associations in which any such rule of action is allowed. The man who should apply in his family or in his citizenship this 'survival of the fittest' theory as it is professed and operated in business would be a monster, and would be speedily made extinct. To divide the supply of food between himself and his children according to their relative powers of calculation would be a short road to the penitentiary or the gallows. In trade, men have not yet risen to the family life of animals. It is a race to the bad, and the winners are the worst."

But all Darwin was actually saying was that the "fittest" were the best adapted to existing conditions at a given historical moment in a specific environmental context. He was primarily addressing the relationship between food supply and population size. Soon other biologists joined the fray, identifying group cohesion and solidarity to be equally as central to survival as competitive advantages.

Peter Kropotkin, the Russian naturalist and philosopher, reported on his studies of animal behavior in his famous book *Mutual Aid*, concluding, "Even in those spots where animal life teemed in abundance, I failed to find—although I was eagerly looking for it—that bitter struggle for the means of existence among animals belonging to the same species. Happily enough, competition is not the rule either in the animal world or in mankind. It is limited among animals to exceptional periods. Better conditions are created by the elimination of competition by means of mutual aid and mutual support. That is the tendency of nature."

But biologists daring to propose that any organism could live in partnership with another were relentlessly ridiculed. When the Swiss botanist Simon Schwendener asserted that lichen were not a single organism, but a symbiotic mix of fungi and algae, he was viciously condemned.

Institutional support for research on symbiosis evaporated in the heat of ideology, channeling official science into the reductionist machine model that led us into flawed mechanistic approaches such as single-action pharmaceutical drugs, pesticides, and GMOs. Orthodox science still celebrates the "selfish gene" and tends to neglect the study of relationships, ecosystems, and interdependence.

It took the genius of microbiologist Lynn Margulis to get symbiosis unstuck. She found what is very likely proof in DNA of an ancient evolutionary innovation between warring kinds of bacteria. After neither side could devour the other, instead they followed the urge to merge, leading to multicellular life as we know it. Evolution is coevolution, navigating by the North Star of symbiosis. Her theory, called *endosymbiosis*, violently rejected at first, is now widely accepted by mainstream science.

What does symbiosis look like?

Leafcutter ants and their fungus farms are a marvel of nature and one of the most closely studied forms of symbiosis, the mutual interdependence of species. As biologist E. O. Wilson wrote:

> The leafcutter colony is a single organism. The superorganism's brain is the entire colony. Through a unique step in evolution taken millions of years ago, the ants captured a fungus, incorporated it into the superorganism, and so gained the power to digest leaves. Or perhaps the relation is the other way around. Perhaps the fungus captured the ants and employed them as a mobile extension to take leaves into the moist underground chambers. In any case, the two now own each other and will never pull apart. The ant-fungus combination is one of evolution's master clockworks, tireless, repetitive and precise, more complicated than any human invention and unimaginably old.

Subsequent research uncovered even more amazing complexity to this wonder of symbiosis. Biologists were puzzled at how the ants could keep their precious fungus safe from pathogens, an especially dire threat to a monoculture. It turns out that their caverns are *not* free from pathogens. In fact, the fungus is very vulnerable to a devastating mold found nowhere else but in ant nests. To keep the mold in check, the ants long ago made a discovery that would send the stock of any pharmaceutical company soaring.

After it was long believed that there was a single fungus, it turns out that the ants have domesticated at least four kinds, which are often cultivated near one another.

When the fungus is threatened by the mold, which happens among 60 percent of colonies within two years, the ants bring in another species, which provides a bacterium that is lethal to the deadly mold as well as being a fertilizer for the fungus. That same bacterium has been the source of over half the antibiotics used in medicine. An Alexander Fleming of ants discovered antibiotics millions of years before people did.

Ants also invented agriculture before people did, by 50 million years, and they are accomplishing two feats beyond the powers of present human technologies. They are growing a monocultural crop year after year without disaster, and they are using an antibiotic so prudently that they have not provoked antibiotic resistance.

This centuries-old battle for the soul of the science of life rages on. Today an ecological Darwinism is ascendant that encompasses the complexity of reciprocal relations in communities of organisms and their interdependence.

By the time of World War I, social Darwinism had been thoroughly discredited in every field of human endeavor except one: the market. The ideological heirs of the robber barons continue to promote the fraud that the extreme concentration of wealth and power is a natural law operating for the greatest good.

So watch out for those belief systems—BS, that is.

THIS IS YOUR BRAIN ON PUBLIC RELATIONS

Lizards from Outer Space

$\mathcal{A}$s the comedian Lily Tomlin remarked, no matter how cynical you are, it's impossible to keep up any more.

A few years ago a friend e-mailed me a link to a website to check out for its sharp political commentary. I was really busy and I never got to it. A couple months later, she e-mailed me again to say, "Don't bother." She had drilled down and discovered the site's core belief: George W. Bush and Dick Cheney are lizards from outer space.

OK, scratch that. But the more I thought about it, what struck me was—yes, indeed, there are lizards among us. In fact, there are lizards *in* us.

From a biological perspective, one of the features that make us unique as human beings is that our brain is composed of three distinct brains. The most ancient is the "lizard brain." It deals with pure survival, encoded with the primeval instincts for breathing, getting food, fight, and flight. Lizards have no emotions. They are disinterested in their young—except, perhaps, to eat them.

Then there's the famed neocortex, the thinking brain that Western civilization has so fervently exalted. It gives us our intellectual abilities for reason, speech, and complex problem solving.

Lastly, there's the limbic brain, which harbors perhaps our most unique qualities as mammals. It gives us feelings, empathy, and the capacity for emotional connection. It's one reason human babies have such long periods of parental nurturance—to wire our emotional intelligence.

So—what if wily, cold-blooded, brain-sucking lizards have somehow learned to pluck our limbic strings? What if they are casting a lizardly spell over us to hijack our thinking and feeling selves with prefactual, fear-driven survival compulsions? What if these lizards are *not* from outer space, but are right here among us?! And what if they have staged a silent, invisible coup d'état, using the single most dangerous technology of the twentieth century—public relations? Is there a way to break the reptilian spell?

George Lakoff, the author and professor of linguistics at the University of California–Berkeley who calls himself a "cognitive activist," says this: "One of the fundamental findings of cognitive science is that people think in terms of frames and metaphors—conceptual structures. The frames are in the synapses of our brains—physically present in the form of neural circuitry. When the facts don't fit the frames, the frames are kept and the facts ignored."

In other words, forget winning on the facts or the science. It's all about the story. And once stories take hold, they're hard to dislodge.

In 2003, the Environmental Working Group, a public-interest nonprofit group based in the Beltway, leaked a fascinating story, a kind of story within a story about how to frame the environmental story. Actually it was about instructing so-called conservative politicians how to lie through their teeth to sucker the public into doing the opposite of what people want. After all, survey after survey shows that Americans care deeply about the environment and are even willing to shell out money to take good care of it. So duping innocent people into harming the environment requires an occult technology of trickery.

The Environmental Working Group managed to obtain documents from a briefing book assembled by Frank Luntz, a top public opinion researcher for corporate lobbyists. Luntz was the architect of Newt Gingrich's Contract with America, and he has a Who's Who client list of top lobbyists as well as many conservative politicians. The briefing book was a playbook on how to frame the wholesale rollback of environmental and public health protections while avoiding a stinging public backlash like what befell Reagan's ignominious Secretary of the Interior James Watt. Watt became a political lightning rod by staring the corporate pillaging of the public trust in the eye and proclaiming: "Bring it on." The country felt otherwise and he went down in flames. So the new improved manual counseled a stealth campaign to buff up a hall of mirrors where nothing is what it seems and no fingerprints are visible.

Luntz sternly warned Republican leaders that they were overreaching on the environment because 62 percent of Americans—and even 54 percent of Republicans—preferred to see Congress do more to protect the environment rather than cut regulations. He further cautioned that they had an image problem to overcome: "A caricature has taken hold in the public imagination: Republicans seemingly in the pockets of corporate fat cats who rub their hands together and chuckle maniacally as they plot to pollute America for fun and profit. I don't have to remind you how often Republicans are depicted as cold, uncaring, ruthless—even downright anti-social. The fundamental problem for Republicans when it comes to the environment is that whatever you say is viewed through the prism of suspicion." Go figure!

Here—in Luntz's own words—is an abbreviated guide to help you decipher the shape-shifting doublespeak. This is your brain on public relations.

The PR headline is "The Environment: A Cleaner, Safer, Healthier Future." These are a few of its eight key messages.

- Number One: First assure your audience that you're committed to "preserving and protecting" the environment, but that "it can be done more wisely and effectively." Since many Americans believe Republicans do not care about the environment, you will never convince people to accept your ideas until you confront this suspicion and put it to rest. Absolutely do not raise economic arguments first.
- Number Two: Provide specific examples of federal bureaucrats failing to meet their responsibilities to protect the environment.
- Number Three: Your plan must be put in terms of the future, not the past or present. The environment is an area where people expect *progress*, and when they do not see progress, they become frustrated.
- Number Six: If you must use the economic argument, stress that you are seeking "a fair balance" between the environment and the economy. Be prepared to specify and quantify the jobs lost because of needless, excessive, or redundant regulations.
- Number Eight: Emphasize common sense. In making regulatory decisions, we should use our best estimates and realistic assumptions, not the worst-case scenarios advanced by environmental extremists.

To fight off the ingrained bad-guy image, Luntz cuts to the chase:

> Indeed it can be helpful to think of environmental and other issues in terms of "story." A compelling story, even if factually inaccurate, can be more emotionally compelling than a dry recitation of the truth. . . . The facts are beside the point. It's all in how you frame your argument.

To do this, Luntz says, "The most important step is to neutralize the problem and bring them around to your point of view by convincing them of your sincerity and concern. Any discussion of the environment has to be grounded in an effort to reassure a skeptical public that you care about the environment for its own sake—that your intentions are strictly honorable."

Luntz goes on to describe "words that work." The three words Americans are looking for in an environmental policy are "safer, cleaner and healthier." The solution to global warming is semantic: "climate change." Global warming sounds scary, but climate change sounds like you're going from New York to Florida. The problem, of course, is that New York is going to be Florida, and Florida's going to be underwater, a deep blue state—but, hey, later for that.

Some other buzzwords to listen for are "conservationist" and "preserving and protecting." And you may recall hearing ad nauseum about Bush's phony "Clear Skies" and "Healthy Forests" initiatives. This is the larger story they're part of, in Luntz's words:

> Americans love the outdoors. The most popular federal programs today are those that preserve and protect our natural heritage through conservation of public lands and water through parks and open spaces. . . . Becoming a champion of national parks and forests is the best way to show our citizens that Republicans can be *for* something positive on the environment.
>
> You must explain how it is possible to pursue a common-sense or sensible environmental policy that "preserves the gains of the past two decades" without going to extremes, and allows for new science and technologies to carry us even further. Give citizens the idea that progress is being frustrated by overreaching government, and you will hit a very strong strain in the American psyche.

So when you hear this stealth story coming at you, you'll know you're being framed. You'll know someone is trying to have public relations with you.

MIGHTY CORPORATE

A Nation of Hustlers

*W*e are a nation of hustlers. So says historian Walter A. McDougall, the Pulitzer Prize–winning author of *Freedom Just Around the Corner.* Of course, being hustlers has a positive side—a nation of "builders, doers, go-getters, dreamers, hard workers, inventors, organizers, engineers and a people supremely generous." But, McDougall points out, "Americans have enjoyed more opportunity to pursue their ambitions, by foul means or fair, than any other people in history. No wonder American English is uniquely endowed with words connoting a swindle."

Here's just a sample of some of the verbs he lists, starting with the *B*s: "Bait, bamboozle, bilk, bite, blackmail, bleed, blindside, bluff, buffalo, burn, caboodle, cheat, chisel, clip, con, connive, conspire . . . "

Now, the list goes on—and on—but it looks to me as if he missed one of the supreme swindling *C*s: *corporation.* Because, if you're looking to defraud, delude, double-cross, dupe, embezzle, fleece, gouge, hoodwink, hornswoggle, mislead, mug, rig, rip off, sandbag, scam, screw, shaft, shortchange, snooker, or just plain sucker the public in the Grand American Tradition, you've got to have a corporation.

Now don't get me wrong. Commerce is great, and business is business. As for free trade, I'm all for it. Let's give it a try sometime. But that doesn't seem to be part of the corporate business model.

When George W. Bush began his first term, the news media heralded his arrival as the first MBA president, a CEO commander-in-chief. W. set the template and the stage for federal administrations to come with the brazen embrace of a corporate Oval Office. This master of the universe trumpeted the depth of his A-list corporate lineup: Dick Cheney from Halliburton; Donald Rumsfeld from Searle Pharmaceutical; Andy Card from General Motors; and of course Condi Rice from Chevron, who even had an oil tanker named after her. Their promise was to run government with the ruthless efficiency of a corporation. This is one promise they delivered on. They were mighty corporate.

When you heard a spokesman for the Interior Department say "We're looking at how we're doing business in the twenty-first century," you knew they were going to give you the business. It started when Deputy Assistant Secretary Paul Hoffman proposed some seemingly "minor word changes" to the Park Service's basic policy document. Kind of a "small is beautiful" approach that would end up clear-cutting environmental protections. "Illegal uses," he said, instead of just harming park resources, must "irreversibly" harm them. Commented a former National Park Service official: "Taken to its extreme, I suppose you could do anything to a wildlife population as long as you preserve the last breeding pair." Why Mr. Hoffman, that was mighty corporate of you.

Are you fed up with all these no-bid corporate contracts the government has been doling out? In retrospect they may look pretty good. Following Saddam's ouster, the U.S. government airlifted $12 billion in cold hard cash to Iraq to take care of business. That's 281 million bills weighing 363 tons headed for American contractors and Iraqi ministries. It turns out several billion bucks are *still* MIA. As the Coalition Provisional Authority reported to a congressional committee, contractors were told to "bring a big bag." Now that's mighty corporate.

You go to war with the army you have, not the army you'd like, right? Given then Secretary of Defense Donald Rumsfeld's famous quip, you'd think that two years into the Iraq War, the Pentagon would have patched the deadly gap with armor-plated vehicles for our troops. Think again. Half of them remained unprotected. Why? The Defense Department relied on just one small Ohio company to armor Humvees. The military offered to buy out the rights, but the company claimed it was a threat to its "current and future competitive positions." That's mightily corporate.

I bet you don't remember the American Jobs Creation Act of 2004. It started as a law to terminate a $5 billion a year corporate tax subsidy the WTO outlawed. Then it magically transformed into $137 billion in *new* corporate tax breaks. Hey, shouldn't our government have shown compassion for the nearly 95 percent of corporations that were paying less than 5 percent in taxes? Commented a former Reagan Treasury Department official: "The only question was whether this was the worst tax bill in our lifetime, or the worst tax bill in U.S. history." Said one tax lobbyist who worked on the bill, "The way you get votes is you buy them." Now *that* is mighty corporate.

Or maybe, in this unstable economy, you're worried about your pension. Businessman Robert Miller wasn't. He's the turnaround artist who took failing companies and pumped up the balance sheet. How? He offloaded their pension liabilities onto a federal safety net program. Then he made a killing selling the newly unburdened companies for a pretty penny. Miller's nifty innovation caught fire as a business strategy. The problem is that the federal pension program was already $23 billion in the red in 2004 and the Congressional Budget Office estimated that the deficit would swell dramatically in years to come. In other words— you're on your own, America. Now is that mighty corporate?

One corporation has reamed, ripped-off, rooked, roped-in, sandbagged and, well, *sacked* better than most. Goldman Sachs has lived up to its name. In the words of Senator Carl Levin, head of the Senate investigations committee, "They bundled toxic mortgages into complex financial instruments, got the credit rating agencies to label them as AAA securities, and sold them to investors, magnifying and spreading risk throughout the financial system, and all too often betting against the instruments they sold and profiting at the expense of their clients." Of the hundreds of billions of dollars of bonds issued with AAA, bet-your-pension-on-it, good-as-a-suitcase-of-C-notes ratings in 2006, 93 percent were later downgraded to junk status.

Turns out it was the old lipstick-on-a-pig routine. While the American people watched their homes, their jobs, and their economy crumple, Goldman Sachs locked the office door at the end of some workdays $50 million richer than it was that morning. Now that might deserve Hall of Mighty Corporate Fame status. Of course, given how hypercompetitive these feral predators are, likely they'd want to grab the number one spot even if it's for Worst Person in the World. As famed football coach Vince Lombardi liked to say, "Winning isn't everything. It's the only thing."

By now you're probably asking yourself, "What kind of person would do these things?" Clearly they're not like you and me. Now obviously, a corporation is not a person. But by law it actually *is* a person. So what kind of corporate person would do such things? According to criminal psychologist Robert Hare, whom you may have seen in the documentary *The Corporation*, there's a name for them: psychopaths. Hare created the psychopathy checklist. It's a personality test that's the gold standard for making clinical diagnoses of that 1 percent of the population that is devoid of conscience.

Hare says psychopaths are callous, cold-blooded individuals with no sense of guilt, remorse, or empathy. He asserts that corporations are psychopathic because they ruthlessly seek their own selfish interests without regard for the harms they cause to others. As he told *Fast Company* magazine, "If I wasn't studying psychopaths in prison, I'd do it at the stock exchange." So he modified his psychopathy checklist to identify so-called subcriminal or corporate psychopaths. Of course, the peril of this new test is that companies will perversely use it to hire the candidates with the highest scores. That would be mighty corporate.

Unlike most other criminals, corporate psychopaths usually grew up in middle- or upper-class families. They attended college and may hold advanced degrees. That's only natural. White-collar crime is worlds more profitable than street crime. Even if you get busted, it's usually a government catch-and-release program. And you'll probably get to keep most of your winnings, too.

One prominent figure who fits Hare's profile is the aspiring bathtub killer Grover Norquist. You probably remember Grover from his famous "reduce government to the size I can drown it in the bathtub" routine. Or perhaps from the time he compared the estate tax to the Holocaust. He's got a really, really serious issue about taxes. On the rich, that is.

Grover is best known as the influential head of Americans for Tax Reform. In his Beltway office, he became famous and powerful by hosting a weekly neoconservative strategy session of government officials, corporate lobbyists, and the think tanks who love them. It was the sizzling ticket in town if you wanted to drown the baby and do business with it at the same time. Grover called it the "Leave Us Alone" coalition.

Grover is hardwired into numerous big business interests and powerful politicians. Maybe a little too hardwired. In fact, Congress subpoenaed his records for the federal investigation into his close ties with the soon-to-be-infamous lobbyist Jack Abramoff, the high-flying K Street wheeler-dealer who was forced to downsize and serve hard time in federal prison (later to emerge with a conversion against his former profession). Abramoff and his associates blatantly defrauded Native American tribes who wanted to avoid taxes on reservation gambling, and he defended "free trade" in the sweatshops of the Northern Mariana Islands by throttling proposed minimum wage laws. But Grover somehow managed to dodge any legal entanglements in the sticky Abramoff affair and remains as influential as ever in Republican and conservative politics.

Now we all have our wounds, and in the wound can sometimes be found in the gift. I searched for Grover's wound, the Rosebud that might illuminate his psychopathic descent into the heart of corporate darkness. There it was—hiding in plain sight on Wikipedia (it has since been removed).

You see, Grover learned his politics by the tender age of ten. His father would liken each bite Grover took out of his ice cream cone to a different type of *tax* levied by the federal government. The horror, the horror.

So next time some corporate psychopath—invisible-hand-in-glove with the government—tries to stiff, sting, trick, trim, wangle, or just plain hustle you out of a bite of your ice cream cone, you'll know what to say: "That's mighty corporate of you. Now leave me alone!"

THE INFOGANDA WARS

The Battle of the Story

*T*he story of the battle is equally the battle of the story. The political prize is to win the hearts and minds of the public. Who the victor is in that contest may determine whether we make it through this shrinking keyhole of human evolution.

In the elegant words of Native American author N. Scott Momaday, "We live in a house made of stories." And as the spiritual seeker and teacher George Gurdjieff once put it, "The best way to keep a sheep a sheep is to convince it that it's an eagle."

During the Bush Lite administration, radio listeners in Iowa heard an inordinate amount of White House Press Secretary Tony Snow's voice—in a promo he previously did when he was still a Fox radio host pitching sponsors and selling Nu-Vu Windows and Siding. Said one AM radio Iowa news director: "Just imagine, you're listening to the radio, Tony Snow has been speaking to you as the spokesman for the leader of the Free World, and then a commercial comes on with him trying to sell you a window." Tony Snow worked hard to kill the ads, commenting, "It's like, you don't have the White House press secretary flacking siding."

Since when? Fake news and "truthiness" selling everything from war to Medicare policy and prescription drugs devour the nation's news media in an all-out invasion of the body snatchers. Government and corporations are having public relations with the press, and it's not pretty. It has spawned a weird new mutant species: infoganda.

The empire of infoganda contemptuously dismisses the so-called "reality-based community" in favor of manufacturing its own reality. Fake newscasters, corporate stealth marketers, and government disinformation shills routinely pose as journalists, or covertly lease them. These actions are illegal under U.S. propaganda statutes, yet they go largely unpunished. Meanwhile on occasion real reporters who speak truth to power have faced prosecution and even prison.

As if that weren't bad enough, the corporate concentration of media has produced more outlets that cover less news. The Federal Communications Commission tried to suppress its own report which documented the fact that media deregulation has led to fewer owners, fewer choices, and less local news. Still hanging in the balance is the battle for the Internet—the last bastion of uncensored, democratic communication, at least in the United States.

As if reality weren't already confusing enough, Big Brother has been supersized. Under cover of 9-11, government agencies began systematically withholding formerly public information in unprecedented volumes. Within a few brief years, the government has classified record-setting amounts of information.

Perhaps the most critical feedback loop in a free society is a free press. As Bill Moyers said, "What's important for the journalist is not how close you are to power, but how close you are to reality. The quality of journalism and the quality of democracy are inextricably intertwined."

In that light, the really big news about the news bubbled up from cable TV's *The Daily Show with Jon Stewart*, the impishly subversive fake news show on the Comedy Central channel. The *Daily Show*'s fake coverage of the first Obama-McCain presidential debate outpolled CNN among young viewers. Fake news is more popular than the fake news that passes for real news.

We live in a national entertainment state, an echo chamber of fast-food news loops, infoganda, and the perennial staples that William Randolph Hearst lovingly called "crime and underwear." At a time when the corporate consolidation of the media is well on its way to ceding control of information to the meaty hands of a half-dozen giant conglomerates, the disconnect between reality and Orwellian newspeak is, well, best reported on a fake news show.

Breaking news—the news is broken.

As the former *New York Times* Chief Political Correspondent Richard Reeves said, "Real news is the news you and I need to keep our freedoms."

Fortunately, despite the corrosive advertising-driven climate, independent journalism that dares to tell the truth is experiencing a dramatic renaissance—from documentary films, to mushrooming independent print and web publications, to web 2.0's user-generated universe. Potent independent reporting is even compelling mainstream media to cover some real news. The rising proliferation of vital alternative media is providing a countervailing force to the corporate memory holes swallowing up both information and democracy.

As the battle of the story escalates, just remember—you're an eagle.

FAMILY VALUES

Why Is It a Crime?

I wanna talk to you about family values.

Family values are under assault. This deplorable situation presents a grave threat to the very fabric of our society. Family values have sustained society since civilization began. People who hold family values have deep convictions. The problem is—more and more of these convictions are felonies. When serving your country means serving time, it's an indictment of our society.

Let's put our cards on the table. What happens in Vegas stays in Vegas, right? The family values we're talking about are crime family values. We're all family here. So let's be frank.

Everybody knows the business of America is business. America is for sale, and America belongs to the people who own it. The rules are simple. Make money. Exercise power. Minimize the bloodshed. That's the way of the world. The question is not *if* we're going to have crime. The question is if we're going to have *organized* crime, or *disorganized* crime. So let's get with the program.

Are you with me?

Now I'm not talking Tony Soprano here. We went corporate a long time ago. It was a racket made in heaven. Actually, in Washington DC. Which brings me to my point—the sorry state of government corruption and corporate crime.

My grandfather's old friend Willie Sutton used to say he robbed banks because "that's where the money is." Well, today old Willie would be robbing the government. Do the math: $1.4 trillion a year. That's real money. And it's OPM, the best kind: Other People's Money.

Think about the mess the government's making, then think about what organized crime does best. Monopolies. Grand theft. Fraud. Bid rigging. Accounting scams. Arms dealing. Drug trafficking. Toxic-waste dumping.

Who better to do these functions than experienced family businesses? We can and must professionalize government.

We say we're against big government, but we're not. Big government provides family value. Think about it. The bigger the government, the more money there is. The more money, the more corruption. The more corruption, the more regulation. The more regulation, the more government. The more government, the more money. It's a perfect system. It's a road-tested formula for permanent unlimited growth and stability.

So I am very, very concerned that certain parties are spoiling the party by degrading family values. I am shocked—shocked!—by the sheer incompetence of our politicians and government officials. Gangster wannabees. Romper-room racketeers. It gives family values a bad name. It breaks my heart.

Are you with me?

Look what's going down.

A very disturbing report came to my attention. It's from some do-gooder group calling themselves Transparency International. They run a scam called the Global Corruption Barometer. It tells how corruption affects ordinary people's lives around the world. It's your usual bleeding-heart public opinion survey. And guess what? Corruption is increasing. Who knew?!

This Global Corruption Barometer says people think political parties are the most corrupt, followed by legislatures. Duh. But really it's all a perception issue. The question I ask you is:

Why do people *think* corruption is getting worse?

Two reasons: a lack of professionalism, and a disrespect for traditional family values.

Everybody knows the appropriations process is a shakedown. Extortion, bribery, whatever you want to call it. Congress is a "pay to play" game. Always has been. A "transactional" Congress, that's the MBA lingo that President George W. Bush made so popular in his salad days.

Take this joker Congressman John Boehner. Some years ago, he's a big party up-and-comer, and he's swinging a tobacco vote on the floor of the House. So far, so good. Until he starts handing out campaign checks from Brown & Williamson tobacco, right there on the House floor. Why? So he can, quote, "get credit." Everybody and their mother sees him doing this. So they have to make a new rule and they name it after him. He wanted credit, he got credit.

Then then the House Majority Leader Tom DeLay gets popped—because he did not launder his campaign contributions clean. End of a brilliant career. So Boehner gets promoted to majority leader! Why, I ask you, are we rewarding incompetence?

Not that the private sector is exactly a role model. Take Brent Wilkes. He's pimping defense contracts to Congress. *Earmarks*, they call them. Stick the pork in some bill in the middle of the night and ride the gravy train home. Everybody wins. It's all good.

Until this dingbat waltzes into meetings with congressmen. In their office, Wilkes tells them what he's buying and he hands them the envelope. We're talking Ethics 101. Any wise guy knows you give them the envelope in the *hallway*. This is the blond leading the blond, as my wife says.

So we have a little talk. OK, Wilkes admits he's a "rookie." But he's teachable. He goes into training to be a "chuck wagon" for Congress. You got expenses? He'll take care of them. Tickets to the game? Skyboxes. You need cowboy boots? Monogrammed. A little golfing in Scotland? Pack your freshly delivered Louis Vuitton bags.

But then Wilkes has to make like a big shot. At parties, he tells people, "If you throw enough dough at Congressman Whoop-De-Doo, you'll get it back 100 times over." He's right. He himself has scored $90 million in earmarks. He's a good earner. This is the shame of it.

But finger pointing at parties? I mean, with earmarks of $64 billion in play, who wants the attention?

So sure as day Wilkes gets popped and it turns into a regular St. Valentine's Day Massacre on the Hill. Jack Abramoff and his whole candy store go up in flames. Then they all start singing to the authorities. Traditional family values simply do not allow this. It's like all Ten Commandments rolled into one.

Wilkes was in a great business, too: defense contracts. What makes it so great? In a word: cost overruns. Oops—a dollar short and a day late! Doesn't matter. We're talking tens of billions short and years late.

I look at it this way. I think you'll appreciate this. It's just as well when these wacko Star Wars weapons never get built. We already got enough to blow up the planet a thousand times over. Thinking long-term, peace is good for business. I'm talking sustainability here.

Are you with me?

The other problem I'm having is this: accountability. The Defense Department says it, quote, "lost visibility" on over $7 billion in the war on terrorism. *Ahem.* "Lost visibility"? Now I know something about things that fell off the back of the truck. But I give you my personal guarantee—in a family business, when things fall off the back of the truck, we know where they land. This is accountability.

It gets worse. I'm sure by now you've heard about the K Street Project. The Republicans decide to wipe out the competition. They tell all the lobbyists on K Street, "If you want government business, you can't give any money to the Democrats."

From the start, I knew this was a lousy idea. Bottom line, a dispute between families is bad for business. Cardinal law.

So sure enough . . . what happens when one family gets control of Congress *and* the White House—and announces it's open for business? The number of lobbyists shoots up from 10,000 to 35,000. And because now there's only one family to do business with, fees go up 100 percent! Sixty-eight lobbyists for every member of Congress, and you get inflation. This is the wisdom of our two-party system. The free market.

As you can tell, I'm smoked about the decline of family values. But for me, rock bottom was this Transparency "Corruption Perceptions Index" whatever. It's a scorecard of all the countries of the world, from the least corrupt to the most corrupt.

As a citizen, I feel ashamed. Out of 160 countries, in 2010 the US of A only rated as the twenty-second least corrupt country in the world! We practically invented white-collar crime. We not only wrote the book, we made the movie. We are number one in corruption. It's our biggest export worldwide. We are not getting the respect we deserve for the American Way.

I see this as a marketing issue. We need to get our story out.

But like my lawyer says, "Get your ducks in a row before you let the cat out of the bag."

So, this is my program. We need to professionalize government. Of course lobbyists should write legislation that affects their industries. Of course politicians should have a revolving door with family businesses. Of course you should hire your relatives and cronies. Of course you should wet your beak at every step. If this is not family values, what is?

These are technical issues with technical solutions. What we need is a crime czar to *regulate* the culture of corruption. If everybody's doing it, how can it be a crime? It's a regulatory issue, pure and simple. No drama.

The way things are now, we are not getting our money's worth. *That* is the real crime.

I am asking for your support. Right here today, I am launching the American Crime Family Values Agenda.

We're calling our program the "Contract on America."

Are you with me?

A PARADE OF DWARVES

Have-Nots and Have-a-Lots

*W*hen figurines of the Virgin of Guadalupe, the revered patron saint of Mexico, flooded that country, they bore the stamp: *Made In China*. This bizarre signature of corporate globalization run amok only adds insult to injury. The injury is that, with China's acceptance into the WTO, this time around the giant sucking sound from the South was jobs leaving Mexico for China. The insult is the homogenization of local cultures that's careening mindlessly around the globe in random acts of manufacturing.

Mobile, global capital migrates wherever labor is cheapest, environmental regulations weakest, and corrupt elites friendliest. In this disembodied world of drive-by investment, gone is any allegiance to people, place, culture, or nation. The political reality is that, as of 2009, 44 of the world's 100 largest economies were corporations rather than nations. The biggest corporations are often far bigger than many national economies, and more powerful.

The great game of free trade, so-called, is rigged. As Tina Rosenberg wrote in the *New York Times*, "No nation has ever developed over the long term under the rules being imposed today on Third World countries by the institutions controlling globalization. The United States, Germany, France and Japan all became wealthy and powerful nations behind the barriers of protectionism." As one UN economist commented, "When the economy opens, you need *more* control mechanisms, not fewer."

But a growing backlash is giving globalization whiplash. The WTO talks essentially collapsed, and corporations are working the rope line one-on-one to gain entry to national economies. Countries across Latin America have generated a political groundswell against the failed experiment of so-called "free-market" capitalism. Popular uprisings have in quite a few places derailed the privatization of state-owned companies and utilities.

The invisible hand behind the divisive political battles around immigration is corporate economic globalization's destruction of national economies worldwide. Poor people from countries destabilized by global forces often flee their own countries or regions as economic refugees to seek work elsewhere: Central Americans to the United States; Africans to Europe; Indians, Pakistanis, Bangladeshis, and Filipinos to the Gulf; and Chinese peasants to that nation's coastal cities.

In fact, the gaping wealth gap worldwide is increasing within every country and also between nations, in turn driving ever-greater environmental and social destruction. Nor has globalization enhanced and distributed democracy. The radical extremes between rich and poor have stretched like Spandex to an untenable and repressive world of have-nots and have-a-lots.

What does this bifurcated world look like? Consider what Clive Crook wrote in "The Height of Inequality" about a striking image from the Dutch economist Jan Pen's 1971 study of income distribution in the UK:

> Suppose that every person in the economy walks by, as if in a parade. Imagine that the parade takes exactly an hour to pass, and that the marchers are arranged in order of income, with the lowest incomes at the front and the highest at the back. Also imagine that the heights of the people in the parade are proportional to what they make: those earning the average income will be of average height, those earning twice the average income will be twice the average height, and so on. We spectators, let us imagine, are also of average height.
>
> Pen then described what the observers would see. Not a series of people of steadily increasing height—that's far too bland a picture. The observers would see something much stranger. They would see, mostly, a parade of dwarves, and then some unbelievable giants at the very end.

As Crook continues, "Back when Pen wrote his book, incomes were already more skewed in America than in Britain. Over the past thirty-five years, and especially over the past ten, that top-end skewness has greatly increased. The weirdness of the last half minute of today's American parade—even more so the weirdness of the last few seconds, and above all the weirdness of the last fraction of a second—is vastly greater than that of the vision, bizarre as it was, described by Pen."

As Kevin Phillips documented in his book *Wealth and Democracy*, the financial bubble bath of bursting bubbles in the United States is hardly a new phenomenon. There have been at least six major boom-bubble-bust economic cycles since the American Revolution, many of them linked to technological innovations. Throughout, the top 1 percent has always held disproportionate wealth and power.

Phillips shows that by 1995 in the United States, the average working person's real income was below 1973 levels, despite working longer hours. By the millennium's end, the share of the top 1 percent grew to nearly its highest level ever. In 2012, the United States has the most inegalitarian and elitist income spread of any industrialized nation. As author E. L. Doctorow said, "We recognize two forms of citizenship, common and preferred."

The ownership society is aptly named. It's principally owned by that pesky 1 or 2 percent of the population, and it comes largely at the expense of American workers. While corporate profits shot up to a forty-year high, real wages and salaries sank to a fifty-nine-year low. Goldman Sachs saw the connection: "The most important contributor to higher profit margins has been a decline in labor's share of national income."

Honey, we shrunk the middle class. Poverty has grown dramatically since the 2008 crash, and it now afflicts somewhere between 13 and 24 percent of the population, depending on which economic criteria one uses. One thing is for sure: a forty-hour workweek at the minimum wage will definitely not get you out of poverty. We have been creating a permanent class of the working poor.

In the face of this assault, U.S. workers have increasingly been losing the right to organize. Every twenty-three minutes, a worker is either fired or harassed for trying to unionize. In 2011 the battle exploded onto the national stage with the declaration of open class war against public employee unions by newly elected Republican governors in several states, including Wisconsin, Ohio, and Indiana.

Phillips finds that great wealth accumulation—despite "free market-laissez-faire" rhetorical camouflage—has throughout U.S. history been made through the manipulation of the political system and through corruption. It has been nearly totally dependent on government policies, and very often on war profiteering. Though new wealthy entrepreneurial elites do arise with booms, old-wealth families have maintained enormous assets and power that has often grown by leaps and bounds.

Phillips says that the decline of great economic powers is historically linked to four factors. The first is the "financialization" of their economies, as speculation replaces real production and commerce. Until the recent crash, a large percentage of U.S. financial activity was speculative, the casino economy—rather than productive investment in tangible businesses or infrastructure.

The second factor is very high levels of debt. The United States is now the biggest debtor nation in the world. As journalist William Greider pointed out, "You can't sustain an empire from a debtor's weakening position. Sooner or later the creditors pull the plug." Even the IMF has called the United States' huge trade imbalances "unsustainable" and a possible source of instability.

The third is extreme economic inequality. The United States economy today rivals the extremes of the Great Depression and Gilded Age.

Lastly, military overreaching usually seals the decline of a fading dominant economy. The United States' adventures in Iraq, Afghanistan, and the "Long War" (the Department of Defense's term) throughout the Middle East are textbook examples. The United States appears likely to lose its undisputed military hegemony as China and other Asian high-tech economies and newly emerging powers flex their muscles in the coming decades.

Although the United States is still the world's biggest economy and only military superpower, the signs point to the fact that we're witnessing the beginning of the decline of the U.S. empire. No American politician would dare speak those words, which would be political suicide. At the same time, the U.S. cash-and-carry political system has engendered a degree of corruption that will be difficult to deconstruct. The fictional renegade political candidate Jay Bulworth said it best in the movie *Bulworth*:

> Ya know it ain't that funny, you contribute all my money
> You make your contribution and you get your solution.
> As long as you can pay, I'm gonna do it all your way.
> Yes, the money talks and the people walks . . .

As mobile global corporations anchor and expand their power world-wide, the global antiglobalization movement does have its inspiring moments, such as those from the best culture jammers in the world, the Yes Men. A shadowy dynamic duo of anticorporate pranksters of political theater, the Yes Men first sprung to life in 2000 when they set up a website which is such a close parody of the official WTO site that they were contacted by a conference of international lawyers to give an official talk. The Yes Men dispatched their fake WTO representative, Andy Bicklbaum, under a nom de guerre. He explained soberly to the stony-faced lawyers that the WTO viewed the Italian siesta as a barrier to trade. He went on to express the WTO's support for allowing citizens to auction their votes to the highest corporate bidder. The lawyers had no idea they were listening to an imposter. They paid sober attention and temporarily swallowed it hook, line, and stinker.

When a group of textile manufacturers then invited the "WTO" to talk to them in Finland, the Yes Men's deadpan WTO man explained carefully that the Civil War had been a waste of time and resources. According to rational economic logic, slavery would have given way to the cheaper and more efficient system of sweatshop labor that we have today. Again they were taken most seriously.

After being exposed, the Yes Men commented, "We think the ethical thing to do is to represent the WTO more honestly than they represent themselves." When WikiLeaks released over five thousand e-mails from the shadowy private intelligence-gathering company Stratfor in 2012, the memos revealed a concerted espionage campaign against the Yes Men, who were clearly not considered a joke by the corporate class.

As big business hijacks the rhetoric of sustainability, we find ourselves in a hall of mirrors. Are we to believe the rap? Or is it just more cynical greenwashing to defuse the pressure and keep on doing business as usual? Or is the whole idea of corporate social responsibility an oxymoron?

Writing about lapping corporate crime waves in the magazine *Business Ethics*, another possible oxymoron, editor Marjorie Kelly, who has long championed the corporate social responsibility movement, had this to say:

> We believed corporate social responsibility was about separating the good guys from the bad guys, and that good guys could be spotted by their exemplary policies and programs and sustainability reports. The lesson is that all the things corporate social responsibility has been measuring and fighting for and applauding may be colossally beside the point, because they fail to tell us what's really going on inside companies: unremitting pressure to get the numbers, by any means possible.

Somebody's profiting from the overwhelming drive to get the numbers, and that somebody is not "everybody." It's the financial elite. They prosper not because they're more productive or virtuous than the rest of us, but because they wield power. We haven't focused enough on system design, particularly on how the system lends power to the financial elite. Because power is what it's all about, not good intentions, or voluntary initiatives, or toothless codes of conduct. Power. We would do well to focus on democratizing structures of power. . . . That means imagining, and then creating, economic democracy.

One of the most successful corporate ploys has been spreading the meme that doing the right thing for the environment means robbing American workers of jobs. Not.

To the contrary, greening industry is emerging as precisely the pathway to a large-scale jobs-creation program and a dynamic opportunity to reinvent business prosperity—a reliable prosperity. Initiatives such as the Apollo Alliance (and now the BlueGreen Alliance) offer new models of economic development friendly to labor, business, and the environment. They marry the creation of good "green-collar" jobs with a national transition to alternative energy, clean technology, "zero waste" systems, green building, and organic farming. This is the unfolding future. It can work and people will work—at good jobs that are meaningful and provide a living wage.

As John de Graaf, founder of Take Back Your Time, points out, we may have the "grossest domestic product in the world," but what are American workers getting for it? Overwork, poor health, isolation from family and friends, and general unhappiness. In contrast, as the World Economic Forum documented, four of the five most competitive economies in the world have the most time-friendly, family-friendly, and worker-friendly policies.

Left to its own devices, the system will continue to create regular crises while further concentrating wealth and distributing poverty. The rich get richer and the poor get poorer. Negative feedback loops perpetuate themselves until there's an intervention.

Fortunately the unlikeliest of people in the unlikeliest of places have launched the next American Revolution . . .

THE UNLIKELIEST OF PEOPLE IN THE UNLIKELIEST OF PLACES

Corporations, Democracy, and the Rights of Nature

Sometimes defending the environment feels like a game of Pop the Gopher, which you may have played at a local carnival. There's a large sort of checkerboard with holes in the squares. A mechanical gopher pops up, and you try to slap it back down with a rubber mallet. The moment you do, another one springs up—and another and another until it's impossible to keep up. The house makes sure Pop the Gopher is a losing proposition for its customers.

That's how Tom Linzey felt about being an environmental lawyer. Working with the group he founded in 1995, the Community Environmental Legal Defense Fund (CELDF), he and his team provided desperately needed legal services to environmental and community groups. As the ones in the white hats, they were among the pitifully few two hundred full-time public interest environmental attorneys in the entire United States at the time. They were simply too small to keep up.

So Linzey and the crew reframed the problem by starting to train citizens in how to bring lawsuits, appeal permits, and all around do it themselves. They gave the citizen apprentices three years of law school in two weeks, and amazingly the folks started winning litigation and permit appeals. Even though everyone else thought the group was really successful, it still wasn't enough. With CELDF's legal training, citizens were better at popping their gophers, but more gophers kept popping up through new holes.

Although Linzey's team gave citizens the education they needed to begin winning their own litigation and permit appeals cases, by the time the appeals reached local administrative hearings in places like Pennsylvania's Environmental Hearing Board, they found the rules had been written in favor of the very ones who would be regulated by them. Guess who? It's not you and me, or the affected communities. It's corporations.

Tom Linzey concluded that the old saw is true: "The only thing environmental regulations regulate is environmentalists."

That's when things started to get interesting. Instead of constantly trying to pop the corporate gopher, Linzey decided to change the terms of engagement. He started sealing the holes.

> In 1998 we got calls from seventy local governments in Pennsylvania. We were originally formed just to help non-profit groups, and helping out local governments that were all elected officials in Pennsylvania was quite a different thing. We practice in central Pennsylvania. In Pennsylvania, we have Pittsburgh on one side, Philadelphia on the other, and Mississippi in the middle. We're talking rural, conservative Pennsylvania in north central and south central Pennsylvania. What were these calls about? Factory farms, hog farms and chicken farms were moving into Pennsylvania. Pennsylvania has a very rich history of family farms, and these communities were very concerned.
>
> A lot of other states had experience with factory farms before we did. In the Midwest, you have factory farms of 100,000 hogs in several buildings. Then a handful of corporations that control agribusiness production in this country decided Pennsylvania was a good place to go.
>
> In the late 1980s, the boards of the largest agribusiness corporations in the country said, "We want to move into Pennsylvania because there's a lot of profit to be made." So what did they do? They got the Pennsylvania legislature to adopt a law called the Nutrient Management Act. Basically it said that, if you are a factory farm corporation and you want to open up a facility in our state, all you have to do is take care of the manure that's produced from the factory farms.
>
> In Pennsylvania we have a unique legacy of democracy. We have close to 3,000 general-purpose municipal governments, 1,400 of which are called rural second-class townships. They're run by three to five elected officials, and most range in size anywhere from 400 people to about 15,000 folks—fairly small. Up to that point, we had a lively discussion in Pennsylvania government and in north central and south central Pennsylvania about whether

these communities wanted factory farms to come into their community at all.

It wouldn't be so bad if the Nutrient Management Act had been adopted because it was a fairly weak regulatory law just dealing with manure disposal. It wouldn't be so bad if it was just a state law, and all the other municipal governments at the sub-state level could have adopted what they wanted. But there was a clause thrown into the Nutrient Management Act that pre-empted local governments from passing any manure disposal laws that were more stringent than the state's.

Tom Linzey found these tactics were not exclusive to Pennsylvania. His group looked to the Midwest, where there are massive factory farms such as million-layer chicken operations and 150,000-head pig farms. There they found hope. They learned that communities in nine states had linked efforts to pass anticorporate farming laws that prohibit agribusiness corporations at large from owning farmland or engaging in farming. They also discovered that the reasons behind such laws are not just to protect the environment and the quality of life. The laws are also about protecting the survival of farmers from things like "output contracts."

These are contracts that family farmers sign to produce livestock for only one company. The farmer no longer even owns the animals. The corporation retains title to the animals— unless of course the animals die and then title transfers to the farmer for disposal. The corporation can terminate the contract at its discretion at any time. What does that mean? A once-independent family farmer, who has to spend a quarter of a million dollars to put in a feeding unit to raise something in these factory farm industrial farming conditions, can be cut at a moment's notice. He no longer has a diversified farm or is feeding product to a bunch of different folks, but to just one corporation. They're stuck, and that's the relationship between the corporation and the farmer.

Today we have a once-independent family farmer struggling to survive in an economy created and manipulated by the four corporations that now control over 80 percent of the production of hogs in the United States. There's no free market in hog production anymore. In North Carolina, 90

percent of all hogs are raised under contract. The corporation pays what it wants. There's no price set by the market.

Did these anticorporate farming laws hold up in court? Linzey
found they had. The U.S. Supreme Court had upheld the ability of
states to adopt such laws in the 1940s, and other courts had upheld
the constitutionality of those laws. The reasoning was based on several
factors, but the compelling argument was that, if a corporation wants to
set up shop and something goes wrong and you sue the corporation, the
corporation's structure serves as a limited liability shield. You can't get
to the wallets and the pocketbooks of the officers and the directors who
made the decisions about putting the operation there. That's the essence
of the corporation: limited liability, accompanied by an arsenal of legal
protections they wield against communities.

What did Linzey and his team do? "Well, we have no pride of author-
ship. We stole some language. We went out and we took South Dakota's
work, where the anticorporate farming law is part of the state constitution. It was driven into the constitution by farmers and activists in South
Dakota who refused to fight things by parts per million, by water pollution, by odor pollution, by end-of-the-pipe measures. And that's what's
wrong with environmental law: It's all end-of-the-pipe. It waits until the
problem is caused, then comes up with a solution. Well, the folks in the
Midwest didn't want to be in that position, and they took these steps to
drive this law and this concept into the constitution through a statewide
initiative process that mandated no corporations in farming."

Using the South Dakota constitution's language as a model, ten
municipal Pennsylvania governments adopted the anticorporate farming laws. Since the laws went into effect, not one factory farm has been
sited in these rural areas.

Linzey says this process taught him how it's possible for communities
and movements to actually win the immediate frontline battles. But
even more important, he recognized that the real issue is to challenge the
underlying assumption—and legal authority—that gives corporations
the right to make decisions that in a democracy are supposed to be made
by the community. As Linzey points out,

> These corporations are not only changing the food system,
> but in the process they are crushing a family farm culture
> that is about much more than simply families raising

vegetables. It's a culture, a family farm culture that supports other businesses and communities in Pennsylvania.

The national statistics are pretty grim. Over the last 20-plus years, 300,000 family farmers in this country have been eliminated. Four corporations now control over 80 percent of both hog and beef production in the United States. Perhaps the most stunning statistic is that death by suicide is now higher than equipment-related deaths among farmers in the United States. It's the number one cause of death for farmers. When folks say we "lost" 300,000 farmers, in truth we didn't lose them—they were extinguished by this rolling behemoth we call agribusiness corporations and a corporate minority of decision makers who control them.

Our work since then has been not just to develop ordinances. It has been grappling with these fundamental issues about power. Whose vision is it going to be to build these regions, whether they are townships, counties or multi-regional areas? Is it going to be the folks that live there, or is it going to be out-of-state corporate interests that are using that community for profit? That's what it came down to in Pennsylvania.

By reclaiming their own power, these Pennsylvania townships prompted a fierce counterreaction by the agribusiness industry—with support from eleven Pennsylvania legislators who introduced Senate Bill 826. It was designed to stop local governments from passing these types of local laws. The ferocious corporate blowback in turn provoked an outright citizen uprising.

Tom Linzey suddenly found himself in the center of another American Revolution. "We did presentations on rainy nights where 500 people in a county of 12,000 showed up to talk about the future of their community. That's when we changed the language and reframed it from dealing with hog manure to talking about democracy and local control and self-governance and all these things that supposedly we have."

In the face of the angry citizen resistance, Senate Bill 826 died. Then at midnight, legislators in the pocket of agribusiness got together again and, instead of amending Senate Bill 826 to try to make it less noxious for the local governments, they renumbered and reintroduced it as Senate Bill 1413. It moved through the Senate Agricultural Committee to the full floor of the Senate and on to the House of Representatives, where it went through two days of consideration—the smallest amount of time for any such legislation ever. Linzey and the communities caught the move, but only at the last minute. They rapidly pieced together a coalition from people as diverse as the United Mine Workers of America, the Sierra Club, the Pennsylvania Association for Sustainable Agriculture, and the Pennsylvania Farmers Union. They managed to stop it again.

Establishment newspapers such as the Harrisburg *Patriot-News* (the capital paper) characterized the bill as an affront to the concept of self-governance, language you don't hear in rural Pennsylvania. The newspapers started talking that talk because the communities were starting to talk it. The pulse was that the communities were speaking very differently from the same old environmental regulatory two-step of the past thirty or forty years.

As Linzey observes, "We're caught in a feedback loop, where our failures are interpreted as simply a message to do the same thing, but do it better. We need another expert. We need ten more people to come to a meeting. We need a lawyer. Oh, if only we had five lawyers, then maybe we would have won. It's that feedback loop that's so dangerous. That's what we've been trying to break out of. Now the conversation has moved beyond that. Whether it's over timber harvesting, a nuclear power plant, quarries, or any single issue that we've probably all been involved in, how do we transform that single issue work into doing the work of democracy?"

One community soon moved the debate over environmental protections and local interests to *the* central question of democracy: *Who's in charge?*

The residents of Porter Township in rural Pennsylvania were well prepared when they had to face off with the Alcosan Corporation. The company was planning to spread human sewage sludge as "fertilizer" on farms located in the southern part of the county. A boy had died from a massive infection after riding an ATV across a field "fertilized" with this human waste sludge ("biosolids") in Berks County, on the other side of the state. This needless tragedy galvanized the community.

During 2002, Porter Township in Clarion County, an hour and a half north of Pittsubrgh, became one of over forty local governments in Pennsylvania to adopt a sludge ordinance that prevents sludge corporations from doing business in particular townships. In December 2002, the Porter Township elected officials also adopted CELDF's Corporate Rights Elimination Ordinance. That ordinance declared that, in *their* neck of the woods, corporations would not be considered as *persons*.

The assertion that a corporation is not a person might seem like a big "duh." But according to a dubious Supreme Court ruling in 1886, corporations were actually declared persons—with full human rights guaranteed by the Constitution. The ruling came without precedent or explanation. In fact, it contradicted the entire body of law that preceded it. Further, no such statement appeared in the actual ruling, but was entered after the fact as a "head note" by a court clerk with no judicial authority. Nevertheless, it became the cornerstone of a vast body of law that has been perfected in the 125 years since.

You may remember the Boston Tea Party. It actually began as a revolt against the East India Company after it enlisted the British Crown to exempt it from paying the tea taxes that applied to merchants in the colonies, thereby destroying any competition from small colonial merchants. The American Revolution began as an anticorporate, anti-monopoly rebellion.

Following the American Revolution, corporations were kept on a tight legal leash. Corporations could be formed only to undertake public projects, and could exist for just a finite period. After that, they could be rechartered only if they could show they existed for the public good. Their directors and officers were held personally liable for the actions and harms of the corporation. All that began to change with the 1886 Supreme Court ruling that corporations were persons.

The Corporate Rights Elimination Ordinances that have been passed in Pennsylvania give communities the right to refuse to recognize these corporate constitutional rights at the municipal level. The argument shifted from contaminated sludge to the Constitution. Linzey recalls:

> We started talking about corporate personhood rights. The fact is that corporations have personhood rights, which means they have Bill of Rights protections under the Constitution. They've organized their law firms to gain these rights through their pure economic power.
>
> In practical terms, because corporations have person-hood rights, you can't have unannounced inspections by regulators of factory farms, because corporations are protected by the Fourth Amendment against unreasonable searches and seizures. The First Amendment of free speech protects agribusiness corporations in Pennsylvania to make contributions to the folks that sit on the House Agricultural

Committee. The Fifth Amendment protects them against "takings," which means that, if you pass an ordinance that impacts some type of corporate property, the corporation has a cause of action against the local government. This isn't some vague pie-in-the-sky academic concept. These are real constitutional rights that our forebears fought, bled and died for to get those protections for us as people. Now corporations are using those same rights against our communities who want to make a sustainable future.

You can design and develop the best tool in the best way with the best language or the best technology, but if this guy, the elephant in the room, is making a profit from doing things exactly the opposite, how the hell are you going to implement it? And what good is having the tool unless you can implement it?

One of our local governments got sued by the agribusiness corporations in an attempt to try to overturn the anti–corporate farming law. People came up to me after it happened and said, "I'm really sorry your anti–corporate farming ordinance might be overturned," to which we responded, "This is great!" because the complaint spelled out everything we had been talking about. We took the complaint and mailed it right off to the local governments. Instead of crouching in a corner, saying "Don't hit me, or please don't bring a lawsuit against this ordinance," bring it on! The paradigm has shifted and people understand it as an anti-democratic maneuver by an anti-democratic entity trying to tell communities how to exist and what their vision is.

We've moved the struggle to a place where we've drafted a Corporate Rights Elimination Ordinance. It strips constitutional privileges from corporations at the local government level. What we do is to use it as a shield for local governments who are going to get sued over the factory farm stuff that they're doing. We make it a whole new hurdle to get over, and then we use that to go up through the courts and start a real discussion in this country about constitutional rights and corporations, at least at the judicial level.

Porter Township elected to stop playing Pop the Gopher. By challenging the "personhood" of corporations, it started plugging the gopher holes in the losing game of environmental ordinances and permit appeals. Twenty Pennsylvania townships then passed similar laws against corporate farming and corporate sludging.

By 2000, several other rural municipal governments had rebelled against the corporate agribusiness forces intent on imposing an unsustainable vision of farming on them. As Linzey observes, "They learned that every single environmental issue isn't a single issue at all, but can be traced directly to the subordination by the law of the rights of communities to the rights of the corporate few. They had learned that the bullies who run the place line their pockets and enhance their power by both stopping majorities from forming, but also when forced, they pull out the Constitution. They wield the law. With that understanding, our rural communities began to create majorities by reframing the otherwise single issues that they were faced with."

Because the communities took a different path, the legislature now had to come at them differently. The lawmakers had to draft and introduce legislation that didn't change the parts per million to allow a little more pollution, but instead sought to strip away the lawmaking power of those rural governments. The rural township governments had written a different script that forced the corporations to respond on the ground of democracy.

For the first time in Pennsylvania in the memories of the lobbyists, the number one Farm Bureau legislative priority—the number one priority of the agribusiness corporations in Pennsylvania—sank in defeat in 2001. It sank again in 2002. Says Linzey, "It went down for another very large reason, not just that they had programmed the legislators to come after them in an anti-democratic piece of legislation, but because the coalition that we reached out to was much different than any other coalition that had ever before been seen in Pennsylvania. Yes, it was cranky but it was big. And who were the members? The United Mine Workers came on board because their workers had gotten sick from sludge being spread on mine reclamation sites. The Pennsylvania Farmers Union, the AFL-CIO, the Pennsylvania Association for Sustainable Agriculture, and yes, the environmental groups came in because they saw it as being more effective. In those townships, not one new teaspoonfull of sludge has been spread. Not one new factory farm has been sited."

A cranky coalition defeats an opposite and *unequal* corporate reaction— on the grounds of democracy. Needless to say, the saga does not end there.

In 2003, a federal appeals court found the South Dakota law barring corporate farming in violation of the Interstate Commerce Clause, on the sole basis of notes scribbled by some of the drafters of the statewide initiative during the drafting process. As Tom Linzey predicted, the battle between democracy and corporate power was heating up. Yet the Pennsylvania story, small as it seemed at the time, may be looked back on as the Boston Tea Party of corporate law.

Linzey's phone started ringing off the hook with calls from other local governments that wanted to ensure the rights of citizens to build safe and secure communities and decide on their own vision of a sustainable future. People were coming to understand what Thomas Jefferson had warned against over two hundred years ago: "I hope we will crush in its birth the aristocracy of our moneyed corporations, which dare already to challenge our government in a trial of strength, and bid defiance to the laws of the country." That moneyed aristocracy of corporations long ago moved beyond defying the laws of the country to writing the laws of the land.

Until, that is, the "unlikeliest of people in the unlikeliest of places" arose to act as wild-card change agents. As Linzey describes,

> They're rural municipal officials whose primary job is to plow the roads in the winter and patch the roads in the summer. They're the folks that wear the steel-toed work boots and the John Deere hats. These folks in rural Pennsylvania have been dumped on for years. After all, rural communities being dumped on and poor communities being dumped on is nothing new. So what happens when the unlikeliest of people in the unlikeliest of places begin to reject notions of regulating factory farms and the land application of sludge because regulating an activity automatically means allowing it to operate? Instead they begin to simply say "no" to the corporate vision of agriculture being imposed upon them. Perhaps most importantly, what happens when people become disobedient by believing they can make law to codify their values, interests, goals and futures and build the types of communities they want and they need?

The communities had come to understand why Linzey had been trying to explain to them the fine points of corporate law. They had gotten a crash course in what had seemed like abstract legal arcana.

Predictably, the corporations picked on the littlest guy—a very small rural township. "They filed a lawsuit," Linzey recalls:

> It said that the anti-farming law that you've adopted as an ordinance violates our corporate constitutional rights. It violates our due process and equal protection rights, because—haven't you heard silly folks?—corporations are persons. On the front page of the complaint it said, "We are corporations, we are persons and, even though you formed a majority to codify your values, interests and goals, your ordinance is unconstitutional." Unconstitutional!
>
> So our folks in Pennsylvania got a copy of the complaint. We made a bajillion-jillion copies of it and spread it over our rural communities. And our rural supervisors, those guys with the John Deere hats, they got a copy of this complaint and they said, "Now we understand what Tom was talking about all those years. It's not abstract, it's not academic, this corporate rights concept. It hits us when we manage to build the majorities to move law forward."
>
> I will always remember, standing in one of those communities giving an update, and a rural township supervisor put up his hand and said, "Mr. Linzey, this is great that we can pass sludge ordinances and factory farm ordinances. And that's good stuff, but what good is it if we pass an ordinance—one of these issue ordinances? We can still get sued and we have to spend $100,000 going through depositions and discovery. We have to go through that whole process of being sued and being defendants." We looked back at him and said, "What do you want us to do? We're a small organization." And they said, "We want to eliminate corporate constitutional rights at the municipal level."
>
> So we said, "Yeah, we could do that." We went back to the office and began drafting the Corporate Rights Elimination Ordinance. After Porter Township, unanimously voted to adopt a binding law as the first in the country to pass a binding ordinance eliminating corporate constitutional rights, another township followed in early 2003. Then another rural municipal government. We were at the beginning of the beginning, and we'd discovered some new tools.

Up till then our job had been drafting ordinances, binding law that municipalities can adopt to put their values, interests and goals into law. Now we've started writing constitutions. We've started drafting local charters under the Home Rule provisions in Pennsylvania, and under similar home rule provisions that exist in 43 states. What does that mean? It means that we're in the business of constitution-making now, not just ordinances, because before that we were defining what a sustainable community looks like by default. We'd been saying that sustainable communities don't look like certain things. They don't have agribusiness corporations operating in them. They don't have sludge corporations operating in them. We'd been defining by default.

When we started the charter-writing process, we had to ask, "What do we want?" We're so used to not asking, "What do we want?" but "What can we get?" This process allowed our rural municipal officials to start talking about what they wanted. For starters, people wanted the inalienable right to stand free on the ground of democracy.

Another tool Linzey and his group have long used is Democracy Schools. When CELDF was first witnessing the limits of training citizen lawyers and getting tangled up in a corporate legal script whose outcome was predetermined, Linzey connected with the work of longtime activist Richard Grossman (who died in 2011). In the early 1990s, Grossman had cofounded a research and education group called the Program on Corporations, Law, and Democracy (POCLAD). Grossman and POCLAD conducted deep research on the legal history of corporations, and in particular on corporate charters. He began organizing and teaching workshops around 1995 to raise the basic question of who's in charge. Linzey began working with him to create more engaged Democracy Schools and take the work from the theoretical to the practical.

These weekend seminars have now operated in more than two hundred communities and graduated over three thousand community members, local elected officials, funders, and activists across the United States and Canada. They teach strategies to reclaim local sovereignty over key economic and political decisions that affect communities, and provide community leaders with effective organizing tools. Says Linzey,

Perhaps, just perhaps, we're in this mess today not only because we don't live in a democracy, but because we've never had a democracy in this country. Indeed, perhaps the corporate cultural I.V. in our arms has been working so well that it's hard for us to even imagine what self-government would look like. We assume that we're working within a framework in which majorities actually make governing decisions.

After all, that's what we've been taught to believe. High-sounding phrases roll off the tongues of judges and legislators, like "consent of the governed" and "majority rule." Yet, as we know, it doesn't quite work that way. Community majorities are overridden on a daily basis. Regulatory agencies legalize projects and actions that communities don't want. Zoning and land-use ordinances are routinely overridden by judicial doctrines like the "fair share doctrine" in which courts can throw out zoning and land-use ordinances if those laws don't allow for the community's fair share of development as compared to communities next door. Local laws are routinely nullified that conflict with state and federal law. When communities really try to practice democracy and refuse to swallow what they've been given, corporate managers write new preemptive laws and use the state legislatures to nullify community lawmaking. When national governments get out of hand, they use international trade agreements to preempt them. Corporate managers using the courts to override communities avail themselves of a bunch of legal doctrines that seem to be manufactured by the day. Things like "limited liability," or "state actor" in which corporations can't legally be held responsible for violating the constitutional rights of people, or the "permit shield defense" that requires that communities exhaust administrative remedies—and on, and on, and on.

Welcome to what some have coined a "corporate state" in which our own governmental institutions, language and even our brains are wielded against our own best interest where the corporate few wield preemptive legal power against the rest of us.

One thing we've learned, however, during our tromping across Pennsylvania over the last ten years is that it's extremely difficult for the people to hear the proposition that we don't have a democracy. After all, one evening of discussion can only do so much to untangle a life's worth of assumptions. And so another tenet of this organizing was born, the understanding that although people can't hear it, that they can certainly see it when it happens in front of them in their own communities.

In 2003, Linzey received a call from St. Thomas Township, a hamlet of 5,800 in the south-central part of Pennsylvania. His contacts were Fred Walls, a native Pennsylvanian and retired dairy farmer, and his wife Pat, a teacher and mother of two. They reported that about two years earlier an apple orchard in town had gone up for sale near the Walls's home. Like other locals, Fred and Pat had considered buying it, but couldn't afford the price. In May 2003 the property was auctioned with little public notice. The 560 acres fell into the hands of a Philadelphia-based firm called the St. Thomas Development Company.

Two months later the company filed a proposal to open a quarry on the site, as Fred Walls remembers all too well:

> That started our neighbors talking. We live right below where the quarry is being put in. There's six or eight houses across there, and we started gathering at the garage between my house and a neighbor's house and started to talk. People wanted to know what was going on and how this could happen. I remember distinctly us talking about what right they had to come in here and to affect our community. That was the start of a group in St. Thomas. From there we decided to make plans to fight the quarry. We decided to start gathering information, planning a public meeting, and see what we could do to affect the permit process on the quarry. The number of people grew slowly, but we planned another meeting and this time about 100 people showed up, which is pretty good for a small township.

The thousands of community groups who have worked to head off potentially damaging development would be familiar with what came next: talk over kitchen tables, new recruits, petitions, and an official name: Friends and Residents of St. Thomas Township (FROST). FROST consisted of a core of 15 people, from an army colonel to a small hobby farmer. Their goal was to convince Pennsylvania's Department of Environmental Protection to deny the quarry's permit. With the help of paid experts, they scoured the permit application for deficiencies. They found, for example, that it neglected to mention the sinkholes on the site, which could be exacerbated by new operations. Pat Walls remembers the scene:

> We researched the impact of quarries on other areas, too. We talked with people from other areas who have quarries next to them. We rallied support against locating a quarry in our township, especially because where they were going to start quarrying was within a thousand feet of our elementary school. As a teacher, I found that appalling that they could do that so close to an elementary school and not really worry about the impact that it would have on young children's lungs, and the dirt and the dust and the pollutants that they would be breathing in.
>
> So, we forwarded this information to Department of Environmental Protection, and their files overflowed with testimony and correspondence from locals who were also concerned. DEP told us that because of all the concern they had gotten, all these letters and things like that, that they would scrutinize this permit a lot more closely and carefully since it did become such a hot-button issue in St. Thomas.

FROST expected that objective scrutiny by the DEP would lead to a permit denial. But Pat and her neighbors soon learned otherwise:

> The deficiencies we thought would stop the quarry, the DEP brought to the attention of the quarry, and they fixed them. As a teacher, if I would give a test, and so many kids failed it, it would be like me giving them back the test and saying correct your answers and then I'll give you an A for it. It didn't make sense to me that the DEP would just keep letting them fix it and fix it and fix it until they got a permit that they would approve.
>
> DEP would also make recommendations to change numbers on the permit, so it would fall into a category where they wouldn't have to do other studies that might

prolong the permitting process. We just couldn't believe it was happening, that they had that kind of control. For DEP, their client is the corporation. We were told that. It's their client and they have to take care of their client, and they work with them so they can permit them eventually.

It seemed that events would go according to the standard corporate script. For years Fred and Pat Walls had worked the official channels of local government in St. Thomas Township to stop a hazardous quarry operation from digging, dynamiting, and hauling next to an elementary school and across the street from their home. Then the project would receive its permit. The residents would watch for permit violations. And if pollution became excessive, the community would spend its meager resources on complaint, protest, and possibly litigation. To FROST, that scenario didn't seem acceptable.

Fred Walls, one of those unlikeliest people in the unlikeliest of places, had a different idea.

As we were forming and trying to fight the quarry and do what we could to stop it, one of our members said he knew an environmental attorney that might help us, might help us with the regulations, might help us with DEP. He mentioned his name—Thomas Linzey. There was a lot of mixed emotions by our group, because Tom's name had been in the paper several times, not always in a good light from the powers that be. But we said we need help—and we were looking for any ally we could find.

We invited Tom to one of our meetings and we weren't ready for what he told us. He said the regulatory path was a path to sure defeat. He said this system was designed to permit quarries. The regulations were written by the mining industry to make sure that permits were granted. In Pennsylvania, the DEP is supposed to stand for Department of Environmental Protection, but everybody calls it the Department of Everything Permitted. One or two quarries have been turned down in the last 30 years and most everything else gets permitted.

He told us that we would waste our time, waste our money, waste our energy—and we would still get the quarry. We needed to do things differently, we needed to get political, and we needed to run a candidate for township supervisor and try to affect the elections in St. Thomas Township. At that point—there was only about eight weeks before the election—there was no time to get anybody on the ballot. If we did anything, it had to be a write-in candidate. The next thing Tom Linzey said to us is, "Win the election and call me," and he left.

After the shock of realization wore off and Linzey's message sank in, the group came up with a candidate, Frank Stearn, and began a cherished American ritual. As Fred Walls recounts:

We started collecting money. We started doing everything we needed to do to get a campaign rolling. It was exactly four weeks till election day when we announced his candidacy. Every Saturday we would go out and beat on doors and hand out literature. We did mailings. We did signs, fundraising. Everybody knows about that. And meetings, they never stopped. We just kept on going to get Frank elected.

November 3rd was election day, and it was an off year, but we had quite a turnout. About 1,200 people turned out to vote in the township. With a write-in candidate, you don't have much of a chance to win, 'cause the deck is stacked against you. There is no party out there that thinks write-in candidates are good—Republicans or Democrats. So you got no help from either one, and we were on our own. But the turnout was good. Frank won the election outright. Then the vote was contested.

Stearn's opponents had found a few ballot-box technicalities, including one involving the spelling of the candidate's name. But a retabulation confirmed Stearn's victory—with even more votes than originally recorded. That was on February 18; it turned out to be Stearn's first day on the job.

Fred Walls, his wife Pat, and the community could hardly believe what happened next. "As Frank gets sworn in," Fred shakes his head,

St. Thomas Township supervisors are served with a letter from St. Thomas Development Company. They threatened the township and Frank, and they said that, if Frank

Stearn voted for any matter that concerned the quarry or any of their actions they needed to do—because of Frank's prior position against the quarry—the township would be violating the corporation's Fifth Amendment rights. They said that, if Frank voted, the township could be liable for monetary damages. Our election was nullified by three people from a corporation out of Philadelphia.

What to do next? There was a lot of questions around. What gives them the rights to do this? We're starting to discuss where's democracy, who controls democracy. Re-enter Thomas Linzey.

This time, FROST was not shocked when Linzey delivered his sober prognosis: A corporation's right to extract stones from their community was superseding their right to self-government. With Linzey's help, they organized an impromptu Democracy School and learned more about the rights of corporations. The group considered filing a civil rights lawsuit, but they knew full well that their financial reserves would prove no match for those of the powerful corporation. Fred Walls recalls the fateful moment of truth:

> I remember the discussions about what would happen if we filed suit and they didn't like it. Well, next thing you know, we're worried about our houses and our homes and our savings accounts. So we learned about asset protection and what it would take to do this stuff, and we decided to file suit. Next thing you know, the quarry corporation threatened us with retaliation. We were all getting worried about what to do and we had some discussions about some strange stuff. What's more important, the law or our township or the stuff we own? We all sat there and thought, "Would Rosa Parks have worried about sitting down in the back of the bus?" We hung tough and kept going until the court came back with a ruling that said, "Silly people, you know you don't have the right to do this; and Mr. Linzey should be lucky he didn't get sanctioned for what he did."
>
> Again we appealed to a higher court. Again it was tossed out, without a hearing. Your rights aren't as important as a corporation is basically what they taught us. We

learned then who wielded the power in this country. We learned the difference between law and justice, which aren't mutually compatible.

Represented by Linzey and CELDF, FROST filed a first-of-its-kind federal class action civil rights suit against the corporation and its directors—charging that the corporation's exercise of its claimed constitutional "rights" actually violated the rights of the residents of the community to govern themselves. Given that corporate constitutional rights were so well established in law, the group knew their effort was a long shot, but they considered just the filing of the lawsuit a victory since it revealed a provocative truth: Corporations possess greater rights than the communities in which they do business.

Pat, Fred, and friends regrouped under the name St. Thomas Alliance for a New Direction (STAND). STAND has continued campaigning for "home rule." Home rule is a provision in many states that allows communities to carve out a measure of sovereignty by writing their own constitutions. STAND is determined not only to win such a charter but also use it to the fullest in St. Thomas Township. It's determined to protect the health and well-being of its schoolchildren and community members, governing according to the priorities of its people, by its people, and for its people.

It has been a long and winding road to stand the ground of democracy for Tom Linzey and these courageous rural Pennsylvania communities. Says Linzey,

> I can still remember a meeting several years ago. One of our elected officials, in response to the town lawyer who had just informed him that the township was powerless to stop sludge from being dumped, pulled out the Pennsylvania Constitution from his desk and read the words from Article One, Section Two: "All power is inherent in the people, and all free governments are founded on their authority and instituted for their peace, safety and happiness."
>
> People are taking self-governance very seriously in the Keystone state, and they're inviting you to get serious with them. Our folks in Pennsylvania have given up hope that the legislature will help them, that the courts will help them, that environmental groups will help them or that state agencies

will help them. Instead they've turned to the same place that the abolitionists and suffragists turned, to the same place that the populist farmers of the 1890s and the American revolutionaries turned—to themselves and to each other.

As Linzey and company kept relentlessly pushing the communities to define what they really wanted, a startling response surfaced—"one of those things that folks in one of our rural communities wanted was to write about the *rights of nature*."

I always get in trouble for saying this, but in the United States we've never had an environmental movement. The reason is that movements in this country drive rights into the Constitution. They drive rights into the fundamental governing frameworks of communities, the country and states. That's what constitutions do. We've never had an environmental movement in this country because the environmental movement has never sought to drive rights for nature into the Constitution. When we look back at other movements, they didn't screw around with regulating things. The abolitionists didn't ask for a Slavery Protection Agency. The abolitionists drove the Thirteenth, Fourteenth and Fifteenth Amendments into the Constitution. The suffragists drove their own amendment into the Constitution. That's what movements do.

In the United States, nature has no rights. Ecosystems have no rights. Rivers have no rights. Bears, cougars, trees—no rights. They're property under the law. There was a point in this country when people were property. So what happens when we start writing charters that recognize the inalienable rights of nature? Not their usefulness to us, or their value to us, but their rights in and of themselves. And what happens when those provisions give people the power to stand in as trustees, to litigate the rights of nature? That's where it gets exciting.

At the dawn of the American Revolution, these famous words in the U.S. Declaration of Independence rang as a beacon of liberty in their day: "We hold these truths to be self-evident, that all men are created equal . . . " Less well known is the fact that in 1776 "equality" and "legal rights" referred to white men of property and wealth—only they could vote, and only they had "legal standing." Civil rights were denied to Native Americans, who became wards of the government as you would treat a foster child. African Americans as slaves were literal property under the law. Women were the legal property of their husbands and had no rights. At the time, the founders considered these logical extensions of a Constitution based at its core on property rights.

Now at the dawn of the twenty-first century, people are asking: What about the rights of nature? Should rivers, mountains, whales, and ecosystems have inalienable rights that guarantee *their* interests—their inherent right to life? If nature had rights, what would it demand from us? And what are our human rights worth if we destroy the healthy functioning ecosystems on which all life depends?

In the twenty-first century, are we ready to move from a Declaration of Independence to a Declaration of Interdependence? To a revolution from the heart of nature? Tom Linzey points out the inevitable logic of a property rights constitution, the norm around the world:

> Forever in this country, as well as in Western law, nature has been held to be property. If you own a ten acre piece of land, you have a deed to it, the law authorizes you, in fact encourages you in some ways to actually destroy that piece of the ecosystem on that piece of land.
>
> We've tried to build an environmental movement on the basis of nature as property. Environmental regulations and laws are all based on Congress's authority under something called the Commerce Clause. In fact, when Congress passed the Clean Air Act, the Clean Water Act, the National Environmental Policy Act and even the Endangered Species Act, they were all done under the Commerce Clause authority, which essentially says that nature is commerce. Western philosophy and law treat nature as property. It's really a shake-up when people start saying that right-less things should have rights, at the very least the right to exist.

After all, we've done this before in American history. In the 1800s, it took a grievous Civil War to guarantee the rights of African Americans in the Constitution. The suffragists fought for women's rights for one hundred years before women won the right to vote in 1920.

In his landmark book *Wild Law: A Manifesto for Earth Justice*, South African environmental attorney Cormac Cullinan asserted that human beings are actually but members of a planetwide community that includes the ecosystems that make all life possible. Without clean water, clean air, healthy soil, fertile habitats, and sufficient wildlife, every member of the Earth community suffers, including us.

Cullinan drew on the thinking and work of other pathfinding thought leaders in this novel legal arena of Earth jurisprudence, including Thomas Berry and the United Nations. He advocates for a new body of law to counter the commodification and corporatization of nature. Its first priority is to protect the ecological community on which all life depends. And what would happen if people could have legal standing on behalf of nature and give voice to the voiceless? Tom Linzey decided to find out, once again transplanting theory into practical reality:

> For example, if somebody pollutes the Spokane River, if you want to step in and try to actually help the Spokane River, the first thing you have to get by is this concept of "legal standing." You have to either live on the river or have some kind of financial interest that's been affected by the pollution of the river. When you go into courts, the first question a judge asks is, "What's your financial interest in the river?" The law doesn't see the river, just like it didn't see the slave, just like it didn't see the woman in court. It sees you. The inquiry is how much you have been damaged by the pollution of the river, and then you're awarded the damages. It doesn't go back to the river, because the river's not seen. Nature and ecosystems are held in that pocket right now as property.
>
> What's fascinating is that over a dozen municipalities in the United States today working with our organization have passed local laws that declare that ecosystems have rights to exist and flourish of their own, and that anyone in the community can step into the shoes of the ecosystem to protect it or vindicate it. Damages have to be measured by the damage to the ecosystem and damage awards have to go back to restoring the ecosystem itself. It's a fundamental shift in the law.

Like previous popular movements, granting rights to ecosystems may seem outlandish or impossible. Yet challenging corporate personhood is helping communities wake up to how corporate rights are on a collision course with environmental well-being as well as with the rights of ordinary citizens, such as those in Nottingham, New Hampshire.

Mari Margil, a graduate of Harvard's Kennedy School of Government who works with Linzey and CELDF as associate director, has helped ground Earth justice and the emerging rights of nature movement in law. "The people of Nottingham had fought for seven years to stop USA Springs Corporation from coming in and privatizing their water. They appealed permits to the state Department of Environmental Services. They circulated petitions. They lobbied their state legislature. They held protests and they filed lawsuits. They did everything right through conventional environmental organizing, but somehow they still weren't winning."

Margil recalls how the citizens of neighboring Barnstead caught wind of the losing struggle in Nottingham. At a Democracy School in Barnstead, a town official asked why the state environmental agency seemed more interested in granting permits to corporations to take their water than helping people in the community protect it. Observes Margil,

> Over a hundred years ago, the first regulatory agency, the Interstate Commerce Commission, was created at the request of the railroad corporations, the Wal-Marts of their day. As the U.S. attorney general Richard Olney told the president of Burlington Railroad back in 1893, the agency "is or can be made of great help to the railroads. It satisfied the popular clamor for government supervision at the same time that that supervision is almost entirely nominal." He went on to say that the agency acts as "a sort of barrier between the railroad corporations and the people."
>
> As one Barnstead resident put it, it seemed as though nothing had changed in over a hundred years. To the folks in Barnstead, it seemed that, if they took the path of Nottingham, it was only a matter of time before a corporation came along and took their water. Because of that, several Select Board members asked us to draft an ordinance that would ban corporations from coming in and siphoning off their water, and which offered the best and highest protection for their aquifer. They also wanted the

ordinances to strip corporations of their ability to override the community's law making. We worked hand in hand with them to draft an ordinance, and the Barnstead ordinance recognizes that ecosystems have legally enforceable rights, and bans certain corporations from carrying out activities the community doesn't want and, lastly, strips corporations of constitutional protections. Adopting the ordinance at a town meeting by a vote of 135 to 1, Barnstead became the first community in the nation to ban corporations from privatizing their water.

Folks struggling to protect their water in neighboring Nottingham soon called CELDF. They wanted an ordinance based on the one written by the citizens of Barnstead. Margil witnessed an extraordinary process unfolding. Gail Mills, who with her husband Chris became leaders in the campaign to pass the ordinance, explained their decision to turn their back on the environmental regulatory system that they'd fought in for so long: "We have to go out and make our own history and not let others define it for us."

Spokane, Washington, then became the first midsize city in the United States with a citizen movement organized and strong enough to attempt to rewrite its governance laws to limit corporate control and legalize the rights of nature. Linzey moved to Spokane to support the community organizing effort:

> Spokane's an interesting place. The second largest city in the state of Washington, it's rural and fairly conservative. The folks that went through the Democracy Schools then started to clump together and they said, "Let's build a campaign here based on some of these principles." Their key issue in Spokane was that the city has 27 neighborhoods. Just like any other city, you have a defined neighborhood you live in. Even though there are those official municipal neighborhoods and there are elected neighborhood councils, people in the communities come together as residents and form their own neighborhood councils. There are 27 of them as well. Under the city's charter, those neighborhood councils have no binding authority whatsoever. They're advisory only. So they do things like issue dump passes.

When Walmart sought to build a store in one of these neighborhoods, a thousand residents rose up in protest. Their attempt to stop it failed because they had no binding authority. Many residents realized that the neighborhood councils were window dressing.

As a result, some neighborhoods came together with graduates of the Democracy School, and other groups started to come into the circle, including labor union locals such as the United Food and Commercial Workers, the Ironworkers Union, the letter carriers, and the plumbers and pipe fitters. Once various labor union locals got interested, the conversation broadened. If the neighborhood councils sought to change the structure of law to give themselves binding decision making authority, what about all the labor issues of the past fifty years that had yet to be realized?

Soon environmental groups, including the Sierra Club and organizations concerned with protecting the Spokane River, joined. Quickly twenty-four organizations gathered, people who had never sat down in a room together.

A citizen group called Envision Spokane formed and spent a year crafting a nine-point Community Bill of Rights addressing issues such as the environment, medical care, low-income housing, prevailing wages and apprenticeship rights on jobs, as well as neighborhood control over local development. The community coalition put Proposition 4 on the November 2009 ballot. It aimed to be the first legally binding, enforceable Community Bill of Rights in a major city within the United States Among its provisions was one that would recognize the rights of nature, as well as override corporate constitutional rights.

An instant flash flood of corporate opposition saturated the electorate with half a million dollars' worth of "free speech." Much of it was out-of-state money, from the likes of the National Association of Home Builders in Washington DC.

The vote was over 75 percent against Proposition 4. Envision Spokane viewed the glass as one-quarter full—a remarkable advance coming from empty. The coalition publicly vowed to keep fighting to successfully amend the city charter. In the next effort in 2011, the Proposition gained 49.12 percent of the vote (28,872 votes) with 50.88 percent against. They'll be back . . .

Linzey sees Spokane as building a true movement. "What's happening in Spokane is the cutting edge of actually using government to make what has previously been reserved as private economic decision making left to a very few number of people. What the folks backing Proposition 4 in Spokane are saying is that that system has caused severe problems in

Spokane, including one in three families being without adequate health insurance, including the Spokane River being one of the most polluted rivers in the United States, including the fact that locally owned businesses have no legal protections against out-of-city corporations coming in and mashing them down."

When the Supreme Court ruled in 2010 that corporate spending on elections constituted "free speech," the battle lines became even more starkly drawn. Local communities simply cannot compete financially against giant deep-pocketed corporations in an age where election campaigns are largely waged in the media, speech is anything but free, and media companies make big bucks off election ads. But when the unlikeliest of people in the unlikeliest of places start rewriting the script, all the ads in the world can't spin their reality-based experience.

In 2009, the first CELDF-drafted ordinances were adopted in Maine banning corporations from massive water withdrawals. By 2012, 142 communities in Pennsylvania, New Hampshire, Maine, and Virginia had adopted CELDF-drafted laws and over 350,000 people were living under these governing frameworks. In late 2010, the city of Pittsburgh adopted one of CELDF's ordinances—becoming the first major municipality in the United States to adopt a Community Bill of Rights and enforce that bill of rights by banning natural gas extraction (fracking) and corporate rights within the municipality.

Innovation always arises locally, and if conditions are right, it spreads—in this case it's moving out globally. It's not only the American system of property law that denies the rights of nature. CELDF began to answer calls for legal assistance from as far away as Nepal and Turkey. In 2007, through a connection made via Bioneers with Rainforest Action Network founder Randy Hayes and the U.S.-based Pachamama Alliance (a leading nonprofit that works on behalf on indigenous peoples in the Amazon), CELDF was invited to meet with delegates of Ecuador's constitutional assembly who were in the process of writing a new constitution. A small South American country was about to emerge as the first in the world to write Earth justice into its national constitution.

CELDF's Mari Margil traveled to Montecristi in Ecuador to assist the delegates in drafting a rights-based system of environmental protection. She stepped into a corrosive environment, literally and figuratively:

> For centuries, the people and landscapes of Ecuador have
> been exploited by outsiders. In recent years, it was revealed

that Texaco had dumped more than 18 billion gallons of toxic wastewater into the Ecuadorian rainforest.

We were not experts in Ecuadorian law, but there are similarities which cut across international lines. There, like here, the law treats nature as property. We told the delegates the stories of Barnstead and other towns, how we worked with them to draft and adopt new laws recognizing legally enforceable rights of ecosystems.

We also had the opportunity to meet with the president of the constitutional assembly, Alberto Acosta. We thought we'd have an uphill battle trying to explain to this former minister of Energy and Mines why communities in the U.S. were adopting laws recognizing ecosystem rights. But before we had a chance to say anything, he told us that, to his mind, the law treats nature as a slave with no rights of its own. We had found a meeting of the minds in one of the most unlikely but most critical of places. We were asked to draft language for the delegates. Over a series of months, they shaped and expanded that language, and in 2009 the people of Ecuador approved the new Constitution, becoming the very first country in the world to recognize in its Constitution the rights of ecosystems to "exist, persist, regenerate and evolve."

In 2010, CELDF became a founding member of the Global Alliance for the Rights of Nature, an international organization formed to build a global movement to recognize nature's legal rights, and is currently chairing its Legislative Assistance Working Group.

As Margil points out, "In 1973, Professor Christopher Stone penned his famous article 'Should Trees Have Standing?' He explained this idea of rights of nature and why it's so hard for us to think about those without rights, the right-less, as possibly having rights, and why every time a movement is launched to recognize rights for the right-less, as the abolitionists did and the suffragists did, the movements and the people involved are deemed treasonous and radical. Stone writes, 'The fact is that each time there is a movement to confer rights onto some new entity, the proposal is bound to sound odd or frightening or laughable. This is partly because, until the right-less thing receives its rights, we cannot see it as anything but a thing for the use of us—"us" being, of course, those of us who hold rights.'"

As Margil reminds us, "In the cherished children's book *The Lorax* by Dr. Seuss, the Lorax asked, 'Who speaks for the trees?' The people of Ecuador, Barnstead, Nottingham and a dozen other communities have answered, 'We do.' And now I ask all of you, 'Will you speak for the trees?' For if not you, then who? And if not now, then when?"

Part 3

VALUE CHANGE
FOR SURVIVAL

REMEMBERING THE FUTURE

Clear Thinking, Justice, and Peace

*A*s the late Richard Deertrack of Taos Pueblo once said: "From the point of view of a plant, all people look pretty much the same." From the point of view of the planet, we are one species.

The challenge we face is not primarily technological. The environmental crisis is more accurately a human crisis. It's political, cultural, and deeply personal. To succeed in this momentous transition, we're being called upon to cooperate on a grand scale. It requires the equivalent of a wartime mobilization, yet its purpose is precisely the opposite: to create peace. To get to the other side, we're going to have to face and heal the deep wounds in our societies and in ourselves.

The world has reached a collective turning point, a burgeoning global awakening. Large numbers of people are recognizing the need to start stepping back from the abyss. Author and student of social movements Paul Hawken describes this unprecedented global movement of movements as "humanity's immune response." He proposes that it's the biggest movement in the history of the world, and it's growing rapidly.

The Mayan people describe this movement of movements as "one 'no' and many 'yeses.'" The "no" is to the concentration of wealth and the distribution of poverty. The "yes" is to "a world where many worlds fit," a global society devoted to health, justice, dignity, diversity, and democracy—to human rights and the rights of nature.

Since 1990 there has been a global explosion of civil society dot orgs and social entrepreneurs. In many cases they have shifted their attention away from governments to businesses, which often have a greater capacity for producing real social change quickly. Dot orgs now span a sprawling social ecology of change, from opponent to partner and all points in between.

We're witnessing the endgame of a civilization at war with the natural world and with ourselves. It is not a winnable war. The overriding issue is how we make peace—with the land, each other, and ourselves.

We have a lot of history to overcome. War is a scarlet river flooding across the ages. The late psychologist James Hillman suggested that war is so deeply embedded in our psyche that we worship it as divine. We have made a religion of war—holy war.

Tribe against tribe. Nation against nation. War against the Earth. War against the poor. War against religious beliefs. War against the indigenous. War against peoples of color. War against women. War against the Other.

The industrialized warfare of the twentieth century was the bloodiest ever. Fear and rumors of war have led us to build vast military-industrial complexes that have caused environmental harm, the magnitude of which will shadow us for generations. The supreme irony is that our security anxiety has made the world perilously insecure.

Today at the dawn of the twenty-first century, modern techno-war could lead to the virtual annihilation of human civilization. Even global warming meets its match in the face of nuclear winter. We are all prisoners of war.

How do we get out of this alive? We are not the first to ask that question.

The late Seneca historian John Mohawk reminded us that the Iroquois Confederacy was forged out of cataclysmic war. He told the story this way.

There was an individual born among the Hurons in the Great Lakes who grew up in a society that was each against all. Blood feuds left not only villages fighting villages, but individual households fighting individual households. Violence ruled the day. Not unlike the twenty-first century, it was a time of absolute horror and degradation of the human soul.

A young man not yet twenty had an insight. He said violence is a really bad idea. He went to the people, and he stated, "You have to stop these cycles of violence." The cycles of violence were embedded deep in the laws and customs of the Indian peoples. They were about revenge, for real and imagined injuries.

This young man, who became known as the Peacemaker, said that war makes people crazy. When people are at war, they're not thinking clearly.

His argument was this: "We don't need to live this way. We have the power in our collective minds to create a world in which people do not use violence, but rather use thinking." He went from village to village and persuaded people that we have to have a pact against violence.

Of course, when you walk into a village and say, "We have to put down our weapons of war and have peace," they're going to say, "Not till the other guys do." To which you say, "Okay, let's go talk to the other guys." Until someone says, "Can't talk to them. They're all crazy."

So the Peacemaker responded, "When you tell yourself your enemy can't think, you destroy your own power to make peace with him. In order to use our minds to solve problems, we have to first acknowledge that the people on the other side of the negotiation probably want their people to live, and probably want a lot of the same things you do." So it starts by looking for common ground with the enemy.

People said, "We're at war with these people because they've harmed us. They've done wrong to us." The Peacemaker replied that the pursuit of peace is not merely the pursuit of the absence of violence. Peace is never achieved until justice is achieved. Justice is not achieved until everyone's interests are addressed. So, he said, you will never actually finish addressing everyone's issues. You can't achieve peace unless it's accompanied by constant striving to address justice. It means your job will never end.

The Peacemaker said we have to build an institution to represent this. He brought together the chiefs of five nations, who formed the Iroquois Confederacy (later to expand to become the Iroquois Six Nations). Its purpose was, and still is, to practice clear thinking, address justice, and sustain peace. Its highly sophisticated government was in fact one of the inspirations for our American democracy.

The Peacemaker did not say we'd kill each other off with weapons. He said that in the end, unless we achieve peace among ourselves, the people of the planet will be eliminated.

The time the Peacemaker foresaw is with us. Our warring ways now threaten the very basis of our sustainability as a species and countless others we're already extinguishing.

Memory is really about the future. The ancient wisdom of First Peoples reminds us of the deepest values of this American land. The Indigenous Environmental Network puts it this way: "The health and well-being of our grandchildren are worth more than all the wealth that can be taken from these lands. The first mandate is to ensure that our decision making is guided by consideration of the welfare and well-being of the seventh generation to come."

To carry us forward, we have this and other rich underlying values in this country: a democratic government of, by, and for the people; ingenious innovation; and rich multicultural diversity. These are precisely what we need to succeed in a global cooperative mobilization to create a truly just and sustainable civilization.

In 2011 the proposed Pentagon budget of $708 billion of our taxes comprised more than all of the rest of the world's military expenditures combined. That did not even include the accrued direct costs of hundreds of billions of dollars for the wars in Iraq and Afghanistan. With about $30 billion, we could protect and conserve all the great remaining threatened centers of biological diversity in the world, and pay the people living there to implement that conservation. As the organization Business Leaders for Sensible Priorities points out, with $60 billion we could put every child in America in Head Start, guarantee health care for every child, rebuild every single American school, and begin to establish energy independence for the United States using renewable fuels.

As human beings, we have one very important trait going for us at this historic turning point. We excel at cooperation. It has been one of our greatest evolutionary advantages. For about 99 percent of our trajectory as a species we lived in small, stable bands of very closely related hunter-gatherers. It was an optimal setting for cultivating close cooperation.

The catch is that we limited our cooperation to our own small groups. Outsiders beware, because we can also be ruthlessly efficient cooperative killing machines. As Stanford neurobiologist Robert Sapolsky observes, a primal xenophobia—a fear of the Other—is hardwired deep in our brain. Brain imaging studies show that the amygdala (the location of our ancient fight-or-flight survival response) is easily stimulated into fear and aggression—for instance by seeing pictures of another race. However, tests show that, in people who have substantial experience with people of different races, the amygdala simply does not become activated. The amygdala also remains quiet when we come to see people as individuals rather than as members of a group.

There are additional proven ways to mitigate our instinctive fear of the Other. One is trade. Another is to maintain porous borders and flows among groups. Sapolsky concludes, "Humans may be hardwired to get edgy around the Other, but our views on who falls into that category are remarkably malleable."

The challenge we face is whether we can soften our clannish cultural borders—in fact expand those borders beyond our very human-ness—to cooperate on a global scale and embrace a culturally diverse and biologically interdependent world.

And what will happen if we take the road to extinction? As Bob Holmes wrote in "Imagine Earth Without People": "It will only take a few tens of thousands of years at most before almost every trace of our present dominance has vanished completely. Alien visitors coming to Earth 100,000 years hence will find no obvious signs that an advanced civilization ever lived here."

Our wounds are deep, like old bad habits. There is much we need to forget. There is also much we need to remember. Above all, we need to remember the future.

Since the atomic bombs fell on Hiroshima and Nagasaki, the quest of the past half-century has been to make peace—not by force of military might—but by rational mutual interest and ethical principles. By clear thinking and by addressing justice.

Vietnam is the most studied example of recent techno-wars where we used fewer soldiers but lethally advanced weaponry to do maximum damage to people and the environment. Babies are still being born deformed by pervasive Agent Orange poisoning from extensive chemical warfare.

Vietnam is begging the rest of the world to come study its experience. Its official policy is this: We have been the most hurt by recent wars. We're not angry. We just want you to see what war does, so we can all stop it together.

Ed Tick is a psychotherapist who began working in the 1970s with Vietnam vets who suffered from post-traumatic stress disorder (PTSD). Most were taking multiple drugs to suppress the personal hell haunting their lives. Tick realized that PTSD was not about stress; it was about trauma. He learned that the Greek word *travma* actually meant a puncture, a hole, a wound. For the Greeks, it was also a spiritual wound: a hole in the soul.

Tick began taking vets back to the scene of their trauma, to face and embrace the Other, to seek redemption in forgiveness. They began to heal the wounds to their souls. They became true warriors. Knowing the horror, now they try to talk people out of war.

On one of these truth and reconciliation journeys to Vietnam, Tick and the veterans visited My Lai. Today My Lai is a beautiful peace garden like Hiroshima where people from all over the world come to learn. Before that, it was the infamous scene of the slaughter of an unarmed village by U.S. soldiers.

At My Lai, Tick and the vets met a woman of seventy-five, the only member of her family to survive the dreadful massacre. She lost her husband, her parents, and all her children. These are Ed Tick's words:

> She expressed her terrible pain at living. I said to her, "Grandmother, we're so sorry for you and your losses. How do you feel about us Americans coming to visit you and see this place when we took so much from you?"
>
> She said: "My pain doesn't matter. It is so important that you come."

And I said, "Grandmother, I can understand that 'thank you.' But how do you feel about our veterans coming back? Maybe they were here. Maybe they took the lives of your family or other Vietnamese people."

She said: "Oh no, no. You misunderstand. It is most important that your veterans come back here, so that I can take their hands and look into their eyes, and forgive them and help them heal."

There is a place in Vietnam called Marble Mountain. It's very sacred. There is an ancient Buddhist temple in it. The Viet Cong used it as a field hospital. We bombed it twice. But the temple is still intact and it wears its scars. Outside that temple on Marble Mountain, there is a simple wooden sign that proclaims in both Vietnamese and English these words, an ancient Buddhist precept:

Hatreds never cease by hatreds in this world.
By love they cease.

This is an ancient law.

The wounds we're inflicting on the Earth and on each other are the same wound.

Blessed are the peacemakers.

THE STAR ROVER

The Law of Love

*O*ur senses are relentlessly assaulted with horrific and heartbreaking images of war, torture, and vicious cycles of escalating revenge. It's hard to see how to break the death spiral of violence and vengeance. But hatred is a candle that burns from both ends. If we don't find our way out, it threatens to destroy us. Where can redemption be found?

I'd like to share with you a story from the past that's a parable for our troubled times. It took place a century ago at San Quentin, the notorious prison that for over 160 years has symbolized brutality and barbarism. It's a story of redemption, and of just how profound a difference one person can make, even against seemingly hopeless odds. It's a fable of how closely inner personal transformation is linked with social transformation. It reminds us that the most important social struggles last for generations across cycles of improvement and regression.

I fell into this story thirty years ago after reading Jack London's last novel, *The Star Rover*. When I learned that the novel was inspired by the true story of Ed Morrell, known as "the dungeon man of San Quentin," I dove into a haystack of research.

Morrell's self-told tale is fantastical. It could easily be taken as the fevered hallucinations of a madman or the exotic concoction of a fabulist. There are basic facts, however, that are beyond dispute and in the historical record. Draw your own conclusions.

In the early 1890s, Morrell was an idealistic young rebel in California's Central Valley who threw his lot in with an insurgent band called the California Outlaws. The Outlaws were battling the giant railroad monopolies that were robbing settlers of their homes and property, and plundering California and the nation. Morrell impulsively assisted a daring jailbreak to free an innocent man imprisoned as the leader of the Outlaws. The two fugitives were finally captured months later, climaxing the biggest manhunt in the state's history that attracted a swarm of three thousand bloodthirsty bounty hunters, the worst cutthroats and thieves in the West from Canada to Mexico.

Morrell's crime should have brought a maximum ten-year sentence, but the railroad monopoly owned state politics. A kangaroo court handed him a life sentence at hard labor in Folsom State Prison, which was run by a former railroad official. He was a marked man.

Morrell was immediately subjected to a grisly catalog of tortures. He was suspended by sharp handcuffs from a derrick, arms extended behind his back until his kidneys bled. He was hosed down in a cell covered with chloride of lime powder until the corrosive fumes choked him into a strangling unconsciousness. The iron of hatred branded his heart. He lived for vengeance. And things were about to get even worse.

After a failed prison rebellion, Morrell was shipped out to San Quentin, infamously known as the country's most murderous jail. Morrell described it as a "fetid mist of sickening odors, a smoldering cauldron." Word came down from the top to crush him.

"Henceforth," Morrell later wrote, "my life was to be one long siege of torture." Following an onslaught of brutal punishments, a stool pigeon trying to curry favor with the warden falsely accused Morrell of knowing where guns for a fictitious jailbreak were hidden. Unable to confess to nonexistent guns, Morrell watched in shock as the authorities condemned him to *solitary confinement for life*.

He was locked in a dark tomb of eight-by-four-and-a-half feet. Invisible guards slipped maggot-ridden slop and water under the steel door once every twenty-four hours. Months, years passed. Only one other prisoner shared solitary for life, and they risked savage beatings each time they tapped out a Morse code of "knuckle talk" in their "ghost world of the living dead."

For three years, not even a guard entered Morrell's cell. He battled madness, but he managed to summon the inner strength to focus his mind with an amazing power of visualization. He "drew plans on the walls of his brain," inventing machines and playing mental checkers. Eventually he learned to hypnotize himself, claiming to consciously project his mind outside the walls to distant lands and loved ones, to go "star roving," as author and prison activist Jack London would later term it. And once again, things were about to get worse.

One day the steel door flung open on the new warden, a one-eyed fiend stinking of whiskey. The warden contemptuously displayed his cherished "overcoat." Reveal where the guns were hidden, or Morrell would meet his fate in the straitjacket.

Guards forced Morrell's hands into two interior pockets and flung him facedown on the stone. They laced up the four-foot canvas overcoat, squeezing the breath from his withered body with the force of a boa constrictor. Pains like millions of sharp needles shot though his tender flesh. Uncontrollable horror seized him. He kicked frantically and wailed until they gagged him with shoe leather and left him. His limbs went numb and dead. On the fifth day, they released him—paralyzed, bruised, shriveled.

Morrell slept—for how long he had no idea. As he later recounted, "I had reached the turning point where I would sink forever into the abysmal depths of despair, or be reborn a new being with a realization that my sufferings had all been for a purpose, that it was necessary for me to go through this veritable Hell upon earth in order to have awakened in me the consciousness of a great inner power, a philosophy of life that would make possible a great future. I did not know that some people are called upon to pay a terrific penalty in order to bring out a true understanding of their inherent goodness; that forces of destruction in the form of intense suffering must be brought into play until the old self is annihilated, especially with those who come here to perform a mission, perhaps a great service to humanity."

It was a strange sleep, a kind of lucid dreaming filled with voices and visions. At last he found himself in a "punishment room" where all those who had tortured him were themselves being subjected to their own atrocities. It was a scene he had long visualized as his ultimate retribution. "Before I went to sleep," he later recalled, "I was seething with hatred for every one of them, cursing them, vowing vengeance. Now I looked at them with deep compassion instead of hatred. I was pained when I gazed upon their suffering. Then came the strangest reaction of all. I went to work releasing them. With a great intensity of purpose, I madly tore at the fetters that bound them in their misery and worked with a terrific speed releasing them from their suffering."

Morrell awoke in a mad whirl of intoxication and great joy. He heard a voice speaking to him from the depths of infinite luminous space: "You have learned the unreality of pain, and hence of fear. You have learned the futility of trying to fight off your enemies with hatred. Your weapon henceforth will be the sword of love, and as time progresses and your power unfolds, this new weapon will cut and hew away all evil forces which now oppose you. Even the straitjacket will have no terrors for you. It will only be a means to greater things. Your life must now be a work of preparation, and when the time is ripe for your deliverance, you will know it. The proof will be a power to prophesy to your enemies, not only the day of your ultimate release from this dungeon but also from the prison, when the governor of the state in person shall bring your pardon to San Quentin."

Slowly Morrell opened his eyes. His shrunken hands no longer trembled. The spasmodic twitching of his mouth and eyes had ceased. He felt the strength of a million men. The dungeon was a place of horror no more. It was the crucible of fate where he was to be reborn.

When the warden and guards returned and threw Morrell back in the jacket, they were confounded by the lack of fear in his eyes and his faint smile. As Morrell later confided, "I was already in the state of belief that my mind was one thing and my body was another, that the intangible self could control the physical. I started concentrating upon the willing to death of my body." Morrell maintained he could hypnotize himself into a kind of suspended animation: dead to all appearances yet mentally awake. (As a boy, he worked in pitch-dark coal mines and said he developed strong powers of visualization, which he refined into meditation techniques in solitary.) After inducing this "little death" on his body, he said he was able to project his consciousness across space and time, frequenting the bustling streets of San Francisco or strange lands with foreign tongues, moving about "as a ghost." He claimed to encounter people who would later play crucial roles in his life, including his liberator and his wife.

When they finally released Morrell from the jacket 126 hours later, he was indifferent to their threat to lace him right back up. Left alone, he lapsed into a slumber and again the dreams came. He found himself on a journey through all the prison hellholes of the world. He saw thousands of men rotting with idleness, being educated in new ways of crime. He saw a million men financially dependent on crime, from judges and police to clerks and officials. He saw billions of dollars expended, paid for by honest taxpayers, for a futile system. He awakened with a vision of what he called the "New Era Penology," a system of rehabilitation instead of punishment. He called it the law of love—to return good for evil.

The warden, maddened at being unable to break Morrell, now ordered a double-jacketing—one on top of the other—to last for ten days. Morrell would confess, or die in the jacket.

On the fourth day, the warden and guards returned unexpectedly. A Senate investigating commission had come to San Quentin unannounced.

Fearing that the truth might leak out if Morrell died, they slashed his ropes. "Dead as a doornail," pronounced the opium-addled prison doctor.

As they lifted Morrell onto the gurney, his eyelids fluttered and opened. In an instant he was smiling into the warden's scarlet face. The mortified warden was lurching out of the cell when Morrell called out in a feeble whisper: "I have a little prophecy to make. This is the last time I will ever be tortured in the jacket! One year from today I will go out of this dungeon, never to return to it; and better still, four years from the day I leave the dungeon I will walk from the prison, a free man with a pardon in my hand. More, the governor of the state will bring that pardon in person to San Quentin."

It was the last time Morrell would see the warden, who was busted in a scandal when it was discovered he had used prisoners to manufacture counterfeit money that he and some guards dispersed all over the Bay Area. The guards now treated Morrell kindly. Never again was the prisoner put in the straitjacket. He worked ceaselessly on his ideas for the New Era Penology.

One year later, the new warden came to his cell. He had determined that indeed a stool pigeon framed Morrell. He had met the day before with the Board of Prison Commissioners to approve his release from solitary.

Morrell's return to health was phenomenal, and within several months the warden appointed him head trusty of the prison, second in power only to the warden himself. Morrell immediately instigated a series of reforms, including an end to corporal punishment. Four years from his release from solitary, he was pardoned by the acting governor of California. He had spent fifteen years in prison, five of them in solitary confinement.

While the primary account of Morrell's experiences in San Quentin is his own, many of the external facts are corroborated by newspapers of the era and other sources. What is certain is that he was released from his tortures in solitary and pardoned from prison, and went on to become a powerful force for prison reform. Sometimes called the "father of the Honor System," he held a series of mass meetings around the Western states from 1908 to 1915. In 1909, his address to the California legislature resulted in a new parole law, and two years later led to the abolition of all forms of corporal punishment in the state's penal, juvenile, and mental institutions. Speaking before a joint legislative session, he exhibited the straitjacket, demonstrating it on several scandalized legislators. About 1,500 men in California prisons had been legally subjected to its horrors until it was finally banned in 1913.

Morrell's reforms spread to Colorado, Oregon, Washington, and the new state of Arizona, whose governor George W. P. Hunt became close with Morrell and wrote on his behalf in 1924: "What happens to these men we put in prison? Does this prison and punishment business for which we pay such tremendously high prices do enough to justify the money we spend on it? Does prison reform men? It may punish them, but does it prevent others from entering lives of crime? Does it either protect us or reform them? Why does it not decrease crime? We want a real solution to this crime business."

Like Governor Hunt and Morrell, a contemporary prison reformer also wanted a real solution to this crime business. When Jeanne Woodford became warden of San Quentin in the year 2000, she brought bold ideas. As David Sheff reported in the *New York Times* on his visit to San Quentin: "The prison was bustling with purposeful activity. In the education building, inmates studied for their high-school equivalency examinations and college degrees. In factories, they learned to operate computer-controlled lathes, printing presses and milling machines . . . Woodford is a warden of the old school—not the really old school of her San Quentin forebears, who considered chaining prisoners in a dungeon useful therapy—but the one that attributed criminality to psychological and social forces and considered it a prison's job to address those factors."

Contrary to the vision of Woodford and Morrell, the trend over the twentieth century has been otherwise. The United States is known as the "land of the free," but it would be more accurate to call it the land of the imprisoned. In 1980, about 220 people were incarcerated for every 100,000 Americans. By 2010, it tripled to 731. The money spent on prisons by states has risen at six times the rate of spending on higher education.

According to the U.S Bureau of Justice Statistics, 2,266,800 adults were incarcerated in U.S. federal and state prisons, and county jails at year-end 2010 — about .7% of adults in the U.S. resident population. Seventy percent of prisoners in the United States are non-whites, including in 2008 one in eleven African Americans (9.2 percent), one in twenty-seven Latinos (3.7 percent), and one in forty-five Caucasians (2.2 percent).

No other society in human history has imprisoned so many of its own citizens for crime control. The quadrupling of the incarcerated population in the United States from 1980 to 2003 is not attributed to violent crimes, which had remained relatively constant or declining over those decades. The prison population swelled primarily because of public policy changes causing more prison sentences and lengthening time served, such as mandatory minimum sentencing, "three strikes" laws, and reductions in the availability of parole or early release. Nearly three quarters of new admissions to state prisons were convicted of nonviolent crimes. Only 49 percent of sentenced state inmates were held for violent offenses. Nor do these statistics reflect white-collar crime, very conservatively estimated at around $400 billion in the United States. Only a small percentage of white-collar criminals do hard time, if they're detected at all, given very lax investigation in this area.

Until the 2008 budget crisis, California had the biggest prison system in the industrialized world, 40 percent bigger than the Federal Bureau of Prisons. That dishonor has since gone to Texas, which holds more inmates in its jails and prisons than do France, Great Britain, Germany, Japan, Singapore, and the Netherlands *combined*. The California Department of Corrections and Rehabilitation has built thirty-three new prisons since 1984 and is still out of beds. As Reginald Wilkinson, director of Ohio's Department of Rehabilitation and Correction, said, "If you build a prison, you are going to find people to put in it."

The prison boom is a relatively recent phenomenon, beginning to climb only in the mid-1970s. Nevertheless, America's prisons are more overcrowded now than when the building spree began. Yet the proportion of offenders sent to prison each year for violent crimes has actually fallen. Many other nonviolent crimes would usually lead in other countries to community service, fines, or drug treatment.

As Eric Schlosser wrote in the *Atlantic Monthly*, "The prison-industrial complex is not a conspiracy, guiding criminal justice policy behind closed doors. It is a confluence of special interests that has given prison construction in the U.S. a seemingly unstoppable momentum." According to the Department of Justice, expenditures for operating the nation's justice system increased from almost $36 billion in 1982 to over $185 billion in 2003, an increase of 418 percent. Private companies see a lucrative market.

The human fodder for this massive privatization of the prison system is mainly people of color, and it is fueled principally by the "war on drugs." The number of incarcerated drug offenders has increased twelvefold since 1980. Although the prevalence of illegal drug use among white men is approximately the same as among African American men, African American men are ten times as likely to be arrested for a drug offense. About 40 percent of inmates in the United States are African

American, though African Americans comprise only about 12 percent of the population. More African-American men are in prison or jail, on probation or parole than were inslaved in 1850, before the Civil War.

As Schlosser concluded, "The lure of big money is corrupting the nation's criminal justice system. The prison-industrial complex includes some of the nation's largest architecture and construction firms, Wall Street investment banks, and companies that sell everything from security cameras to padded cells available in a 'vast color selection.' The line between the public interest and private interests has blurred."

When Governor Arnold Schwarzenegger appointed Jeanne Woodford to head the California Department of Corrections in 2004, her philosophy was straightforward: "Same man, same result; changed man, changed result." She was convinced that when you treat people like human beings, they respond accordingly. Studies show that the more education and rehabilitation programs prisoners have while incarcerated, the less likely they are to commit another crime. Woodford moved on, but she left yet another vivid footprint in the long lineage seeking genuine reform of the justice system—including Ed Morrell's lingering vision.

People are complicated creatures. We seem to be of two minds.

On the one hand, research shows that pleasure centers in our brains light up when we exact retribution. We also know that under certain conditions such as those in prisons, ordinary people are routinely and predictably capable of doing monstrous things.

But as human animals we are also hardwired for empathy. We are equally capable of extraordinary acts of compassion and altruism.

We have a choice. In a world where nation-states no longer have a monopoly on weapons of mass destruction, where religious conflicts can inflame the entire globe, where ancient vendettas can overwhelm the future, the choice is chillingly clear.

In a straitjacket in the dungeon of San Quentin, Morrell learned that freeing himself from the prison of his hatred liberated him from actual prison walls and inspired him to change the system and free others.

From San Quentin to Abu Ghraib, the words of Ed Morrell ring out across space and time. "What was possible for me—a raving lunatic bent on vengeance—is possible for anyone."

VALUE CHANGE FOR SURVIVAL

Six Degrees of Climate Separation

*W*hen the world's national governments came together in Copenhagen in 2009 to fashion a global climate treaty, the most ambitious goal even mentioned was to reduce CO_2 emissions by 80 percent by 2050. Even if the governments had agreed (which predictably they did not) and were to succeed in hitting that target, the global average temperature would be at or well on its way to 4°C (about 7°F) above current averages.

What does 4°C look like?

Author Mark Lynas tried to answer that question in his book *Six Degrees*. He pored over tens of thousands of scientific papers that used advanced computer modeling, as well as studies of the fossil and geologic records—because it has all happened before.

After giving a talk about his book, Lynas overheard an audience member apologizing for dragging a companion to so depressing a lecture. "Depressing?" wondered Lynas. The thought had not occurred to him. He knew the impacts he presents are *terrifying*. "But," he wrote, "they are also, in the main, still avoidable. Getting depressed about the situation now is like sitting inert in your living room and watching the kitchen catch fire and then getting more and more miserable as the fire spreads throughout the house—rather than grabbing an extinguisher and dousing the flames."

Consider some of what Lynas found.

Once upon a time by midcentury, when it's hotter by 4°C, Earth is becoming unrecognizable. With seas three to four feet higher and rising faster, parts of low-lying coastal cities worldwide are periodically underwater—including Boston, New York, and the submerging archipelago of islands formerly known as the United Kingdom. Capital markets have collapsed, and rebuilding cities twice or three times has given way to mass migrations. The major project in the United States is moving 150 million coastal city dwellers inland, but interior cities are balking at the unbearable strain of millions more climate refugees.

It's all happening too fast. Adaptation takes time—for people and species. With climate change, speed kills.

It's the savage temperatures that dominate, hotter than anything in our species' evolutionary history. The temperate Mediterranean climate has turned North African at 113°F on a summer day. Summer is the dreaded season, haunted by perennial fires and scalding heat waves.

Food production is crashing worldwide and water shortages are chronic. The 60 percent of the world's population whose crops depended on the failing Asian summer monsoon are starving and thirsty. Climate chaos has put nuclear-armed India, Pakistan, and China on hair triggers.

The thawing permafrost in Alaska, Canada, and Siberia is unleashing mammoth stores of methane. This greenhouse gas, twenty times more potent than CO_2, will double the rate of warming. The ecosystems that create and mediate a climate favorable to life are so radically damaged they can no longer regulate the climate.

The world is unraveling. Megadroughts. New Category 6 hurricanes called "hypercanes." Mass starvation. Cascading economic crises. Failed states. Tropical diseases migrating north. Entire populations fleeing the tropics toward the northern climates. Stretched beyond adaptation, it's a civilization in fast-forward collapse.

Anger and blame spike with climate chaos. Virulent ideologies take aim at the rich nations whose fossil-fueled industrial juggernaut caused the cataclysm—then despite their wealth, failed to deal with it in time.

But really the deal was sealed when the climate crossed the bright line of a 2°C temperature increase, and self-reinforcing positive feedback loops triggered *runaway climate change*. By 3°C the Amazonian rain forest dried up and burned to ashen desert, driving the world's weather haywire. Biodiversity plummeted into freefall. As biologist E. O. Wilson had forewarned, we fell upon "the Age of Loneliness."

That 3° inexorably triggered 4, then 5 and 6. At 6°C (10.6°F), Earth resembled the "Mother of All Disasters" that occurred 250 million years ago; it's known as the time when "life nearly died." Fireballs of methane dwarfing nuclear explosions engulfed hellish skies. Monsoons carrying deadly sulfuric acid annihilated most remaining vegetation and creatures living above ground. About 95 percent of all terrestrial and marine species went extinct. The only large terrestrial vertebrate that we know survived was *Lystrosaurus*, a piglike animal that may have wandered the planet alone for a few million years. Life's diversity did regenerate to prior levels. It took 50 million years.

This is what six degrees of separation looks like. Terrifying. As Mark Lynas wrote, "If we had wanted to destroy as much of life on Earth as possible, there would have been no better way of doing it than to dig up and burn as much fossil hydrocarbons as we possibly could."

Time to grab the fire extinguishers.

The daunting global imperative is to arrest the temperature rise below 2°C or face the certainty of runaway climate destabilization. If we're really lucky, we may have until around 2020 to make a dramatic shift.

But make no mistake—the 2°C we've virtually assured is plenty bad enough, and we're buying time to adapt to a radically altered world.

The reality-based goal is 80 percent CO_2 reductions by 2020, not 2050. We can do it with existing technologies without using nuclear energy or biofuels, according to the esteemed environmental policy analyst Lester Brown, energy guru Amory Lovins, and many other credible and respected experts who show that we can get there with state-of-the-shelf technologies and wise policies.

It's 2020 or Bust. Can we do it?

On the technological plane, yes we can. Energy efficiency improvements alone can reduce emissions by as much as 50 percent by 2030 with no net cost. Despite fossil fuel subsidies, wind energy is close to becoming price-competitive with coal, and solar also is likely to be competitive in the foreseeable future. Numerous game-changing technological breakthroughs are almost ready for prime time, including biomimicry innovations.

But the problem is it's not fundamentally a technological problem. As David W. Orr points out, climate change represents the biggest *political failure* in the history of civilization. It's a crisis of governance and leadership.

Can we rapidly realign our policies, politics, and economy at a large enough scale to stabilize the climate?

One sterling energy success story has been California. As the world's eighth largest economy, the Golden State instituted a succession of policy innovations such that it now emits about half as much carbon per dollar of economic activity as the rest of the country. It's first among the states in promoting energy efficiency. The result has been savings of $56 billion for customers, while obviating the need for twenty-four new large-scale power plants. The gains are so impressive that its rules have been adopted by other states and into federal standards. Next came building codes, which several other nations have adopted.

California registers more clean energy patents than any other state and in 2009 was attracting about 60 percent of all U.S. clean tech venture capital. California has passed the first-ever tailpipe regulation of CO_2 and greenhouse gases, in tandem with other states and Canadian provinces. In April 2011, Gov. Jerry Brown signed a mandate into law that 33 percent of electricity in California must come from renewable sources by 2020. The new law, known as a renewable portfolio standard, is the most aggressive by any state. The new mandate also requires utilities to draw some of their power from distributed generation.

The Golden State is proving that a lower-carbon, more energy-efficient economy benefits the larger economy. According to George Soros, "There is no better potential driver that pervades all aspects of our economy than a new energy economy." There are plenty of livelihoods and profits to be had, including in the labor-intensive enterprise of rebuilding our decrepit infrastructure. Financial investment in solar and wind creates 50 percent more jobs than the same amount in coal and generates four times as many jobs as the equivalent in the oil industry. The current market for the restoration of ecosystems and the built environment is already at $2 trillion, with a potential market of $100 trillion.

Big business seems ready to act. Of the $250 billion global investors spent on new power capacity in 2008, for the first time the majority went to renewables. Clean-energy markets continued to expand rapidly in 2011, despite adverse economic and political climates, increased industry consolidation, and downward pricing pressures on manufacturers. Combined global revenue for solar PV, wind power, and biofuels rose 31 percent over 2010 growing from $188.1 billion in 2010 to $246.1 billion.

Clean energy expert Amory Lovins portrays the reinvention the U.S. electricity system as another electrifying opportunity. "We examined four scenarios for the U.S. electricity system over the next 40 years. One is business as usual, the official forecast. Another is a new nuclear build and clean coal, so-called, technology using the best that the industry knows how to do. That would have about a trillion dollars extra cost in capital. It would save some more fuel, and it's one way to hedge climate risks, but it would greatly concentrate the technological and financial risks that are already pretty acute, especially financial risks to the present utility system. It wouldn't do anything about the national security risks of potentially nation-shattering, cascading blackouts.

"We then looked at a centralized renewable scenario. If you quintuple the utility-scale renewables that the United States has right now, that's enough to meet 80 percent of our electricity needs when combined with efficiency. That is another way to hedge the climate risk. It turns out to have less technological and financial risk, because you have a diversified portfolio of pretty mature technologies that are already succeeding beyond our wildest dreams. Half of all the new generating capacity in the world for the past three years has been renewable, because it has lower cost and lower financial risks than the big thermal power plants.

"But then there's a fourth scenario where you let renewables compete at all different sizes. Half your generation becomes distributed, and that's what enables you to restructure the grid in a very resilient fashion so those major failures can't happen. That distributed renewable scenario costs about the same as business as usual, and it turns out to manage best all of the risks, including climate and security, and it has the best opportunities for innovation, entrepreneurship, and customer choice. So we think it very well fits what's actually happening in the market."

Lovins's research, detailed in his book *Reinventing Fire*, offers an integrated design strategy that combines the electricity and oil revolutions with efficient buildings and factories, and efficiently using directly burned fuels. "Business, enabled and sped by smart policies in mindful markets in co-evolution with civil society, can lead the United States completely off oil and coal by 2050, saving $5 trillion dollars, much risk and insecurity, and 82-86 percent of the fossil carbon emissions. Our energy future is not fate but choice.

"Humans are inventing a new fire, not dug from below but flowing from above, not scarce but bountiful, not local but everywhere, not transient but permanent, not costly but free. Except for a little biofuel grown in ways that sustain and endure, this new fire is flameless. Please consider how we can together help make the world fairer, richer, cooler and safer by reinventing fire."

Some of the world's biggest global investors, who collectively manage over $13 trillion in assets, have called for "long, loud and legal signals from governments"—in other words, astute policies. It's worth noting that the driver behind most great American fortunes since the Civil War has largely been government policies.

The Pentagon has embraced climate change as a top national and global security issue and its outsize budget could radically advance clean energy security and market competitiveness. The military is actively modifying its own operations to run on 50 percent renewable energy by 2020, excepting certain combat operations. As such, it is funding and developing technologies and approaches that can be transferred to society at large—not unlike its original development of computers.

Because climate change is not one issue but the result of an entire way of living, it requires a comprehensive redesign of our civilization. We need what Buckminster Fuller called for in 1961—a World Design Science Decade. Design goals include a far greater localization of our basic needs, from distributed energy to more localized foodsheds and bioregional watershed management.

So what stands in the way?

Vested interests will continue to vigorously promote "inertiatives" to delay real change. At the same time, as we have witnessed the biggest bank robbery in history—*by the banks*. The storied revolving door between big business and government has morphed into the interlocking directorate of a corporate state.

In the words of reporter Matthew Taibbi, "The reality is that the worldwide economic meltdown and the bailout that followed were together a kind of revolution, a coup d'état . . . : the gradual takeover of the government by a small class of connected insiders, who used money to control elections, buy influence and systematically weaken financial regulations."

The compelling question is, rather than a bank bailout, why didn't we restructure the "too big to fail" banks that nearly destroyed the global economy as public banks that fund clean technology, green infrastructure, and transportation? In the wake of the crash and looming bankruptcies, professor Gerald Epstein of the University of Massachusetts–Amherst proposed a "Green Bank of America" and "Green Citi Bank." That would be a real public option.

Inherent in our current bind is also the paradox of scale. Although a colossal transformation needs to occur, huge centralized systems concentrate the risk of catastrophic failure, while further concentrating wealth and power. These systems are too big not to fail.

Resilience comes from having many smaller-scale decentralized systems. Distributed energy systems provide much greater efficiency as well as security, in part because huge amounts of energy are lost in long-distance transmission. The leading model is Denmark, where distributed networks generate half the country's electricity and have cut carbon emissions by nearly half from 1990 levels.

Local systems can also operate as publicly owned nonprofit utilities that provide revenues and jobs for cities and states, with rates up to

30 percent cheaper. Instead of corporate megagrids, we can build a decentralized, local energy economy for about the same cost.

What else can we do?

- Turn education into action. Climate leadership by our schools and universities is already mobilizing clean energy initiatives and green development in their institutions and communities. Project-based learning enables students, teachers, and institutions to solve problems while studying them by doing the actual work in the field. As David W. Orr points out, restructuring the academy as part of a bolder effort to redesign urban communities for sustainability can leverage 4,100 colleges and universities, including about 18 million students and 2.7 million faculty and staff as the advance guard of the new green economy.
- Create a Green Civilian Conservation Corps national service program. Realistically even under the best of scenarios, there's no way we're going to create enough green jobs in the foreseeable future to meet the magnitude of the work that needs to be done. Mobilizing the citizenry through government programs and diverse volunteer efforts will be crucial.
- Desubsidize fossil fuels and nuclear energy.
- Publicly fund elections.
- Provide developing nations—who'll be responsible for two-thirds of emissions by 2020—with an annual investment by developed nations for them to transition to renewables, as the United Nations proposes. This is the worthy "bailout" the world needs and deserves, the payment on the global North's ecological debt.
- Give nature legal rights with a constitutional amendment and in local constitutions and ordinances.

At a meeting of global spiritual leaders, Chief Oren Lyons of the Iroquois Six Nations recalls the words of a Japanese elder who distilled the essence of the crisis we face into four words: value change for survival.

Encoded in the deep empirical knowledge of First Peoples for how to live on Earth in a lasting way is a deeper set of values sometimes called "the Original Instructions." They teach us how to be human beings.

- Take only what you need, and give back as much as you take.
- Take responsibility for sustaining the web of life.
- Because all life is connected and related, respect your relatives and each other.
- Pursue peace through justice in a process that never ends.
- Be grateful.
- Enjoy life.

If we respect these instructions, says the Iroquois Law of the Seed, life will go on and on in cycles of continuous creation.

It's a value change for survival. By restoring the web of life, we will restore ourselves and provide a legacy for future generations.

At last, we can become fully human. At last, we get to come home.

It's 2020 or Bust.

THE REVOLUTION HAS BEGUN

"The Shift Hits the Fan"

*T*he Bottleneck. The Great Disruption. The Great Turning. Peak Everything.

Whatever you call it, it's the big enchilada. Or in the words of filmmaker Tom Shadyac, "The shift is about to hit the fan."

We're experiencing the dawn of a revolutionary transformation. This awkward tween state also marks the end of prehistory—the sunset of an ecologically illiterate civilization. Like a baby being born, a new world is crowning.

The revolution has begun—but in fits and starts. The challenge is that it's one minute to midnight—too late to avoid large-scale destruction. We have to fan the shift to ecoliterate societies at sufficient speed and scale to dodge irretrievable cataclysm. This game of beat the reaper can't be won with incremental change. It demands transformation—a great leap of punctuated evolution.

From breakdown to breakthrough, this revolution from the heart of nature leads with a basic shift in our relationship with nature: from resource and object to mentor, model, and partner. Game-changing breakthroughs in biomimetic science, technology, and design are revolutionizing our very ways of knowing.

The global Rights of Nature movement is recognizing the inalienable rights of the nonhuman world of ecosystems and critters, radically widening our circle of compassion and kinship in an expansion of rights that forever transforms the terms of engagement. Greater decentralization and localization are building resilience from the ground up, shaped by ancient indigenous wisdom of becoming native to our place: planet Earth as well as our local zip codes.

The digital communications revolution is crackling on the scale of the invention of radio, TV, film, and the Internet—primed to spread solutions without borders at texting speed. Historic demographic shifts are fertilizing the landscape—from the ascendancy of women's leadership to the worldbeat of cultural and racial pluralism. Empires and dynasties are waning and waxing with sudden shifts in the balance of global power.

Wild times ahead. Unexpected. Unpredictable. Disruptive. Sudden. Widespread innovation and experimentation. An unstoppable drive for freedom. Artistic and intellectual breakthroughs. A shared will toward a new vision and world.

The pushback will be equally fierce—shadows of widespread destruction and violence, mass dislocations, virulent ideologies, and ethnic strife. When a chrysalis turns into a butterfly, the caterpillar's immune system attacks the very first of the butterfly's cells as invaders. Yet in the end, the big, hairy caterpillar audaciously becomes a beautiful butterfly.

What does this shock-and-flow revolution look like on the ground?

Despite aggressive climate-denier PR campaigns, nature keeps breaking our records for the hottest and driest years in many regions. Half the world's coral reefs are bleaching, threatening the collapse of marine food webs and critical fishing grounds. The catastrophic flooding of 20 percent of Pakistan that dislocated 20 million people further undermined a potentially failed nuclear state and region highly vulnerable to ongoing climate shocks. Russia's record-breaking temperatures in 2010 resulted in epic forest fires and the catastrophic loss of one-quarter of its grain harvest. The United States was walloped by ravaging serial floods and scalding heat waves like LA's record-breaking 113°F, while record-shattering tornados killed hundreds in the Southeast United States in 2011 and 2012 and epic droughts plagued vast parts of the Southwest. Physical reality is just getting too hard to ignore, and any residual "skepticism" can't persist much longer. You don't find global warming deniers in China or Europe.

As climate shocks rock the planet, renewable energy is reaching a tipping point and going mainstream. Since 2009, the United States and Europe have both added more power capacity from renewables than from coal, gas, and nuclear combined. Worldwide, renewables have accounted for half of new generating capacity. In total, they constitute a quarter of global power capacity, and 18 percent of electricity supply.

Europe has snatched the leading position globally in great part because of government policy. EU business leadership sees green products as its Silicon Valley. The European Union is aiming for 25 percent of global green products market share by 2020.

China has leapfrogged the world in pursuit of a low-carbon economy. It's now the largest manufacturer of wind turbines, solar panels, and the most efficient grids and coal plants. It has created a national energy "superministry," and the president has stated China must "seize preemptive opportunities in the new round of the global energy revolution." Chinese R&D has been growing at 20 percent a year for twenty years. Do the math to see where the future will reside.

The exponential expansion of wind power is moving it from boutique to industrial scale. England installed the world's largest offshore wind farm, sufficient to power 200,000 homes, with more on the way. Massachusetts gained the first U.S. federal approval for a major offshore wind project, a week after the BP offshore oil blowout, though it continues to face both political resistance and economic hurdles related to swings in the price of natural gas.

Electric cars are heading for the mass market worldwide. McKinsey & Company estimates that 23 percent of U.S. emissions can be cut just by energy efficiency by 2020, offsetting gains in energy usage. Massachusetts and California lead the nation with efficiency standards expected to bring billions in savings to customers and create tens of thousands of new jobs.

Job creation and new businesses are key drivers of renewables. Germany now employs almost as many people in clean energy as in its largest manufacturing sector of automobiles, despite the European financial crisis. Leadership in manufacturing is spreading from Europe to China, India, and South Korea, which will lower the costs of renewable technologies and mitigate emissions. While the United States dithers, we've been bleeding manufacturing jobs and losing the industrial infrastructure necessary to compete.

The spread of renewables is starting to reduce CO_2 emissions in some places. Germany has reduced its emissions by nearly 30 percent since 1990. In the wake of the BP Gulf oil disaster, the oil and gas industry faces steeper regulation while being forced by the decline of existing oil fields to drill in ever gnarlier places using increasingly risky technologies such as fracking, which is now associated with earthquakes. Oil prices will rise along with insurance premiums, further driving the rise of renewables.

However, as a result of the economic crisis that began in 2008, governments have reduced subsidies that helped drive the clean energy boom and rapid pace of innovation. Simultaneously the shale-gas boom has unexpectedly impacted the further expansion of clean energy. Several major solar companies went out of business, and the 2011 MAC Global Solar Energy Index fell precipitously by 65 percent. Yet, as McKinsey & Company observed in its 2012 report "Solar Power: Darkest before

Dawn:" "There is little doubt in the near term that existing players will face difficulties. But these are natural growing pains, not death throes. The industry is entering a period of maturation that is likely to set the conditions for more stable and expansive growth after 2015."

Sweden, which has vowed to eliminate fossil fuels for electricity by 2020 and gasoline-powered cars by 2030, commissioned a research study showing the country could cut emissions by 20–50 percent by changing the national diet. An estimated 25 percent of emissions produced by people in industrialized nations can now be linked with the foods they eat. Sweden has instituted a national food policy using emissions labeling on foods and restaurant menus. The principal Scandinavian organic certification program will require low-carbon farming methods. Sweden's carefully researched dietary recommendations are now circulating throughout the European Union. The country has led the world in making these kinds of previously overlooked connections.

The European Union's ambitious renewables targets have backing from the sovereign wealth funds of China and Abu Dhabi. The European Investment Bank, the US Department of the Treasury, and the World Bank have issued green bonds. Prior to the Eurozone fiscal crisis, national infrastructure banks were being seriously considered by world leaders. Germany's Deutsche Bank has redirected some of its $700 billion in assets to address global warming, including a $7 billion climate investment fund. (Given the financial instability in Europe, these kinds of initiatives have been stymied by the one-step-forward, two-steps-backward shuffle.)

The Government Pension Fund of Norway, the world's second largest sovereign wealth fund, started a Water Disclosure Project as part of its investment criteria to awaken investor awareness about water risks and opportunities. The US Securities and Exchange Commission is calling on public companies to disclose serious risks global warming may pose to their businesses.

Some leading figures in the banking industry have teamed up with economists and mathematical biologists to study natural ecosystems for lessons about resilience. A Bank of England report said that the banking industry will be reshaped by studies that treat global finance as a "complex adaptive system," like a living ecosystem.

A parallel sea change is occurring in the engineering mentality, led by giant firms such as CH2M Hill, which have embraced climate adaptation. Instead of steel and concrete, they're recommending "soft infrastructure"—flexible ecological systems such as wetlands, oyster beds, barrier islands, water retention, wastewater recycling, and water efficiency. The Federal Emergency Management Agency and the U.S. Army Corps of Engineers are even beginning to explore these concepts. The bywords are reliability, local self-sufficiency, and decentralization.

As the nation's largest user of electricity and fuel, the U.S. government has targeted 28 percent reductions in its energy use by 2020. But in the absence of a national clean energy policy, the main action is coming from cities and states. Some visionary mayors and governors are developing ambitious climate strategies and policies while creating jobs, businesses, and living laboratories for innovative low-carbon development. The Pacific Coast states are working to jettison coal within a decade, led by vanguard municipal leadership in LA, San Francisco, Seattle, Portland, and San Diego.

Sounds great, right? But of course, there's more to the story. The successes are tenuous—vulnerable to the vagaries of politics and market oscillations. And we're still losing ground anyway. Global emissions will almost certainly rise by 40 percent by 2030—more than half of which will come from China and the balance from other developing countries. If China fails to green its economy, there's little chance for the world. In truth, the world is reaching "peak everything," in Richard Heinberg's phrase. A global economy built on massive resource use and reduced labor is heading for necessary contraction.

As Groucho Marx put it, "Why should I care about future generations? What have they ever done for me?"

A major barrier in the United States is the annual military budget of over $1 trillion. Although the Defense Department has embraced climate change as a national security issue, national sustainability must move front and center. As David W. Orr observes, "A larger vision of security includes the internal resilience, health and sustainability of the nation for self-renewal. True security is inseparable from issues of education, preservation of soils, forests, waters and broadly based sustainable prosperity. In this perspective, America is less secure that at any time in its history. Sustainability is the core of a national development strategy that is designed to enhance our security, build prosperity from the ground up, *and* reduce ecological damage, risks of climate destabilization and the necessity of fighting endless wars over dwindling resources. The concept of sustainability should be the new organizing principle for both domestic and foreign policy."

In fact, what's needed is the national and global equivalent of a wartime mobilization as occurred during World War II. Some say only catastrophe will precipitate this shift in national purpose to make sustainability magnetic north. Plans are already developing in multiple institutions to create emergency climate war plans, with aggressive milestones and mass mobilization scenarios. Paul Gilding's 1° War Plan foresees a "Coalition of the Cooling" composed of the United States, China, and the European Union, who produce 50 percent of emissions. By leveraging their economic, military, and diplomatic pressure, such a coalition could engage Russia, India, Japan, and Brazil to hit 67 percent of global GHG emissions.

In the United States, governments at the local and regional level have shown it's possible to act rapidly to develop ambitious climate strategies and policies while creating jobs, businesses, and living laboratories for low-carbon development.

But for now, the United States is being left behind. Green jobs are not being generated fast enough because of the lack of a national clean energy policy and reluctance by banks to lend to renewables projects. Public spending on preparedness and adaptation remain pitifully low. As a leader at Germany's Deutsche Bank, referring to the United States, stated, "They're asleep at the wheel on climate change, asleep at the wheel on job growth, asleep at the wheel on this industrial revolution taking place in the energy industry."

How much catastrophe do we need for the United States to get serious? Given the national political stalemate and the "original sin" of oil in American politics, business competitiveness may prove the compelling driver. A National Academies report on U.S. competitiveness said flatly, "We fear the abruptness with which a lead in science and technology can be lost—and the difficulty of recovering a lead once lost, if indeed it can be regained at all."

The supreme challenge of global interdependence is to foster meta-cooperation in a full world. The winners must complement each other's strengths while at the same time developed nations fund developing nations to help them transition.

As Einstein said, we cannot solve the problem with the same mentality that created it. Brother, can you spare a paradigm?

Our collective fate hangs from the cliff by three intertwining ropes: systems, power, and story.

Shifting the mindscape starts with systems thinking. Complex systems by nature are unpredictable, nonlinear, and cannot be controlled. The key to building resilience is to foster the system's capacity to adapt to dramatic change. As the late systems thinker and author Dana Meadows observed, "A diverse system with multiple pathways and redundancies is more stable and less vulnerable to external shock than a uniform system with little diversity."

A paradigm is the hardest thing to change, but it can happen fast. As Meadows advised, "Keep pointing at anomalies and failures in the old paradigm. Keep speaking loudly and with assurance from the new one. Insert people with the new paradigm in places of public visibility and power. Don't waste time with reactionaries; work with active change agents, and the vast middle ground of open people."

At the core of power is the transformation to a restoration economy.

Europe's model of "social capitalism" may be the most important innovation in the world economy since the rise of the corporation as the world's greatest wealth generator. The twenty-seven-nation European Union is collectively the world's largest economy, producing over a quarter of global GDP, a tad more than the U.S. economy and still nearly three times the size of China's. The European Union has more Fortune 500 companies than the United States or China.

Among its structural innovations are two policies: works councils and codetermination, which go right to the heart of power. Works councils give employees significant input on working conditions, as well as codecision rights on some aspects of finances and some consultation rights on new technologies, mergers, and layoffs. They contribute to efficiency by improving the quality of decisions and worker buy-in.

With codetermination, workers elect representatives to supervisory boards. It has fostered cooperation with management and benefitted businesses. Most EU nations use the practice in at least some sectors. As Steven Hill wrote, "Co-determination has proved crucial to the EU's economic success and broadly distributed wealth. It's a culture of consultation and a vibrant small business sector that produces two-thirds of EU jobs, compared with one-half in the U.S."

Ironically the unique European Union model arose in Germany following World War II as the Allies sought to stymie the concentrated wealth and power of the big German corporations that had powered the Nazi regime. The Allies, especially the United States, insisted on real worker participation on company boards to blunt the economic power of the traditional business elites.

Needless to say, Europe's promising trajectory hit the wall with the global banking crisis of ricocheting global over-interconnectedness, and it's far from a worker-run paradise, often hit even in good times with frequent strikes and labor disputes. It's beset by high youth unemployment and social safety nets are eroding. While it appears more likely than not the European Union will make the deeper changes necessary to more closely unify its economic and political ties, it could certainly fail. In either case, the models it has developed remain a lighthouse for what some call Capitalism 2.0.

What's afoot globally today is the reinvention of the economy and the redesign of the corporation, the most powerful institution on the planet, into diverse business ownership and governance structures that go beyond the relentless pursuit of the bottom line by any means necessary. As author and business consultant Marjorie Kelly documents, forms such as large-scale cooperatives, social businesses, and foundation-owned companies are reinventing what Bill Gates calls "creative capitalism." Kelly terms them "emergent new organizational species"—enterprises that are designed like living systems and deliver human and ecological benefits as well as profits.

Group Danone partnered with Grameen Bank in a joint social benefit venture to provide malnourished children in Bangladesh with affordable nutrition at a 1 percent profit. The General Anthroposophical Society, the foundation that carries on the legacy of the Austrian spiritual and ecological teacher Rudolf Steiner, owns Triodos Bank, named the world's greenest bank in 2009. Interface carpet is a billion-dollar "mission-controlled company" whose goal is zero emissions by 2020. Organic Valley, the $500 million farmers' co-op, delivers returns of 2 percent while meeting its mission of saving the family farm. Spain's Mondragon Corporation, the nation's seventh-largest industrial enterprise, is partnering with the United Steelworkers union to create manufacturing co-ops. Holland's large Rabobank Group, founded in the 1800s, operates on cooperative principles and is owned by shareholder customers and employees. The data show that employee-owned firms tend to outperform their peers, and foundation-owned ones perform at least as well or better. In Europe, co-ops contribute 12 percent of GDP.

Another systemic metatrend transforming the economy and society is what writer Hanna Rosin calls "the end of men." As she points out,

"Those societies that take advantage of the talents of all of their adults, not just half of them, have pulled away from the rest." One study measuring the economic and political power of women in 162 countries found with few exceptions that the greater the power of women, the greater the nation's economic success.

In the United States, women now comprise a majority in the workforce for the first time. Women dominate colleges and professional schools, with three women for every two men getting BA degrees. Women are obtaining 60 percent of master's degrees, half of all law and medical degrees, and a bit over one-third of MBAs. Women are beginning to gain ascendancy in middle management and many professional careers, including half of all banking and insurance jobs. Companies with women in top positions perform better, especially those pursuing an innovation-intensive strategy in which "creativity and collaboration" are important. Of the fifteen job categories projected to grow in the next decade, only two are primarily male. Rosin characterizes the emerging U.S. economy as a "traveling sisterhood."

A number of studies have found that male investors as a group appear overconfident, whereas women are more likely to acknowledge when they don't know something. In relation to markets, men tend toward the side of the irrational and overemotional, whereas women are more often cool and levelheaded. At least this was the conclusion of Brad Barber, Gallagher professor of finance at the University of California–Davis, coauthor of a 2001 study titled, "Boys Will Be Boys: Gender, Overconfidence, and Common Stock Investment." Data indicate a strong correlation between risk-taking and testosterone. Following the crash of Iceland's male-directed banking system, the new female prime minister campaigned and won by promising the end of "the age of testosterone."

Because the most important elements in any human system are its purpose and goals, the deeper question is "What is the economy for?" If building resilience is the goal, the priority shifts from growth and expansion toward sufficiency and sustainable prosperity. And we know that economic relocalization creates three times as many jobs, earnings, and tax collections—as well as far greater security through local food and energy systems than through absentee ownership.

Also gaining traction are new metrics, such as the Genuine Progress Indicator (GPI) and various "wellness indicators" of economic, environmental, physical, mental, workplace, social, and political health. Bhutan's Gross National Happiness (GNH) indicators are attracting serious interest worldwide and beginning to be considered in several cities including Seattle. In multiple surveys and studies, happiness is above all tied to the quality of social relationships, not to wealth.

In the context of shifting paradigms, it's worth revisiting the operating instructions for natural systems that determine the baseline. As biologist Janine Benyus has summarized them: Nature runs on current sunlight. Nature banks on diversity. Nature rewards cooperation. Nature builds from the bottom up. Nature recycles everything. Life creates conditions conducive to life.

Benyus's "Life's Principles" also provide basic design elements for appropriate human organization within a very different paradigm. Life designs by optimizing for the good of the whole system instead of maximizing for any one element. It's keyed to the local and it builds resilience through diversity, decentralization, and redundancy. It uses feedback loops to keep learning and responding.

"What makes a difference," said Dana Meadows, "is redesigning the system to improve information, incentives, disincentives, goals, stresses and constraints that have an effect on specific actors."

How then do we set about redesigning human systems? Who's in charge? Who has the real decision-making power?

In practice, the design of the U.S. economic system concentrates wealth and distributes poverty, and economic power translates directly into political power. The wealth gap has reached the notorious extremes of the Roaring '20s. The super-rich .01 percent of the population earn as much as the bottom 120 million. The richest 10 percent control over 90 percent of all financial assets in the country. The richest 1 percent own over half of all the stocks and bonds.

Simultaneously, unemployment is the highest since the Great Depression. As of 2011, close to 50 million Americans live in poverty; although national productivity leaped in the past decade, wages stayed flat. Joblessness and low wages are the new normal.

Washington DC had 11,195 officially registered corporate lobbyists in 2009, and they spent six times what all the environmental, consumer, labor, and other noncorporate entities spent combined on lobbying efforts. The single biggest lobbying and campaign spender is the financial services sector, with banks being the most powerful. As Senator Dick Durbin commented, "Frankly they own the place." It's no wonder. The estimated lobbying return on investment is a 100 to 1. Remember that $13 trillion in public bailout funds for the banking sector?

No wonder there's a Tea Party. Call me traditional, but the Tea Party needs to get back to its roots. The Boston Tea Party was a rebellion against the same kind of money power: a government-backed corporate monopoly. The current "Occupy" movement is actually much closer to the spirit of the original Boston Tea Party.

As author Thom Hartmann recounts, the Pilgrims sailed on a ship chartered and owned by Britain's East India Company. As the corporation's largest shareholder, Queen Elizabeth granted the company "legal freedom from liability," the basis of the corporate structure as we know it.

The East India Company staked its claim on parts of North America and got military protection from the British Crown to help exploit the rich new colony. Already hugely powerful in India and China, the East India Company had gained control over almost all international commerce to and from North America. Still, it was bedeviled by colonial small businessmen and entrepreneurs, who operated their own small ships to bring in tea and other goods and dared to buy tea wholesale from Dutch trading companies. Predictably, the company lobbied for and got laws to put its competition out of business, which included the death penalty for operating without a license.

As Hartmann points out, "'Taxation without representation' meant hitting the average person and small business with taxes while letting the richest and most powerful corporation in the world off the hook for its taxes. It was government sponsorship of one corporation over all competitors."

A year and a half after the Boston Tea Party, there exploded the "shots heard 'round the world." It's appropriate to reclaim the true story of the Tea Party as an antimonopoly rebellion that fundamentally informed the American Revolution, the Constitution, and the first century of highly restrictive American governance and jurisprudence over corporations. That theme is resurfacing today in the growing movement to revoke corporate constitutional rights and create a 28th Amendment that gives free speech rights to people, not to corporations.

Here she comes, Myth America. Rebirth of a nation.

The story of today's battle is above all the battle of the story. As scholar Richard Tarnas observes, "Worldviews create worlds."

The ruling story according to Western civilization took hold about five hundred years ago with the birth of the scientific revolution and exaltation of human reason. When the Copernican revolution showed the Earth revolves around the sun, science redefined humanity's place in the natural order and the cosmos.

Perhaps the defining characteristic of the modern mind is the belief in a radical separation between the human self and the external world. According to the modern mind, Tarnas observes, "Apart from the human being, the cosmos is seen as entirely impersonal and unconscious . . . mere matter in motion, mechanistic and purposeless, ruled by chance and necessity. It is altogether indifferent to human consciousness and values. The world outside the human being lacks conscious intelligence—it lacks interiority—and it lacks intrinsic meaning and purpose. . . . For the modern mind, the only source of meaning in the universe is human consciousness."

The modern mind stands in radical contrast with the primal worldview, exemplified by indigenous cultures. As Tarnas continues, "Primal experience takes place within a world soul, an anima mundi, a living matrix of embodied meaning. Because the world is understood as speaking a symbolic language—direct communication of meaning and purpose from world to human can occur."

The linear, mechanistic, reductionist worldview has yielded to a vastly more complex view of interdependence and other ways of knowing. From complexity and chaos theory to the Gaia hypothesis, a new cosmology is unfolding. In this scientific revolution, the Earth does not revolve around us.

Tarnas frames the battle of the cosmic story in this way:

> Imagine for a moment that you are the universe. But for the purposes of this thought experiment—that you are not the disenchanted, mechanistic universe of conventional modern cosmology—but rather a deep-souled, subtly mysterious cosmos of great spiritual beauty and creative intelligence. And imagine that you are approached by two different epistemologies—two suitors, as it were—who seek to know you. To whom would you open your deepest secrets? To which approach would you be most likely to reveal your authentic nature?
>
> Would you open most deeply to the suitor—the way of knowing—who approached you as though you were essentially lacking in intelligence or purpose—as though you had no interior dimension to speak of—no spiritual capacity or value; who thus saw you as fundamentally inferior to himself (let us give the two suitors, not entirely arbitrarily,

the traditional masculine gender); who related to you as though your existence were valuable primarily to the extent that he could develop and exploit your resources—to satisfy his various needs; and whose motivation for knowing you was ultimately driven by a desire for increased intellectual mastery, predictive certainty, and efficient control over you for his own self-enhancement?

Or would you, the cosmos, open yourself most deeply to that suitor who viewed you as being *at least* as intelligent and noble—as worthy a being—as permeated with mind and soul—as imbued with moral aspiration and purpose—as endowed with spiritual depths and mystery, as he? This suitor seeks to know you not that he might better exploit you—but rather to unite with you and thereby bring forth something new—a creative synthesis emerging from both of your depths. He desires to liberate that which has been hidden by the separation between knower and known. His ultimate goal of knowledge is a more richly responsive and empowered participation in a co-creative unfolding of new realities. He seeks an intellectual fulfillment that is intimately linked with imaginative vision, moral transformation, empathic understanding, aesthetic delight. His act of knowledge is essentially an act of love and intelligence combined—of wonder as well as discernment—of opening to a process of mutual discovery. To whom would you be more likely to reveal your deepest truths?

Which suitor shall we choose? Which do you choose?

ENTANGLED IN UNITY

Poets, Seers, Science, and Oneness

Perhaps the most powerful sight of the twentieth century was the iconic view from outer space of the whole Earth. Our collective worldview changed when we saw that magical image of a shimmering blue and white ball floating in space.

Naturalist author Diane Ackerman captured that vision in her luminous book *A Natural History of the Senses*:

> Picture this: Everyone you've ever known, everyone you've ever loved, your whole experience of life floating in one place, on a single planet underneath you. On that dazzling oasis, swirling with blues and whites, the weather systems form and travel. You watch the clouds tingle and swell above the Amazon, and know the weather that develops there will affect the crop yield half a planet away in Russia and China. Volcanic eruptions make tiny spangles below. The rain forests are disappearing in Australia, Hawaii and South America. You see dust bowls developing in Africa and the Near East. Remote sensing devices, judging the humidity in the desert, have already warned you there will be plagues of locusts this year. And though you were taught about them one by one, as separate parts of a jigsaw puzzle, now you can see that the oceans, the atmosphere and the land are not separate at all, but part of an intricate, recombining web of nature. Like Dorothy in *The Wizard of Oz*, you want to click your magic shoes together and say three times, "There's no place like home."
>
> Most of all, the twentieth century will be remembered as the time when we first began to understand what our address was. . . . Learning our full address may not end all wars, but it will enrich our sense of wonder and pride. It will remind us that the human context is not tight as a noose, but large as the universe we have the privilege to inhabit. It will change our sense of what a neighborhood is. It will

persuade us that we are citizens of something larger and more profound than mere countries, that we are citizens of Earth, her joyriders and caretakers, who would do well to work on her problems together. The view from space is offering us the first chance we evolutionary toddlers have had to cross the cosmic street and stand facing our own home, amazed to see it clearly for the first time.

We human beings are likely here to tell the tale by virtue of the genius-grade chemistry of ancient blue-green algae. As far as we know, they invented photosynthesis—the transformation of light into food and energy that provided the oxygen that allowed people to exist. As Ackerman observes, "We're bastards of witless one-celled organisms. No matter how politely one says it, we owe our existence to the farts of blue-green algae."

On this symbiotic planet, the key to positive long-term symbiotic success is diversity, life's living repertoire of adaptive possibilities. The daunting context today is that the gene pool is evaporating to a gene puddle, radically limiting our options just at the time we're going to have to adapt to dramatically heightened change. We're not playing with a full deck, and the joker is getting wilder all the time. One of the hot-button agendas is conserving what's left and halting the human enterprises destroying it. The iconic naturalist Aldo Leopold early in the twentieth century spoke of a land ethic, or the absence of it:

> All ethics so far evolved rest on a single premise: That the individual is a member of a community of interdependent parts. His instincts prompt him to compete for his place in that community, but his ethics prompt him to cooperate. A land ethic then reflects a conviction of individual responsibility for the health of the land.
>
> A thing is right when it tends to preserve the integrity, stability and beauty of the biotic community. It is wrong when it tends otherwise. The last word in ignorance is the man who says of an animal or plant, "What good is it?" If the land mechanism as a whole is good, then every part is good, whether we understand it or not. If the biota, in the course of aeons, has built something we like but don't understand, then who but a fool would discard seemingly

useless parts? To keep every cog and wheel is the first precaution of intelligent tinkering.

Of course, life is seldom simple, and symbiosis can be problematic, too. Evan Eisenberg in his book *The Ecology of Eden* makes the case that we human beings have made some dubious alliances that are leading to disaster. The partnership people made long ago with annual grasses and cattle was originally a mutually beneficial arrangement, but it wound up sweeping the planet to the exclusion of wider food webs with greater resilience. This kind of unstable system can expand much faster than stable ones, and we humans are double trouble because we are both clever mutualists when it's opportune, and omnivore generalists who can prey on many species—not to mention each other. Symbiotic alliances are not inherently beneficial. It depends whose back you're scratching.

Author and consciousness researcher Larry Dossey sees the connections as radically more profound and mysterious than merely creatures in cooperation with one another. He tells it this way:

> We usually view our body as a solid, here-and-now object, but this view of the body is false. Modern physics tells us that there are no concrete bits from which bodies are made, only endlessly changing patterns of energy and matter.
>
> The amount of actual "material" inside an atom is roughly that of a baseball inside the Astrodome. Our bodies therefore are mostly nothing, almost total emptiness. Moreover, the particles that make up our mostly empty body are not hard bits of matter, but evanescent phenomena that cannot be pinned down to specific points in space and time. The particles are smeared across space, showing only "tendencies" to exist more at one point than another.
>
> All our tissues are in motion, coming and going at different rates. But at the end of a year 98 percent of the matter in the body has been exchanged, and after five years 100 percent has been totally renewed. Part of the material we incorporate into our new body has already been part of the bodies of others; and a part of the substance we shed will enter others' bodies. "Body," therefore, is not a thing but a collective process. We might refine the Golden Rule to state, "Do good unto others because they *are* you."

A process of connectedness also unites us at the subatomic level. Particles, including those of the body, are seen as fields of influence that overlap in never-ending webs of interaction. This means that everything is connected. We know that when particles that have been in contact are separated, when one is changed, the other changes also—instantly and to the same degree, no matter how far apart they may be. No actual "signal" is involved. It's as if the distant particles "know" what the other is doing, and they dance together as a single whole. What's more, this "entanglement" is contagious. No limit exists on the number of particles that can become entangled.

For millennia poets and seers have spoken about the unity and oneness of the world. The verdict is now in, and the poets were right. The unity was there all along.

At the heart of these awesome mysteries, the innate ancient wildness of life stirs the cauldron of evolution. Its complexity is beyond our comprehension. There's a dimension to wildness that some call unknowable, others call sacred. Whatever your perspective—science or spirit—self-willed nature takes the same freedom she gives us: a place to tell her own creation story.

What a gift to reside at such a grand address.

FROM HERE TO INFINITY

The Great Mystery

Some years ago the annual global essay contest sponsored by Royal Dutch Shell and the *Economist* magazine posed this question: Do we need nature?

The winner was Diane Brooks Pleninger of Anchorage, Alaska. Her essay was titled "Interview with a Fungus." Here are some highlights from the interview between Diane Pleninger (D.P.) and *Pilobolus crystallinus* (P.C.).

D.P.   Our guest is *Pilobolus crystallinus*, author of the award-winning bestseller, "Do We Need Mankind? A Fungal Perspective." He is a scholar, lecturer, dung-dweller and author. Mr. Pilobolus, your most recent book raises tantalizing questions about the future of the biosphere and the role that you and other inhabitants will play in it. Tell us how you came to write it.

P.C.   The book resulted from a series of symposia I attended over the past two centuries under the sponsorship of the World Federation of Fungi, on the topic, "What Does Nature Need?"

D.P.   The 19th, 20th and 21st centuries have been a revolutionary period in the biosphere. How have fungi been affected by the events of modern history?

P.C.   The modern history of the fungi, which I date from about 400 million years ago, has been a remarkable success story. The fungi occupy two vital niches in nature whose importance has never been challenged. In one niche, we are drivers of the carbon cycle, elite teams of detritivores whose mission is to digest organic matter and return the component parts to the ecological system. Without our work, life on Earth would long since have ground to a halt for lack of raw materials. In another niche, we act in partnership with the roots of plants to extend their reach into the soil environment and enhance their uptake of water and nutrients. Animals in turn feed on plants and benefit from this arrangement. Both roles are critical to maintaining the biosphere.

D.P.   As you see it, what has been the human purpose during recent centuries?

P.C.   With the advantage of hindsight, I think we can summarize it as a failed experiment in individualism. The idea of the individual—and there is no fungal equivalent—arose during a period of rapid change in human society. In the abstract, individualism looked defensible, even appealing. The ideal individual was to be educated and enlightened, someone we'd all like to know. However, as a practical matter, the culture of enlightened individualism reformed itself after a brief period into a cult of personal freedom. Over the next several centuries, unbridled personal freedom and chance distributions of natural resources led to the creation of certain wealthy and isolated colonies of humans. Their prosperity excited envy, and the rest of the world did what they could to emulate them. Large populations of humans moved from a very simple experience of the natural world to the expectation of a lifestyle similar to what the exploiters were enjoying. This clamor for plenitude put enormous stress on the biosphere.

D.P.   How do you describe the present relationship between nature and mankind?

P.C.   I can only speak for the fungi, who characterize mankind as expendable. After intensive analysis of the data, the Academy was not able to identify even one indispensable human-fungus transaction.

Is the honorable *Pilobolus crystallinus* right? Are we new kids on the evolutionary block a failed experiment as a species? Taking the long view of the fungus among us, human history has repeated itself to the point of stuttering. What is our problem?!

Phoenix, Arizona, which pre–Great Recession was the country's fifth largest and fastest-growing city, doubled its population in the last twenty-plus years. This Sunbelt metropolis named itself after the mythical bird that arose from its own ashes to symbolize death and rebirth. Recently the city's warp-speed sprawl over the fragile Sonoran desert has unearthed a cautionary tale of historical stuttering.

As Craig Childs reported in *High Country News*, because the Native American Graves Protection and Repatriation Act requires a thorough audit of any digging around archeological remains, the construction boom has revealed a ghostly mirror image: a failed prior civilization built along virtually identical lines of development. The empire of the Neolithic people who once lived in the Salt River Valley expanded until they could no longer sustain themselves. They are known as the Hohokam—a Pima Indian word that means "all used up."

As Childs points out, "When archeologists study the Hohokam, they see a civilization that finally collapsed under the weight of drought, overpopulation and ensuing disarray. When they look at Phoenix, they see the same." The Hohokam's unbridled growth finally met its match with climate change—erratic extremes of floods and droughts compounded by impossible demand.

The Hohokam deserted their last remaining settlements in the fifteenth century, leaving only ghostly shadows of their former grandeur. New settlers built over their ruins and cheerily dubbed it Phoenix.

When Childs departed an archeological dig on one of the city's endless new construction sites, he was struck by cheerful banners flapping with environmental bromides such as "Think, Build and Live Sustainably" and "The Future Looks Green." Indeed, the city has enacted groundwater management regulations that are relatively progressive, and it's starting to put in light rail and public transportation. Green buildings are springing up, despite Paleolithic regulations. Will it be a stitch in time? It's worth remembering the Hohokam lasted for 1,500 years. Phoenix, which was officially incorporated in 1881 with a population of 2,500, has about 1,360 years to go, *más o menos*.

Green builder John Abrams says we need to redesign not just the architecture of our homes and buildings, but the very architecture of our communities and businesses. He says we need to start thinking like the cathedral builders who knew their work could not be completed in one lifetime.

If building things to last is the grail, then what else might nature tell us? Although science is an essential ally in our path forward, scientists are increasingly aware of how limited our knowledge of nature really is. Our old-growth cultures of indigenous peoples have thought about such things for a long, long time. As the late Seneca historian John Mohawk saw it,

> What I mean when I say "nature" is everything that supports life on the planet. Nature is so complex, its interactions so dynamic, and it is so non-static that the idea that science

could ever understand it all is utterly laughable. We can understand the more simple things that we do to interfere with it: to degrade it, to wreck it. But we can never understand it. It is beyond our comprehension. In the Indian cultures that I know, they have said that it is a great mystery. It is so complex, so great, so above us that we should never be so arrogant to think that we can understand even a little bit of it.

The culture that I came from saw the universe as the fountain of everything, including consciousness. In our culture we're scolded for being arrogant if we think that we're smart. An individual is not smart according to our culture. An individual is merely lucky to be a part of a system that has intelligence that happens to reside in them. In other words, be humble about this always. The real intelligence isn't the property of an individual or a corporation or something— the real intelligence is the property of the universe itself.

If we had humility, we'd have everything, eh? Mohawk, who served on the Bioneers board for twelve years and was a mentor to me, had the kind of humility that can only be earned intergenerationally through the collectively accumulated wisdom of ancestors in a largely unbroken lineage of transmissions over cycles of vast change as well as continuity. He was deeply encouraged to see the rise of what he called "natural world scientists" who are now grasping what ancient cultures have long known. As Mohawk once said,

Imagine that we can fly at many billions of times the speed of light. That we can rise out of our seats and go in a straight line through the ceiling, and in a second our solar system is behind us and we're racing toward the Milky Way. In a minute, the Milky Way breaks up and we're racing toward places where we can see other galaxies. We're speeding along on this journey, seeing galaxies—not dozens, not hundreds, not thousands, but hundreds of thousands of them, in clusters. If we're going fast enough, we'll notice that we leave one cluster of galaxies only to enter another.

We're told that eventually, if we go far enough, we'll get to the end of all the clusters. Imagine: We're going on and on at almost infinite speed and now have passed all those galaxies and can't see them anymore. When are we going to get to the end? We're not. Maybe there are other clusters. Maybe there are even other universes out there. We can't know, can we? We can't know because we can't get to the end. If we came to another one, we wouldn't know where the end is because the one thing we do know is it doesn't end. It goes on and on and on. Can I suggest that our minds are not capable of truly grasping the infinite? We can imagine it, but we can't really grasp it because we don't have any way to measure that. That's the universe.

Imagine for a moment, with eyes closed, that we want to go back in time, as far as we can go. We're sailing through time in a time machine that clips off a billion years per second. They tell us that if we go further back there is nothing. Yet we don't know if there was nothing or not, because no matter how far back we go in time, we can't get to the beginning. We can't get to the beginning because there was no beginning. There was never a beginning in time, and there's never an end in space. We know that intellectually, but it's very hard to grasp.

Spirit is a word that has a lot of complex meaning. It's very powerful. But imagine yourself being part of that—something of a spirit addressing another part of a spirit that has as its source the infinite intelligence or wisdom that is the very process of creating life on Earth, the process of creating planets and stars and galaxies. This is what is addressed by many cultures as the Great Mystery, the Great Creation. They address it as something other than anthropomorphic, as something that takes our own anthropocentrism and casts it away because, spirit to spirit, it doesn't mean anything. The relation is spirit to spirit, you to plant—the essence of humankind to the essence of everything else. All we can really do about that idea in our conscious minds is have a profound respect for it.

Spirituality is a form of consciousness. Almost all of the world's indigenous cultures, until they become extremely damaged, perceive that they have relationships at some level with special groups of plants and animals or trees. Then they celebrate this relationship, which I propose is a consciousness. It's not only the human who has the consciousness; it's also the plant, the tree, the birds and all the other things. When you address that plant, you're addressing its consciousness in time and space. How it came to be and where it came to be, you don't know. What you know is that you're part of whatever it is that brought the plant into being. You're related in this way.

The ancient Seneca thought about this stuff. They believed that creation is infinite. The Creation or the Creator doesn't wear a beard or walk around on a cloud, carrying a staff. The Creator is the force that gave that plant consciousness, as manifested in its compounds and in its shape at that moment. When you're talking to that plant, you're talking to the essence of the spirit of life in the universe, not just on the Earth. Whatever it is is not confined to here. You can look up in the sky and see that we're not the only place that's occupied. There are other beings in the universe besides us. That's the old spirituality. Acquire that consciousness, and it becomes extremely difficult to rationalize pollution. Acquire that consciousness and it becomes very difficult to rationalize cutting down trees to make board-feet worth of dollars out of them.

I propose to you that spirituality is the highest form of political consciousness.

Knowing the scale of destruction we face, feeling the depth of pain and suffering that the life of the world is experiencing today—we need to ask ourselves some very difficult questions about just how we got here. Ignorance? You bet. Stupidity? Duh. Greed? Big time. But is there some deeper, even more terrible flaw in our nature, some depraved congenital shadow that drives us to annihilate the web of life and extinguish each other and ourselves?

The late visionary biologist Lyall Watson in his book *Dark Nature: A Natural History of Evil* took a penetrating look at the idea of evil from the perspective of a naturalist.

Watson defined evil in much the same spirit as Aldo Leopold: "If good can be defined as that which encourages the integrity of the whole, then evil becomes everything which disturbs or disrupts such completeness. Anything unruly or over the top. Anything in short that is bad for the ecology. Good is not necessarily the opposite of evil, but one part of the field in which they both exist."

Watson suggests that evil always has been and always will be a part of the field. He cautions that trying to suppress it serves only to feed its power. He points out that there is an exquisite dynamic balance in nature where things are "just right." He calls this ecological razor's edge the "Goldilocks" effect. If you remember the fairy tale, Goldilocks wanted her porridge not too hot and not too cold, her bed not too hard and not too soft—everything had to be just right. When that exquisitely just-right balance of nature is disturbed, very bad things happen.

Watson identifies three principle sources of this disruptive evil in ecology:

- a loss of connection to place
- a loss of balance between both numbers and distribution
- a lack of diversity

The takeaway is both simple and complex. We need to restore our connection to place, in the biggest sense as a species to our home, Earth, as well as to our local communities and ecologies. We need to restore balance to numbers and distribution in the world. We need to cultivate and enhance diversity, both biologically and culturally.

We have the knowledge. Now it needs to move out much more widely—very rapidly. But as Chief Oren Lyons asks, how do we educate 7 billion people (and rising) really fast?

A hundred years ago, the futurist and author H. G. Wells said, "We are in a race between education and catastrophe." He could well have foreseen our current destruction of the biosphere. We're unraveling the weave of the web of life itself—on which our own survival depends—yet we barely understand it. Or perhaps *because* we barely understand it.

Is the environmental crisis primarily a crisis of education? If so, we could be in luck, because the answers to how to sustain human communities are embedded in the 3.8-billion-year-old school of natural history called Life on Earth. The facts of life are all around us, if only we pay attention.

Educator David W. Orr says the first step is to become ecologically literate. After all, the origin of the word "ecology"—*oikos* in Greek—means "household." Ecological literacy is the study of the Earth household. As author and physicist Fritjof Capra adds, "In this century, ecological literacy will be a critical skill for politicians, business leaders and professionals in all spheres. It will be the most important part of education at all levels."

Orr suggests that all education is environmental education, by virtue of what we include or exclude about how people are part of the natural world. Curriculum is any place where learning happens. What all education is finally about is how we are to live in this interdependent world.

Orr believes the most important thing we can teach our children is what Rachel Carson called "a sense of wonder." Orr says our capacity to experience that wondrous feeling of being part of the wholeness of creation requires childhood experience in nature, constant practice, and early validation by adults. Falling in love with nature may just be our best hope for the future—especially for the children who *are* the future.

Buckminster Fuller, arguably the greatest designer of the twentieth century, was among the first to advance sustainability and a systemic worldview. He designed breakthrough principles for energy and materials efficiency in the fields of design, architecture, and engineering. He explored strategies for human survival to transform the global human social and economic systems driving the destruction of what he called "Spaceship Earth."

Fuller was convinced that knowledge is our real wealth, that we have enough knowledge to make the world work for everyone.

This was his mission statement for humanity:

> To make the world work
> For 100 percent of humanity
> In the shortest possible time
> Through spontaneous cooperation
> Without ecological offense
> Or the disadvantage of anyone.

This vision is spreading more and more quickly all over the world, aided by the vast array of communications technologies now widely distributed around this beautiful blue and white globe.

How can any one person accomplish this mission? Fuller asked for an unusual memorial on his tombstone: "Call me trim-tab." Here's why, in his words:

> Something hit me very hard once, thinking about what one little man could do. Think of the Queen Mary [ocean liner]—the whole ship goes by and then comes the rudder. And there's a tiny thing on the edge of the rudder called

a trim-tab. It's a miniature rudder. Just moving that little trim-tab builds a low pressure that pulls the rudder around. Takes almost no effort at all. So I said that the little individual can be a trim-tab. Society thinks it's going right by you, that it's left you altogether. But if you're doing dynamic things mentally, the fact is that you can just put your foot out like that and the whole big ship of state is going to go. So, I said, "Call me trim-tab."

Our individual actions can and do make a decisive difference. Yet in the end, like *Pilobolus crystallinus*, humanity's destiny is collective. Our fate will be determined by our ability to cooperate and create peaceful coexistence across vast differences, stretching us to expand our compassion to not only to those suffering the deepest wounds and burdens of history, but to the entirety of the web of life.

But hey—as the naturalist and author Diane Ackerman suggests, we're evolutionary toddlers who've had to cross the cosmic street and stand facing our own home in order to learn there's no place like home . . .

Welcome home.

ACKNOWLEDGMENTS

First and foremost, I give boundless thanks to my daughter, Ramona Ausubel, a gifted writer and editor. She took a tangle of talks and writing I'd done over about the past decade for the Bioneers conference and cut, sculpted, and combed them into a shapely flow. She sounded lovely notes of her own voice that harmonized invisibly with mine. This book would not exist without her, and it's an honor and joy to have her voice here as well.

I also deeply thank my longtime Bioneers colleague J. P. Harpignies, who helped immeasurably on extensive fact-checking and resources, as well as by providing sanguine reality checks on overdoses of attitude or optimism.

I am most grateful to Margo Baldwin and Chelsea Green for including this book in such fine company, and to Joni Praded for her skillful and astute editing.

I thank all the bioneers whose work has inspired and educated me in a permanent graduate school of learning, and those who contributed to getting their stories right in this book.

I bow to my executive assistant and program codirector, Nikki Spangenburg, for her unwavering support, attention to detail, and steady hand in making sure all the elements came together on time. I thank Marita Prandoni for her essential and meticulous help in finalizing the resources.

I honor the entire Bioneers staff and board, a remarkable and dedicated team who do the work every day, thank goodness, that's reflected in these pages.

RESOURCES

*T*his section lists many of the main individuals, organizations, and books mentioned in the text, as well as a few additional organizations working in related domains.

FOREWORD:
It's All Alive, It's All Connected!

David W. Orr. http://davidworr.com/

David W. Orr, "Introduction" in *Ecological Literacy: Educating Our Children for a Sustainable World*, ed. Michael K. Stone and Zenobia Barlow (San Francisco: Sierra Club Books, 2005), ix–xi.

David W. Orr, "Place and Pedagogy," in Stone and Barlow, *Ecological Literacy*, 85–95.

David W. Orr, "Recollection," in Stone and Barlow, *Ecological Literacy*, 96–106.

David W. Orr, *The Nature of Design: Ecology, Culture, and Human Intention* (New York: Oxford University Press, 2002).

David W. Orr, *Down to the Wire: Confronting Climate Collapse* (New York: Oxford University Press, 2009).

David W. Orr, *Earth in Mind: On Education, Environment, and the Human Prospect* (Washington DC: Island Press, 2004).

INTRODUCTION:
Slouching Toward Sustainability

Paul Gilding, *The Great Disruption: Why the Climate Crisis Will Bring On the End of Shopping and the Birth of a New World* (New York: Bloombury Press, 2011).

Kenny Ausubel. *Hoxsey: When Healing Becomes a Crime*. Wellspring Media 2005. (DVD) 83 minutes.

Kenny Ausubel, *When Healing Becomes a Crime: The Amazing Story of the Hoxsey Cancer Clinics and the Return of Alternative Therapies* (Rochester, VT: Healing Arts Press, 2000).

Paul Hawken, *Blessed Unrest: How the Largest Movement in the World Came into Being and Why No One Saw It Coming* (New York: Viking Penguin, 2007).

Paul Hawken. http://paulhawken.com/

It's All Alive . . .

CLOSE ENCOUNTERS OF THE BIOLOGICAL KIND:
Earth Hospitality

Lynn Margulis, *Symbiotic Planet: A New Look at Evolution* (New York: Basic Books, 1998).

Encyclopedia of Life, a free, online collaborative encyclopedia intended to document all of the 1.9 million living species known to science. http://eol.org.

THE REENCHANTMENT OF EARTH:
A Cocreation Story

Malcolm Margolin (http://www.heydaybooks.com) is executive director of Heyday, an independent nonprofit publisher. His California Indian Publishing Program celebrates Indian culture through its quarterly magazine, *News from Native California*, and in the more than forty books it has published.

Dennis Martinez, is founder of the Indigenous Peoples' Restoration Network, a working group of the Society for Ecological Restoration International. http://www.ser.org/iprn/default.asp

TWENTY-FIRST CENTURY BLUES:
The Dim Ages

Gregory D. Foster and Louise B. Wise, "Sustainable Security," *Harvard International Review* 21, no. 4 (1999): 20-23.

THE CLASH OF CIVILIZATIONS:
Disposability or Sustainability?

Peter Schwartz and Doug Randall, "An Abrupt Climate Change Scenario and Its Implications for U.S. National Security," (California Institute of Technology, Pasadena, CA, October 2003) http://www.gbn.com/consulting/article_details.php?id=53

HONEY, WE SHRUNK THE PLANET:
Regime Change and Resilience Thinking

The Resilience Alliance. http://www.resalliance.org/

The Resource Renewal Institute. http://www.rri.org/

Carl Anthony. http://breakthroughcommunities.info/

Majora Carter. http://www.majoracartergroup.com/

Sustainable South Bronx. http://www.ssbx.org/

Peggy Shepard, WE ACT for Environmental Justice. http://www.weact.org

Omar Freilla, Green Worker Cooperatives, a South-Bronx-based organization dedicated to incubating worker-owned green businesses in order to build a strong local economy rooted in democracy and environmental justice. http://www.greenworker.coop/

NATURE'S OPERATING INSTRUCTIONS:
The True Biotechnologies

Janine Benyus, *Biomimicry: Innovation Inspired by Nature* (New York: HarperCollins Publishers, 1997).

Janine Benyus. http://www.janinebenyus.com

Biomimicry Institute. http://www.biomimicryinstitute.org, http://www.biomimicry.net, http://www.asknature.org

Elaine R. Ingham, *Soil Biology Primer* (Ankeny, IA: Soil and Water Conservation Society, 2000).

Elaine Ingham is a soil biology researcher and the founder of Soil Foodweb Inc. (http://www.soilfoodweb.com/), recognized as a leading expert on soil microbiology and the soil food web. She was named chief scientist at the Rodale Institute (http://rodaleinstitute.org/) in 2011.

Andrew Kimbrell. http://www.andrewkimbrell.org

Center for Food Safety. http://www.centerforfoodsafety.org

Andrew Kimbrell, *The Human Body Shop: The Engineering and Marketing of Life* (New York: HarperCollins Publishers, 1993).

Andrew Kimbrell, *Your Right to Know: Genetic Engineering and the Secret Changes in Your Food* (Washington, D.C.: Center for Food Safety, 2006).

Andrew Kimbrell, ed. *Fatal Harvest: The Tragedy of Industrial Agriculture* (Washington, D.C.: Island Press, 2002).

Jay Harman. http://www.jayharman.com/, http://www.paxscientific.com/

Paul Stamets. http://www.fungi.com/

Randall Von Wedel. http://www.tssconsultants.com, http://cytoculture.com/

Dave Foreman. http://rewilding.org/rewildit/

Dan Dagget, *Beyond the Rangeland Conflict: Toward a West that Works* (Layton, UT: Gibbs Smith Publishers, 1995).

Eco-Results. http://ecoresults.org/

Tree People, with Andy and Katie Lipkis, *The Simple Act of Planting a Tree: A Citizen Forester's Guide to Healing Your Neighborhood, Your City, and Your World* (Los Angeles: Jeremy P. Tarcher, Inc, n.d.).

Andy Lipkis. http://www.treepeople.org/

Paul Hawken. http://paulhawken.com/

Paul Hawken, *The Next Economy* (New York: HarperCollins Publishers, 1983).

Paul Hawken, *Growing a Business* (New York: Simon & Schuster, 1988).

Paul Hawken, *The Ecology of Commerce: A Declaration of Sustainability* (New York: HarperCollins Publishers, 1993).

Paul Hawken, *Blessed Unrest: How the Largest Movement in the World Came into Being and Why No One Saw It Coming* (New York: Viking Penguin, 2007).

Paul Hawken, Amory Lovins, and L. Hunter Lovins, *Natural Capitalism: Creating the Next Industrial Revolution* (New York: Little, Brown, 1999).

Natural Capital Institute. http://www.naturalcapital.org/

One Sun, Inc. http://www.onesuninc.com/

Wiser Earth. http://wiserearth.org/

Oren Lyons et al., *Exiled in the Land of the Free: Democracy, Indian Nations and the U.S. Constitution* (Santa Fe, NM: Clear Light Books, 1992).

John Mohawk, *Utopian Legacies: A History of Conquest and Oppression in the Western World* (Santa Fe, NM: Clear Light Books, 1999).

Luisah Teish. http://luisahteish.org/

Luisah Teish, *Jambalaya: The Natural Woman's Book of Personal Charms and Practical Rituals, Carnival of the Spirit* (New York: Harper & Row, 1985).

Jump Up: Good Times Throughout the Season with Celebrations from Around the World (Berkeley, CA: Conari, 2000).

ECOLOGICAL MEDICINE:
One Notion Indivisible

Carolyn Raffensperger. http://sehn.org/

Carolyn Raffensperger, *Precautionary Tools for Reshaping Environmental Policy* (Cambridge, MA: MIT Press, 2006).

Carolyn Raffensperger, *Protecting Public Health and the Environment: Implementing the Precautionary Principle* (Washington, D.C.: Island Press, 1999).

Laurie Garrett, *The Coming Plague: Newly Emerging Diseases in a World Out of Balance* (New York: Farrar Straus & Giroux, 1994).

Theo Colborn. http://www.tedx.org/home.php

Paul Anastas. http://warnerbabcock.com/

John Warner. http://learngreenchemistry.com/Learn_Green_Chemistry.html

Paul T. Anastas and John C. Warner, *Green Chemistry: Theory and Practice* (New York: Oxford University Press, 1998).

Health Care Without Harm. http://noharm.org/

DREAMING THE FUTURE:
Empire Crash in the Age of Nature

J. R. McNeill, *Something New Under The Sun: An Environmental History of the Twentieth-century World* (New York: W.W. Norton, 2000).

Jared Diamond, *Guns, Germs and Steel* (New York: W.W. Norton, 1997).

Jared Diamond, *Collapse: How Societies Choose to Fail or Succeed* (New York: Viking Penguin, 2005).

Hazel Henderson. http://www.hazelhenderson.com/

Ethical Markets Media. http://www.ethicalmarkets.com/

Hazel Henderson and Simran Sethi, *Ethical Markets: Growing the Green Economy* (White River Junction, VT: Chelsea Green Publishing, 2006).

Kevin Phillips, *Wealth and Democracy: A Political History of the American Rich* (New York: Broadway Books, 2002).

Kevin Phillips, *American Theocracy: The Peril and Politics of Radical Religion, Oil, and Borrowed Money in the 21st Century* (New York: Viking Penguin, 2006).

Kevin Phillips, *Bad Money: Reckless Finance, Failed Politics, and the Global Crisis of American Capitalism* (New York: Viking Penguin, 2008).

Fred Block, "A Moral Economy," *The Nation*, March 20, 2006: 16-19.

Novomer. http://novomer.com/

Gar Alperovitz. http://www.garalperovitz.com/

Gar Aperovitz, *America Beyond Capitalism: Reclaiming Our Wealth, Our Liberty, and Our Democracy* (Hoboken, NJ: John Wiley & Sons, 2004).

Democracy Collaborative. http://democracycollaborative.org/

Transition Towns. http://www.transitionnetwork.org/

Business Alliance for Local Living Economies (BALLE). http://www.livingeconomies.org/

David Oates, "Imagine," *High Country News*, April 16, 2007. http://www.hcn.org/issues/344/16957

The Rocky Mountain Institute. http://www.rmi.org/

Hungry Ghost Stories

THE STING:
The Role of Fraud in Nature

David Livingstone Smith, *Why We Lie: The Evolutionary Roots of Deception and the Unconscious Mind* (New York: St. Martin's Press, 2004).

The Yes Men. http://theyesmen.org/

Yes Lab. http://www.yeslab.org/

The Yes Men. 2003.
The Yes Men Fix the World. 2009.

THE ROBBER BARONS:
Déjà Vu All Over Again
Frederick Townsend Martin, *The Passing of the Idle Rich* (New York: Ayer Publishing, 1911).

SURVIVAL OF THE FATTEST:
The Mythology of Greed
Peter Kropotkin, *The Conquest of Bread* (New York and London: G. P. Putnam's Sons, 1906).
Peter Kropotkin, *Fields, Factories and Workshops* (London: Thomas Nelson & Sons, 1912).
Peter Kropotkin, *Mutual Aid: A Factor of Evolution* (London: William Heinemann, 1902).

THIS IS YOUR BRAIN ON PUBLIC RELATIONS:
Lizards from Outer Space
George Lakoff, *Moral Politics: What Conservatives Know That Liberals Don't* (Chicago,
    IL: University of Chicago Press, 1996).
George Lakoff, *Don't Think of an Elephant: Know Your Values and Frame the Debate*
    (White River Junction, VT: Chelsea Green Publishing, 2004).
George Lakoff, *The Political Mind: Why You Can't Understand 21st-Century American
    Politics with an 18th-Century Brain* (New York: Viking Penguin, 2008).
Environmental Working Group. http://ewg.org/

MIGHTY CORPORATE:
A Nation of Hustlers
Walter A. McDougall, *Freedom Just Around the Corner: A New American History,
    1585–1828* (New York: HarperCollins, 2004).
The Corporation. http://thecorporation.com/ Big Picture Media Company, Directed by
    Mark Achbar and Jennifer Abbott, 2003 DVD: 124 minutes.
Robert Hare. http://hare.org/
Robert Hare, *Without Conscience: The Disturbing World of the Psychopaths Among Us*
    (New York: Guilford Press, 1999).
Corporate Accountability International. http://stopcorporateabuse.org/
Multinational Monitor. http://multinationalmonitor.org/
CorpWatch. http://corpwatch.org/
Public Citizen. http://citizen.org/

THE INFOGANDA WARS:
The Battle of the Story
Fairness and Accuracy in Reporting (FAIR). http://www.fair.org/
The Mother Jones/Nation Institute Investigative Fund. http://www.theinvestigativefund.org/
The Fund for Investigative Journalism. http://fij.org/
Democracy Now! http://www.democracynow.org/

FAMILY VALUES:
Why Is It a Crime?
Transparency International. http://transparency.org/

Citizens for Responsibility and Ethics in Washington (CREW). http://www.citizensforethics.org/

A PARADE OF DWARVES:
Have-Nots and Have-a-Lots

Clive Crook, "The Height of Inequality," *The Atlantic*, September 2006: 36-37. http://www.theatlantic.com/magazine/archive/2006/09/the-height-of-inequality/5089/

The BlueGreen Alliance. http://www.bluegreenalliance.org/

Zero Waste Alliance. http://www.zerowaste.org/

Zero Waste Network. http://zerowastenetwork.org/

Zero Waste Institute. http://zerowasteinstitute.org/

Zero Waste International Alliance. http://zwia.org/

Reuse Alliance. http://www.reusealliance.org/

John de Graaf. http://timeday.org/

John de Graaf, David Wann, and Thomas H. Naylor, *Affluenza: The All-Consuming Epidemic* (San Francisco: Berrett-Koehler Publishers, 2001).

International Forum on Globalization (IFG). http://ifg.org/

David Cay Johnston, *Free Lunch: How the Wealthiest Americans Enrich Themselves at Government Expense (and Stick You With the Bill)* (New York: Penguin Group, 2007).

David Cay Johnston, *Perfectly Legal: The Covert Campaign to Rig Our Tax System to Benefit the Super Rich—and Cheat Everybody Else* (New York: Penguin Group, 2005).

Bruce Bartlett, *The New American Economy: The Failure of Reaganomics and a New Way Forward* (Basingstoke, UK: Palgrave MacMillan, 2009).

Bruce Bartlett, *The Benefit and the Burden: Tax Reform—Why We Need It and What It Will Take* (New York: Simon & Schuster, 2012).

THE UNLIKELIEST OF PEOPLE
IN THE UNLIKELIEST OF PLACES:
Corporations, Democracy, and the Rights of Nature

Community Environmental Legal Defense Fund (CELDF). http://celdf.org/

Nick Robins, *The Corporation That Changed the World: How the East India Company Shaped the Modern Multinational* (London: Pluto Press, 2006).

Cormac Cullinan, *Wild Law: A Manifesto for Earth Justice* (White River Junction, VT: Chelsea Green Publishing, 2011).

The Forum on Religion and Ecology at Yale. http://fore.research.yale.edu/

Envision Spokane. http://envisionspokane.org/

Pachamama Alliance. http://pachamama.org/

The Rainforest Action Network. http://ran.org/

The Global Alliance for the Rights of Nature. http://therightsofnature.org/

Christopher D. Stone, *Should Trees Have Standing? Law, Morality, and the Environment* (New York: Oxford University Press, 2010).

Value Change For Survival

REMEMBERING THE FUTURE:
Clear Thinking, Justice, and Peace

James Hillman, *A Terrible Love of War* (New York: Penguin Press, 2004).

James Hillman, *Re-visioning Psychology* (New York: Harper & Row Publishers, 1975).

James Hillman, *The Soul's Code: In Search of Character and Calling* (New York: Warner Books, 1997).

Business Leaders for Sensible Priorities. http://www.americanprogress.org/

Bob Holmes, "Imagine the Earth Without People," *New Scientist*, October 2006: 36-41. http://www.newscientist.com/article/mg19225731.100

Edward Tick. http://soldiersheart.net/

Edward Tick, *War and the Soul: Healing Our Nation's Veterans from Post-Traumatic Stress Disorder* (Wheaton, IL: Quest Books, 2005).

Edward Tick, *The Golden Tortoise: Journeys in Viet Nam* (Pasadena, CA: Red Hen Press, 2005).

Edward Tick, *Sacred Mountain: Encounters of the Vietnam Beast* (Velarde, NM: Moon Bear Press, 1989).

Edward Tick and Stephen Larsen, *The Practice of Dream Healing: Bringing Ancient Greek Mysteries into Modern Medicine* (Wheaton, IL: Quest Books, 2001).

James Gordon, MD. http://jamesgordonmd.com/

The Center for Mind–Body. http://www.cmbm.org/

The Multidisciplinary Association for Psychedelic Studies (MAPS). http://www.maps.org/

THE STAR ROVER:
The Law of Love

Jack London, *The Star Rover* (New York: Grosset & Dunlap, 1915).

Eric Schlosser, *Fast Food Nation* (New York: Houghton Mifflin, 2002).

Eric Schlosser, *Reefer Madness: Sex, Drugs and Cheap Labor in the American Black Market* (New York: Houghton Mifflin, 2003).

The Drug Policy Alliance. http://www.drugpolicy.org/

VALUE CHANGE FOR SURVIVAL:
Six Degrees of Climate Separation

Mark Lynas, *Six Degrees: Our Future on a Hotter Planet* (New York: HarperCollins, 2008).

Mark Lynas, *The God Species: How the Planet Can Survive the Age of Humans* (New York: Fourth Estate, 2011).

Rocky Mountain Institute. http://www.rmi.org/

Amory Lovins, *Soft Energy Paths: Towards a Durable Peace* (San Francisco: Friends of the Earth International, 1977).

Amory Lovins, *Reinventing Fire: Bold Business Solutions for the New Energy Era* (White River Junction, VT: Chelsea Green Publishing, 2011).

Amory Lovins, *Winning the Oil Endgame* (Snowmass, Co: Rocky Mountain Institute, 2004).

Paul Hawken, Amory Lovins, and L. Hunter Lovins, *Natural Capitalism: Creating the Next Industrial Revolution* (New York: Little, Brown, 1999).

Worldwatch Institute. http://www.worldwatch.org/

Earth Policy Institute. http://www.earth-policy.org/

Lester R. Brown, *Plan B: Rescuing a Planet Under Stress and a Civilization in Trouble* (New York: W.W. Norton, 2003).

Lester R. Brown, *Plan B 2.0: Rescuing a Planet Under Stress and a Civilization in Trouble* (New York: W.W. Norton, 2006).

Lester R. Brown, *Plan B 3.0: Mobilizing to Save Civilization* (New York: W.W. Norton, 2008).

Lester R. Brown, *Plan B 4.0: Mobilizing to Save Civilization* (New York: W.W. Norton, 2010).
Lester Brown, *World on the Edge: How to Prevent Environmental and Economic Collapse* (New York: W.W. Norton, 2011).
The Buckminster Fuller Institute. http://bfi.org/
Matt Taibbi. http://www.rollingstone.com/politics/blogs/taibblog
Gerald Epstein. http://www.umass.edu/research/research-units-facilities/political-economy-research-institute-peri

THE REVOLUTION HAS BEGUN:
"The Shift Hits the Fan"

Richard Heinberg. http://www.postcarbon.org/
Donella H. Meadows, Dennis L. Meadows, Jørgen Randers, and William W. Behrens III, *The Limits to Growth* (New York: Universe Books, 1972).
Donella H. Meadows, Jørgen Randers, and Dennis L. Meadows, *Limits to Growth: The 30-Year Update* (White River Junction, VT: Chelsea Green Publishing, 2004).
Stephen Hill. http://www.europespromise.org/
Stephen Hill, *Europe's Promise: Why the European Way Is the Best Hope in an Insecure Age* (Berkeley, CA: University of California Press, 2010).
Jeremy Rifkin. http://foet.org/
Jeremy Rifkin, *The European Dream: How Europe's Vision of the Future Is Quietly Eclipsing the American Dream* (New York: Tarcher, 2004).
Marjorie Kelly. http://tellus.org/, http://corporation2020.org/, http://business-ethics.com/
Marjorie Kelly, *The Divine Right of Capital: Dethroning the Corporate Aristocracy* (San Francisco, CA: Berrett-Koehler Publishers, 2001).
Two European banks known for their ethics and progressive policies are Triodos Bank (http://www.triodos.co.uk/) and Rabobank (http://www.rabobank.com/).
Organic Valley. http://www.organicvalley.coop/
Hanna Rosin, "The End of Men," *The Atlantic*, July/August 2010. theatlantic.com/magazine/archive/2010/07/the-end-of-men/8135/
Thom Hartmann. http://www.thomhartmann.com/
Thom Hartmann, *Rebooting the American Dream: 11 Ways to Rebuild Our Country* (San Francisco, CA: Berrett-Koehler Publishers, 2011).
Richard Tarnas, *The Passion of the Western Mind: Understanding the Ideas That Have Shaped Our World View* (New York: Random House, 1991).
Richard Tarnas, *Cosmos and Psyche: Intimations of a New World View* (New York: Viking Penguin, 2006).

ENTANGLED IN UNITY:
Poets, Seers, Science, and Oneness

Diane Ackerman. http://www.dianeackerman.com/
Diane Ackerman, *A Natural History of the Senses* (New York: Random House, 1990).
Aldo Leopold, *A Sand County Almanac* (New York: Oxford University Press, 1949).
Aldo Leopold Foundation. http://aldoleopold.org/
Evan Eisenberg. http://www.evaneisenberg.com/
Evan Eisenberg, *The Ecology of Eden: An Inquiry into the Dream of Paradise and a New Vision of Our Role in Nature* (New York: Alfred A. Knopf, 1998).
Larry Dossey, MD. http://www.dosseydossey.com/

Larry Dossey, *Healing Words: The Power of Prayer and the Practice of Medicine* (New York: HarperCollins, 1993).

FROM HERE TO INFINITY:
The Great Mystery

Craig Childs. http://houseofrain.com/

John Abrams. http://www.southmountain.com/

John Abrams, *Companies We Keep: Employee Ownership and the Business of Community and Place* (White River Junction, VT: Chelsea Green, 2008).

Fritjof Capra. http://fritjofcapra.net/

Center for Ecoliteracy. http://www.ecoliteracy.org/

Fritjof Capra, *The Tao of Physics: An Exploration of the Parallels between Modern Physics and Eastern Mysticism* (London: Wildwood House, 1975).

Fritjof Capra, *The Web of Life: A New Scientific Understanding of Living Systems* (New York: Random House, 1996).

Fritjof Capra, *The Hidden Connections: Integrating the Biological, Cognitive, and Social Dimensions of Life Into a Science of Sustainability* (New York: Doubleday, 2002).

Lyall Watson, *Supernature* (Garden City, NY: Anchor Press, 1973).

Lyall Watson, *Dark Nature: A Natural History of Evil* (New York: HarperCollins, 1996).

INDEX

ABOUT BIONEERS

*B*ioneers highlights breakthrough solutions for restoring people and planet. Since 1990, Bioneers has acted as a fertile hub of social and scientific innovators with nature-inspired approaches for the world's most pressing environmental and social challenges. Bioneers connects people with solutions and each other. The national and local conferences are complemented by extensive media outreach—including an award-winning radio series, book series, and source for media projects such as Leonardo DiCaprio's film *The 11th Hour* and Michael Pollan's book *The Omnivore's Dilemma.*

Bioneers has been officially honored by the California state Senate, Marin County Board of Supervisors (California), and Governor Bill Richardson of New Mexico, where Bioneers is based. The Bioneers radio series has won dozens of awards, including multiple gold medals in international and New York festivals. The Bioneers Dreaming New Mexico project won second place in the international Buckminster Fuller Challenge Award in 2009 and semifinalist in 2011. Bioneers and founders and Co-CEOs Kenny Ausubel and Nina Simons have received awards and honors, including from Global Green and Rainforest Action Network. Bioneers is a Knowledge Partner of the Tällberg Forum in Sweden.

Bioneers programs include:

ECOLOGICAL LITERACY EDUCATION
Changing the Mindscape: Public Education and Media Outreach
Education for Action: Formal Education

RESILIENT COMMUNITIES
Resilience from the Ground Up: Localization
Wisdom at the End of a Hoe: Restorative Food Systems
Becoming Native to Place: Indigeneity
Bioneers Global: An International Community of Leadership

THE BIONEERS COMMUNITY OF LEADERSHIP
Moonrise: Women's Leadership
The Bioneers Community of Mentors: Intergenerational Leadership
Wild Relatives: The Bioneers Network of Networks

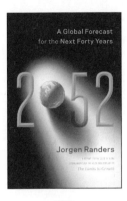

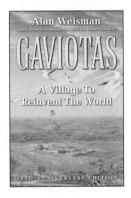
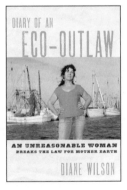

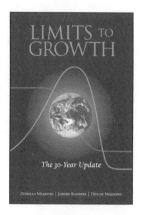

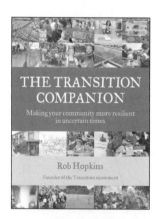
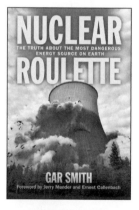